W9-DAR-876

NT Workstation 4

The Cram Sheet

This Cram Sheet contains the distilled, key facts about NT Workstation 4. Review this information last thing before you enter the test room, paying special attention to those areas where you feel you need the most review. You can transfer any of these facts from your head onto a blank sheet of paper before beginning the exam.

INSTALLATION AND CONFIGURATION

1. Know these WINNT and WINNT32 switches:
   - **/O** Creates boot floppies, beings install.
   - **/OX** Creates boot floppies, does not start install.
   - **/B** Installs NT using boot floppy diskettes.
   - **/UDF, /U, and /I** Used for unintended and automated installs.

2. How to plan for, create, and use unattended installation files—UNATTEND.TXT and UDFs.

3. The SYSDIFF utility:
   - /snap [/log:<log_file>] <snapshot_file> creates an image of the base installation
   - /diff [/log:<log_file>] <snapshot_file> <difference_file> creates an image of the changes
   - /apply [/log:<log_file>] <difference_file> applies the difference file to a base installation
   - /inf [/log:<log_file>] <sysdiff_file> <oem_root> creates an .INF file for automating application install along with NT
   - /dump [/log:<log_file>] <difference_file> <dump_file> creates a document detailing the activity of the difference file

4. Setting up a dual-boot system: install DOS or Windows 95, then install Windows NT Workstation.

5. Install, configure, and remove hardware components using Control Panel applets: Network, SCSI Adapters, Tape devices, UPS, Multimedia, Display, Keyboard, and Mouse.

6. When upgrading an existing version of NT, the following information stays intact:
   - Any edits made to Registry using Registry Editor
   - Custom program groups, desktop layout, setting, and Control Panel preferences
   - Local security accounts (users and groups)
   - Network adapter, protocol, service configurations, and addresses (including RAS)
   - Preferences for Accessories and Administrative Tools

MANAGING RESOURCES

7. There are two types of groups: local and global. Local groups are only available on local domains; global groups are available across domains. Local groups can contain

users and global groups, global groups contain users only. You can't place groups within global groups, nor can you place local groups within other local groups.

8. For group permissions, the least restrictive right takes precedence, except No Access always wins! When combining NTFS and share permissions, the least restrictive wins for each kind (except No Access), when combining resulting NTFS and share permissions, the most restrictive wins.

9. You can perform the following in User Manager For Domains:
   - Produce, change, duplicate, and remove user and local group accounts.
   - Enable account policies (assign defaults for passwords, account lockouts, disconnect status, and so on).
   - Create user rights and audit policies.

10. Profiles are local only by default. Made roaming through System applet.

11. Mandatory profiles: change NTUSER. DAT to NTUSER.MAN.

12. Create directory or printer share: set sharing, define share name, set permissions.

13. All new directory shares have default rights of Full Access to Everyone.

14. All new printer shares have Print access to Everyone, Full Control to Administrator and PowerUsers, and Manage Documents to the owner.

15. Attach to printer share: New Printer, Network Printer Server.

16. Attach to directory share: Map Drive or Network Neighborhood.

17. Each shared logical printer can be set to different priorities and access times.

18. Review Disk Administrator menus and options.

19. NT Workstation does not have any fault tolerant partition configurations.

20. Only primary partitions can be active: Select Mark Active from the Partition menu in Disk Administrator.

21. NTFS file and directory permission settings and issues: Read, Change, Full Control, No Access; set by group or user.

22. Vital statistics for FAT and NTFS:

	FAT	NTFS
Maximum volume size	2 GB	16 EB
Maximum file size	2 GB	16 EB
File-level security	No	Yes
Long file name support	No	Yes
Self-repairing	No	Yes
Transaction logging capabilities	No	Yes
File-level compression	No	Yes
File-level security	No	Yes

23. Use FAT for 50 MB partitions or smaller, NTFS for partitions 400 MB or larger.

24. Rules for Permissions on NTFS Move and Copy operations:
   - If you move or copy files within same NTFS partition, they *retain* original permissions.
   - If you create, copy, or move files from one NTFS partition to another, they *inherit* parent folder permissions.
   - All NTFS permissions disappear when files moved or copied from NTFS to FAT.

25. Convert FAT partitions into NTFS using CONVERT.EXE; HPFS not supported in Windows NT 4.

26. Two Registry editors: REGEDIT.EXE (search features) and REGEDT32.EXE (security features).

BOOT FACTS

27. Boot files—NTLDR, BOOT.INI, NTDETECT.COM, and so on—reside on the system partition, Windows NT OS files—including NTOSKRNL.EXE—reside on the boot partition. BACKWARDS!

28. Most important Windows NT boot process components:
   - **BOOT.INI** Describes Windows NT boot defaults, plus OS location, settings, menu selections. It resides in the root directory of the system partition. (Required for NT boot floppy.)
   - **BOOTSECT.DOS** Used if NTLDR permits boot to some other Microsoft OS like DOS or Windows 95. It resides in the root directory of system partition. (Not required.)

Are You Certifiable?

That's the question that's probably on your mind. The answer is: You bet! But if you've tried and failed or you've been frustrated by the complexity of the MCSE program and the maze of study materials available, you've come to the right place. We've created our new publishing and training program, *Certification Insider Press*, to help you accomplish one important goal: to ace an MCSE exam without having to spend the rest of your life studying for it.

The book you have in your hands is part of our *Exam Cram* series. Each book is especially designed not only to help you study for an exam but also to help you understand what the exam is all about. Inside these covers you'll find hundreds of test-taking tips, insights, and strategies that simply cannot be found anyplace else. In creating our guides, we've assembled the very best team of certified trainers, MCSE professionals, and networking course developers.

Our commitment is to ensure that the *Exam Cram* guides offer proven training and active-learning techniques not found in other study guides. We provide unique study tips and techniques, memory joggers, custom quizzes, insights about trick questions, a sample test, and much more. In a nutshell, each *Exam Cram* guide is closely organized like the exam it is tied to.

To help us continue to provide the very best certification study materials, we'd like to hear from you. Write or email us (craminfo@coriolis.com) and let us know how our *Exam Cram* guides have helped you study, or tell us about new features you'd like us to add. If you send us a story about how an *Exam Cram* guide has helped you ace an exam and we use it in one of our guides, we'll send you an official *Exam Cram* shirt for your efforts.

Good luck with your certification exam, and thanks for allowing us to help you achieve your goals.

Keith Weiskamp

Keith Weiskamp
Publisher, Certification Insider Press

NT Workstation 4

Ed Tittel

Kurt Hudson

J. Michael Stewart

Certification Insider™ Press

An imprint of

 CORIOLIS GROUP BOOKS

an International Thomson Publishing company I(T)P®

Albany, NY • Belmont, CA • Bonn • Boston • Cincinnati • Detroit • Johannesburg • London
Madrid • Melbourne • Mexico City • New York • Paris • Singapore • Tokyo • Toronto • Washington

MCSE NT Workstation 4 Exam Cram

Copyright © The Coriolis Group, 1998

Limits of Liability and Disclaimer of Warranty

Trademarks

The Coriolis Group, Inc.
An International Thomson Publishing Company
14455 N. Hayden Road, Suite 220
Scottsdale, Arizona 85260

602/483-0192
FAX 602/483-0193
http://www.coriolis.com

Printed in the United States of America
ISBN: 1-57610-193-2
10 9 8 7 6 5 4 3 2 1

Publisher
Keith Weiskamp

Project Editor
Jeff Kellum

Technical Editors
Amy Horowitz
Kim Shivler

Production Coordinator
Kim Eoff

Cover Design
Anthony Stock

Interior Design
Jimmie Young
April Nielsen

(From L. to R., Ed Tittel, J. Michael Stewart, Kurt Hudson)

About The Authors

Ed Tittel

Ed Tittel recently worked as an instructor and course developer for American Research Group, where he developed and taught from a set of materials on Windows NT 4, both Workstation and Server. Ed is also a regular contributor to *Windows NT* magazine and an instructor for Softbank Forums at its Interop and NT Intranet tradeshows. Prior to going out on his own in 1994, Ed worked at Novell for six years, starting as a field engineer and departing as the director of technical marketing.

Ed has written over 40 computer books, including *HTML for Dummies* (with Stephen N. James, IDG Books Worldwide, 3rd ed., 1997); *Networking Windows NT 4.0 for Dummies* (with Mary Madden and Dave Smith, IDG Books Worldwide, 1996); and a variety of titles on Windows NT, NetWare, networking, and Web-related topics.

Ed has written over 200 articles for publications such as *Byte, InfoWorld, LAN Magazine, LAN Times, The NetWare Advisor, PC Magazine,* and *WindowsUser.* At present, Ed also writes a biweekly column for *Interop Online.* You can reach Ed by email at etittel@lanw.com or on the Web at www.lanw.com/etbio.htm.

Kurt Hudson

Kurt Hudson is a technical author, trainer, and consultant in the field of networking and computer-related technologies. For the past six years, he has focused his energy on learning and teaching technical skills. He has written several training manuals and books for government and private industry on topics ranging from inventory control to network administration.

As a former trainer for the U.S. Air Force, Kurt worked on high-security government projects employing technologies most people see only in the cinema. During his six-year engagement with the military, he earned three medals for improving systems efficiency, training excellence, and increasing national security. After departing the U.S. Air Force, he worked for a variety of private corporations, including Unisys and Productivity Point International, where he continued to learn and teach technical topics.

Since achieving Microsoft Certified Systems Engineer (MCSE) and Microsoft Certified Trainer (MCT) ratings, he has been writing books and conducting training sessions that have helped many individuals succeed in their pursuit of professional certification. You can reach Kurt on the Internet at kurtlh@onr.com or on the Web at www.onr.com/user/kurtlh.

James Michael Stewart

James Michael Stewart is a full-time writer focusing on Windows NT and Internet topics. In addition to working on the *Exam Cram* series, he has recently co-authored the *Intranet Bible* (IDG Books Worldwide, 1997) and the *Hip Pocket Guide to HTML 3.2* (IDG Books Worldwide, 1997). He also contributed to *Windows NT Networking for Dummies* (IDG Books Worldwide, 1997), *Building Windows NT Web Servers* (IDG Books Worldwide, 1997), and *Windows NT, Step by Step* (Microsoft Press, 1995).

Michael has written articles for numerous print and online publications, including C|Net, *InfoWorld*, *Windows NT* magazine, and *Datamation*. He is also the moderator for a Softbank online forum focusing on NT, located at http://forums.sbexpos.com/forums-interop/get/HOS_3.html and a former leader of an NT study group at the Central Texas LAN Association. He is currently an MCP for Windows NT Server 4, Workstation, and Windows 95.

Michael graduated in 1992 from the University of Texas at Austin with a bachelor's degree in Philosophy. Despite his degree, his computer knowledge is self-acquired, based on almost 14 years of hands-on experience. Michael has been active on the Internet for quite some time, where most people know him by his nom de wire, McIntyre. You can reach Michael by email at michael@lanw.com or through his Web pages at www.lanw.com/jmsbio.htm or www.impactonline.com/.

Acknowledgments

Ed Tittel

Thanks again to Keith Weiskamp at The Coriolis Group for backing the *Exam Cram* series. I'd also like to thank the Coriolis team that helped turn our idea into a real deal, including Shari Jo Hehr, Josh Mills, Brad Grannis, and many others. Finally, thanks again to Jeff Kellum, our stalwart project editor, for bringing two more titles to a successful conclusion.

Once again, everybody at LANWrights—including David (DJ) Johnson, who's not quite on board yet—pitched in and made good on some tough deadlines that were made even tougher by tightening up the schedule. Thanks also to my co-authors, Kurt Hudson and James Michael Stewart, who came through when it counted. There's no way we could've finished this project on time without Dawn Rader, our writer, editor, and project manager who kept us moving, even when we had no clue about our final destinations. Likewise, Mary Burmeister, our Jill of all trades, and Natanya Pitts, Webmistress and HTML Goddess without compare, produced screen shots, graphics, tables, and the glossary. Thanks a million to each and every one of you. I'm also truly sad to report that my beloved Yellow lab, Dusty, passed away during this project, and cut a huge hole into my life (and heart). I hope you're always walking and that your tail is wagging, pup, wherever you may be. I miss you!

Kurt Hudson

I would like to thank the following people for their professional contributions to this book: Julie A. Hudson, Doug Dexter, and Lori Marcinkiewicz.

James Michael Stewart

Thanks to my boss and co-author, Ed Tittel, for including me in this book series. Thanks to Dawn Rader, without you this book would have never been complete. A warm howdy to Mary Burmeister and Natanya Pitts (our other work slaves). To my parents, Dave and Sue, thanks for always being there and making it clear how much you care. To Dave and Laura, buy the $20,000 home theater and I'll camp on our couch and cook your meals! To Mark, the cult of the Pocketgods will come back to haunt you, it is already noted in your permanent record. To HERbert, you are the only cat I know that likes to get a buzz. And finally, as always, to Elvis—its wasn't the drugs, the alcohol, or the women, it was those darn fried peanut butter and banana sandwiches. Are you just weird or what?

Contents

. . . .

Introduction

Welcome to *MCSE NT Workstation 4 Exam Cram!* This book aims to help you get ready to take—and pass—the Microsoft certification test numbered "Exam 70-073," titled "Implementing and Supporting Microsoft Windows NT Workstation 4." This introduction explains Microsoft's certification programs in general and talks about how the *Exam Cram* series can help you prepare for Microsoft's certification exams.

Exam Cram books help you understand and appreciate the subjects and materials you need to pass Microsoft certification exams. *Exam Cram* books are aimed strictly at test preparation and review. They do not teach you everything you need to know about a topic. Instead, we (the authors) present and dissect the questions and problems that we've found that you're likely to encounter on a test. We've worked from Microsoft's own training materials, preparation guides, and tests, and from a battery of third-party test preparation tools. Our aim is to bring together as much information as possible about Microsoft certification exams.

Nevertheless, to completely prepare yourself for any Microsoft test, we recommend that you begin your studies with some classroom training, or that you pick up and read one of the many study guides available from Microsoft and third-party vendors. We also strongly recommend that you install, configure, and fool around with the software or environment that you'll be tested on, because nothing beats hands-on experience and familiarity when it comes to understanding the questions you're likely to encounter on a certification test. Book learning is essential, but hands-on experience is the best teacher of all!

The Microsoft Certified Professional (MCP) Program

The MCP Program currently includes four separate tracks, each of which boasts its own special acronym (as a would-be certificant, you need to have a high tolerance for alphabet soup of all kinds):

➤ **MCPS (Microsoft Certified Product Specialist)** This is the least prestigious of all the certification tracks from Microsoft. Attaining MCPS status requires an individual to pass at least one core operating system exam. Passing any of the major Microsoft operating system exams, including those for Windows 95, Windows NT Workstation, or Windows NT Server, qualifies an individual for MCPS credentials. Individuals can demonstrate proficiency with additional Microsoft products by passing additional certification exams.

➤ **MCSD (Microsoft Certified Solution Developer)** This track is aimed primarily at developers. This credential indicates that individuals who pass it are able to design and implement custom business solutions around particular Microsoft development tools, technologies, and operating systems. To obtain an MCSD, an individual must demonstrate the ability to analyze and interpret user requirements; select and integrate products, platforms, tools, and technologies; design and implement code and customize applications; and perform necessary software tests and quality assurance operations.

To become an MCSD, an individual must pass a total of four exams: two core exams plus two elective exams. The two core exams are the Microsoft Windows Operating Systems And Services Architecture I and II (WOSSA I and WOSSA II, numbered 70-150 and 70-151). Elective exams cover specific Microsoft applications and languages, including Visual Basic, C++, the Microsoft Foundation Classes, Access, SQL Server, Excel, and more.

➤ **MCT (Microsoft Certified Trainer)** Microsoft Certified Trainers are individuals who are deemed capable of delivering elements of the official Microsoft training curriculum, based on technical knowledge and instructional ability. Thus, it is necessary for an individual seeking MCT credentials (which are granted on a course-by-course basis) to pass the related certification exam for a course and successfully complete the official Microsoft training in the subject area, as well as demonstrate an ability to teach.

This latter criterion may be satisfied by proving that one has already attained training certification from Novell, Banyan, Lotus, the Santa Cruz Operation, or Cisco, or by taking a Microsoft-sanctioned work shop on instruction. Microsoft makes it clear that MCTs are an important cog in the Microsoft training channels. Instructors must be MCTs to teach in any of Microsoft's official training channels, including its affiliated Authorized Technical Education Centers ATECs), Authorized Academic Training Programs (AATPs), and the Microsoft Online Institute (MOLI).

➤ **MCSE (Microsoft Certified Systems Engineer)** Anyone who possesses a current MCSE is warranted to possess a high level of expertise with Windows NT (either version 3.51 or 4) and other Microsoft operating systems and products. This credential is designed to prepare individuals to plan, implement, maintain, and support information systems and networks built around Microsoft Windows NT and its BackOffice family of products.

To obtain an MCSE, an individual must pass four core operating system exams, plus two elective exams. The operating system exams require individuals to demonstrate competence with desktop and server operating systems and with networking components.

At least two Windows NT-related exams must be passed to obtain an MCSE: Implementing and Supporting Windows NT Server (version 3.51 or 4) and Implementing and Supporting Windows NT Server (version 3.51 or 4) in the Enterprise. These tests are intended to indicate an individual's knowledge of Windows NT in smaller, simpler networks and in larger, more complex, and heterogeneous networks, respectively.

Two more tests must be passed. These tests are networking and desk top operating system related. At present, the networking requirement can only be satisfied by passing the Networking Essentials test. The desktop operating system test can be satisfied by passing a Windows 3.1, Windows For Workgroups 3.11, Windows NT Workstation (the version must match whichever core curriculum is pursued), or Windows 95 test.

The two remaining exams are elective exams. The elective exams can be in any number of subject or product areas, primarily BackOffice components. These include tests on SQL Server, SNA Server, Exchange, Systems Management Server, and the like. But it is also possible to test out on electives by taking advanced networking topics like Internetworking with Microsoft TCP/IP (here again, the version of Windows NT involved must match the version for the core requirements taken).

Whatever mix of tests is completed toward MCSE certification, individuals must pass six tests to meet the MCSE requirements. It's not ncommon for the entire process to take a year or so, and many individuals find that they must take a test more than once to pass. Our primary goal with the Exam Cram series is to make it possible, given proper study and preparation, to pass all of the MCSE tests on the first try.

Finally, certification is an ongoing activity. Once a Microsoft product becomes obsolete, MCSEs (and other MCPs) typically have a 12 to 18 month time frame in which they can become recertified on current product versions (if individuals do not get recertified within the specified time period, their certification is no longer valid). Because technology keeps changing and new products continually supplant old ones, this should come as no surprise.

The best place to keep tabs on the MCP Program and its various certifications is on the Microsoft Web site. The current root URL for the MCP program is titled "Certification Online" at www.microsoft.com/Train_Cert/mcp/default.htm.Microsoft's Web site changes frequently, so if this URL doesn't work, try using the Search tool on Microsoft's site with either "MCP" or the quoted phrase "Microsoft Certified Professional Program" as the search string. This will help you find the latest and most accurate information about the company's certification programs. You can also obtain a special CD that contains a copy of the Microsoft Education And Certification Roadmap. The Roadmap covers much of the same information as the Web site, and it is updated quarterly. To obtain your copy of the CD, call Microsoft at 1-800-636-7544, Monday to Friday, 6:30 a.m. through 7:30 p.m. Pacific Time.

Taking A Certification Exam

Alas, testing is not free. You'll be charged $100 for each test you take, whether you pass or fail. In the United States and Canada, tests are administered by Sylvan Prometric. Sylvan Prometric can be reached at 1-800-755-3926 or 1-800-755-EXAM, any time from 7:00 a.m. to 6:00 p.m. (Central Time), Monday through Friday. If this number doesn't work, try 1-612-896-7000 or 1-612-820-5707.

To schedule an exam, call at least one day in advance. To cancel or reschedule an exam, you must call at least 12 hours before the scheduled test time (or you may be charged regardless). When calling Sylvan Prometric, please have the following information ready for the telesales staffer who handles your call:

➤ Your name, organization, and mailing address.

➤ Your Microsoft Test ID. (For most U.S. citizens, this is your social security number. Citizens of other nations can use their taxpayer IDs or make other arrangements with the order taker.)

➤ The name and number of the exam you wish to take. (For this book, the exam number is 70-073, and the exam name is "Implementing and Supporting Windows NT Workstation 4.")

➤ A method of payment must be arranged. (The most convenient approach is to supply a valid credit card number with sufficient available credit. Otherwise, payments by check, money order, or purchase order must be received before a test can be scheduled. If the latter methods are required, ask your order taker for more details.)

When you show up to take a test, try to arrive at least 15 minutes before the scheduled time slot. You must bring and supply two forms of identification, one of which must be a photo ID.

All exams are completely closed-book. In fact, you will not be permitted to take anything with you into the testing area, but you will be furnished with a blank sheet of paper and a pen. We suggest that you immediately write down the most critical information about the test you're taking on the sheet of paper. *Exam Cram* books provide a brief reference—The Cram Sheet located inside the front cover—that lists the essential information from the book in distilled form. You will have some time to compose yourself, to record this information, and even to take a sample orientation exam before you must begin the real thing. We suggest you take the orientation test before taking your exam; because they're all more or less identical in layout, behavior, and controls, you probably won't need to do this more than once.

When you complete a Microsoft certification exam, the software will tell you whether you've passed or failed. All tests are scored on a basis of 1,000 points, and results are broken into several topical areas. Even if you fail, we suggest you ask for—and keep—the detailed printed report from the test administrator. You can use the report to help you prepare for another go-round, if needed. If you need to retake an exam, you'll have to call Sylvan Prometric, schedule a new test date, and pay another $100.

Tracking MCP Status

As soon as you pass any Microsoft operating system exam, you'll attain Product Specialist (MCPS) status. Microsoft also generates transcripts that indicate the exams you have passed and your corresponding test scores. You can order a transcript by email at any time by sending an email addressed to mcp@msprograms.com. You can also obtain a copy of your transcript by downloading the latest version of the MCT Guide from the Web site and consulting the section titled "Key Contacts" for a list of telephone numbers and related contacts.

Once you pass the necessary set of six exams, you'll be certified as an MCSE. Official certification normally takes anywhere from four to six weeks, so don't expect to get your credentials overnight. When the package arrives, it will include a Welcome Kit that contains a number of elements, including:

➤ An MCSE certificate, suitable for framing, along with an MCSE Professional Program membership card and lapel pin.

➤ A license to use the MCP logo, thereby allowing you to use the logo in advertisements, promotions, and documents, and on letterhead, business cards, and so on. Along with the license comes an MCP log sheet, which includes camera-ready artwork. (Note: before using any of the artwork, you must sign and return a licensing agreement that indicates you'll abide by its terms and conditions.)

➤ A one-year subscription to TechNet, a collection of CDs that includes software, documentation, service packs, databases, and more technical information than you can possibly ever read. In our minds, this is the best and most tangible benefit of attaining MCSE status.

➤ A subscription to *Microsoft Certified Professional* magazine, which provides ongoing data about testing and certification activities, requirements, and changes to the program.

➤ A free Priority Comprehensive 10-pack with Microsoft Product Support, and a 25 percent discount on additional Priority Comprehensive 10-packs. This lets you place up to 10 free calls to Microsoft's technical support operation at a higher-than-normal priority level.

➤ A one-year subscription to the Microsoft Beta Evaluation program. This subscription will get you all beta products from Microsoft for the next year. (This does not include developer products. You must join the MSDN program or become an MCSD to qualify for developer beta products.)

Many people believe that the benefits of MCSE certification go well beyond the perks that Microsoft provides to newly anointed members of this elite group. We're starting to see more job listings that request or require applicants to have an MCSE, and many individuals who complete the program can qualify for increases in pay or responsibility. As an official recognition of hard work and broad knowledge, MCSE certification is indeed a badge of honor in many IT organizations.

How To Prepare For An Exam

At a minimum, preparing for a Windows NT Workstation-related test requires that you obtain and study the following materials:

➤ The Microsoft Windows NT Workstation (or online documentation and help files, which ship on the CD with the product and also appear on the TechNet CDs).

➤ The *Microsoft Windows NT Workstation Resource Kit* (for Microsoft NT Server Version 4), published by Microsoft Press, Redmond, WA, 1996. ISBN: 1-57231-344-7. Even though it costs a whopping $69.95 (list price), it's worth every penny—not just for the documentation, but also for the utilities and other software included (which add considerably to the base functionality of Windows NT Workstation 4).

➤ The exam prep materials, practice tests, and self-assessment exams on the Microsoft Training And Certification download page (www. microsoft.com/Train_Cert/download/downld.htm). Find the materials, download them, and use them!

➤ This *Exam Cram* book! It's the first and last thing you should read before taking the exam.

In addition, you'll probably find any or all of the following materials useful in your quest for Windows NT Workstaion expertise:

➤ **Microsoft Training Kits** Although there's no training kit currently available from Microsoft Press for Windows NT Workstation 4, many other topics have such kits. It's worthwhile to check to see if Microsoft has come out with anything by the time you need the information.

➤ **Study Guides** Publishers like Sybex, New Riders Press, Que (in cooperation with Productivity Point, a well-known training company and Microsoft ATEC), and others all offer so-called MCSE study guides of one kind or another. We've looked at them and found the Sybex and Que titles to be fairly informative and helpful for learning the materials necessary to pass the tests.

➤ **Classroom Training** ATECs, AATPs, MOLI, and unlicensed third-party training companies (like Wave Technologies, American Research Group, Learning Tree, Data-Tech, and others) all offer classroom training on Windows NT Workstation 4. These companies aim to help prepare network administrators to run Windows NT installations and pass the MCSE tests. Although such training runs upwards of $350 per day in class, most of the individuals lucky enough to partake (including your humble authors, who've even taught such courses)find them to be quite worthwhile.

➤ **Other Publications** You'll find direct references to other publications and resources in this book, but there's no shortage of materials available about Windows NT. To help you sift through some of the publications out there, we end each chapter with a "Need To Know More?" section that provides pointers to more complete and exhaustive resources covering the chapter's information. This should give you an idea of where we think you should look for further discussion.

➤ **The TechNet CD** TechNet is a monthly CD subscription available from Microsoft. TechNet includes all the Windows NT BackOffice Resource Kits and their product documentation. In addition, TechNet provides the contents of the Microsoft Knowledge Base and many kinds of software, white papers, training materials, and other good stuff. TechNet also contains all service packs, interim release patches, and supplemental driver software released since the last major version for most Microsoft programs and all Microsoft operating systems. A one-year subscription costs $299—worth every penny, even if only for the download time it saves.

By far, this set of required and recommend materials represents a nonpareil collection of sources and resources for Windows NT Workstation topics and software. We anticipate that you'll find this book belongs in this company. In the section that follows, we explain how this book works, and we give you some good reasons why this book counts as a member of the required and recommended materials list.

About This Book

Each topical *Exam Cram* chapter follows a regular structure, along with graphical cues about especially important or useful material. Here's the structure of a typical chapter:

➤ **Opening Hotlists** Each chapter begins with lists of the terms, tools, and techniques that you must learn and understand before you can be fully conversant with that chapter's subject matter. We follow the hotlists with one or two introductory paragraphs to set the stage for the rest of the chapter.

➤ **Topical Coverage** After the opening hotlists, each chapter covers a series of at least four topics related to the chapter's subject title. Throughout this section, we highlight material most likely to appear on a test using a special Exam Alert layout, like this:

This is what an Exam Alert looks like. Normally, an Exam Alert stresses concepts, terms, software, or activities that will likely appear in one or more certification test questions. For that reason, we think any information found offset in Exam Alert format is worthy of unusual attentiveness on your part. Indeed, most of the facts appearing in The Cram Sheet (inside the front cover of this book) appear as Exam Alerts within the text.

Occasionally, you'll see tables called "Vital Statistics." The contents of vital statistics tables are worthy of an extra once-over. These tables contain informational tidbits that might well show up in a test question.

Even if material isn't flagged as an Exam Alert or included in a vital statistics table, *all* the contents of this book are at least tangential to something test-related. To focus on quick test preparation, this book is lean; you'll find that what appears in the meat of each chapter is critical knowledge.

We have also provided tips that will help build a better foundation of NT-based knowledge. Although the information may not be on the exam, it is highly relevant and will help you become a better test taker.

This is how tips are formatted. Keep your eyes open for these, and you'll become an Workstation test guru in no time!

➤ **Exam Prep Questions** This section presents a series of mock test questions and explanations of both correct and incorrect answers. We also try to point out especially tricky questions by using a special icon, like this:

Ordinarily, this icon flags the presence of an especially devious question, if not an outright trick question. Trick questions are calculated to "trap" you if you don't read them more than once, and carefully, at that. Although they're not ubiquitous, such questions make regular appearances in the Microsoft exams. That's why we say exam questions are as much about reading comprehension as they are about knowing Windows NT Workstation material inside out and backwards.

➤ **Details And Resources** Every chapter ends with a section titled "Need To Know More?". This section provides direct pointers to Microsoft and third-party resources that offer further details on the chapter's subject. In addition, this section tries to rate the quality and thoroughness of the topic's coverage by each resource. If you find a resource you like in this collection, use it. But don't feel compelled to use all the resources. On the other hand, we only recommend resources we us on a regular basis, so none of our recommendations will be a waste of your time or money.

The bulk of the book follows this chapter structure slavishly. But, there are a few other elements that we'd like to point out. There is an answer key to the sample test that appears in Chapter 19, and a reasonably exhaustive glossary of Windows NT and Microsoft terminology. Finally, look for The Cram Sheet, which appears inside the front cover of this *Exam Cram* book. It is a very valuable tool that represents a condensed and compiled collection of facts, figures, and tips that we think you should memorize before taking the test. Because you can dump this information out of your head onto a piece of paper before answering any exam questions, you can master this information by brute force—you only need to remember it long enough to write it down when you walk into the test room. You might even want to look at it in the car or in the lobby of the testing center just before you walk in to take the test.

How To Use This Book

If you're prepping for a first-time test, we've structured the topics in this book to build on one another. Therefore, some topics in later chapters make more sense after you've read earlier chapters. That's why we suggest you read this book from front to back for your initial test preparation. If you need to brush up on a topic or you have to bone up for a second try, use the index or table of contents to go straight to the topics and questions that you need to study. Beyond the tests, we think you'll find this book useful as a tightly focused reference to some of the most important aspects of Windows NT. (For us, several chapters have already come in handy while working with our own in-house Windows NT network.)

Given all the book's elements and its specialized focus, we've tried to create a tool that you can use to prepare for—and pass—Microsoft Certification Exam 70-073, "Implementing and Supporting Microsoft Windows NT Workstation 4." Please share your feedback on the book with us, especially if you have ideas about how we can improve it for future test-takers. We'll consider everything you say carefully, and we'll respond to all suggestions. You can reach us via email at etittel@lanw.com (Ed Tittel), hudlogic@worldnet.att.net (Kurt Hudson), and michael@lanw.com (James Michael Stewart). Please remember to include the title of the book in your message; otherwise, we'll be forced to guess which book you're making a suggestion about. And we don't like to guess—we want to KNOW!

Thanks, and enjoy the book!

Microsoft Certification Tests

1

Terms you'll need to understand:

√ Domain Model

√ Radio button

√ Checkbox

√ Exhibit

√ Multiple-choice question formats

√ Careful reading

√ Process of elimination

Techniques you'll need to master:

√ Preparing to take a certification exam

√ Practicing to make perfect

√ Making the best use of the testing software

√ Budgeting your time

√ Saving the hardest questions until last

√ Guessing as a last resort

As experiences go, test-taking is not something that most people anticipate eagerly, no matter how well they're prepared. In most cases, familiarity helps ameliorate test anxiety. In plain English, this means you probably won't be as nervous when you take your fourth or fifth Microsoft certification exam as you will be when you take your first one.

But no matter whether it's your first test or your tenth, understanding the exam-taking particulars (how much time to spend on questions, the setting you'll be in, and so on) and the testing software will help you concentrate on the material rather than on the environment. Likewise, mastering a few basic test-taking skills should help you recognize—and perhaps even out-fox—some of the tricks and gotchas you're bound to find in some of the Microsoft test questions.

In this chapter, we explain the testing environment and software, as well as describe some proven test-taking strategies you should be able to use to your advantage. We've compiled this information based on the 30-plus Microsoft certification exams we have taken ourselves, and we've also drawn on the advice of our friends and colleagues, some of whom have also taken more than 30 tests each!

The Testing Situation

When you arrive at the Sylvan Prometric Testing Center where you scheduled your test, you'll need to sign in with a test coordinator. He or she will ask you to produce two forms of identification, one of which must be a photo ID. Once you've signed in and your time slot arrives, you'll be asked to deposit any books, bags, or other items you brought with you, and you'll be escorted into a closed room. Typically, that room will be furnished with anywhere from one to half a dozen computers, and each workstation is separated from the others by dividers designed to keep you from seeing what's happening on someone else's computer.

You'll be furnished with a pen or pencil and a blank sheet of paper, or in some cases, an erasable plastic sheet and an erasable felt-tip pen. You're allowed to write down any information you want on this sheet, and you can write stuff on both sides of the page. We suggest that you memorize as much as possible of the material that appears on The Cram Sheet (inside the front of this book), and then write that information down on the blank sheet as soon as you sit down in front of the test machine. You can refer to it any time you like during the test, but you'll have to surrender the sheet when you leave the room.

Most test rooms feature a wall with a large picture window. This is to permit the test coordinator to monitor the room, to prevent test-takers from talking to one another, and to observe anything out of the ordinary that might go on. The test coordinator will have preloaded the Microsoft certification test you've signed up for—for this book, that's Exam 70-073—and you'll be permitted to start as soon as you're seated in front of the machine.

All Microsoft certification exams permit you to take up to a certain maximum amount of time to complete the test (the test itself will tell you, and it maintains an on-screen counter/clock so that you can check the time remaining any time you like). Exam 70-073 consists of between 50 and 65 questions, randomly selected from a pool of questions. You're permitted to take up to 90 minutes to complete the exam.

All Microsoft certification exams are computer generated and use a multiple-choice format. Although this might sound easy, the questions are constructed not just to check your mastery of basic facts and figures about Windows NT Workstation, but also require you to evaluate one or more sets of circumstances or requirements. Often, you'll be asked to give more than one answer to a question; likewise, you may be asked to select the best or most effective solution to a problem from a range of choices, all of which technically are correct. It's quite an adventure, and it involves real thinking. This book will show you what to expect and how to deal with the problems, puzzles, and predicaments you're likely to find on the test.

Test Layout And Design

A typical test question is depicted in Question 1. It's a multiple-choice question that requires you to select a single correct answer. Following the question is a brief summary of each potential answer and why it was either right or wrong.

Question 1

Which of the following is not a directory or file permission?

○ a. Read

○ b. List

○ c. Create Directory

○ d. Change

○ e. Add

Read is both a directory and a file permission. Therefore, answer a is incorrect. List is a directory permission. Therefore, answer b is incorrect. **Create Directory is not a permission. Therefore, answer c is correct.** Change is both a directory and file permission. Therefore, answer d is incorrect. Add is a directory permission. Therefore, answer e is incorrect.

This sample question corresponds closely to those you'll see on Microsoft certification tests. To select the correct answer during the test, you would position the cursor over the radio button next to answer c and click the mouse to select that particular choice. The only difference between the certification test and this question is that the real questions are not immediately followed by the answer key.

Next, we'll examine a question that requires choosing multiple answers. This type of question provides checkboxes, rather than the radio buttons, for marking all appropriate selections.

Question 2

When you create a copy of an existing user account, what pieces of information are reset or left blank? [Check all correct answers]

❑ a. User Must Change Password At Next Logon

❑ b. User Name

❑ c. Account Disabled

❑ d. Password Never Expires

❑ e. Profile settings

❑ f. Password

❑ g. Group memberships

The items that are reset or left blank when a user account is copied are **User Must Change Password At Next Logon, User Name, Account Disabled, and Password. Therefore, answers a, b, c, and f are correct.** Password Never Expires, profile settings, and group membership options remain as they were set in the original account. Therefore, answers d, e, and g are incorrect.

For this type of question, one or more answers must be selected to answer the question correctly. As far as we can tell (and Microsoft won't comment), such questions are scored as wrong unless all the required selections are chosen. In other words, a partially correct answer does not result in partial credit when the test is scored. For Question 2, you would have to position the cursor over the checkboxes next to items a, b, c, and f to obtain credit for a correct answer.

Although there are many forms in which these two basic types of questions can appear, they constitute the foundation upon which all the Microsoft certification exam questions rest. More complex questions may include so-called "exhibits," which are usually screen shots of some Windows NT utility or another. For some of these questions, you'll be asked to make a selection by clicking a checkbox or radio button on the screen shot itself; for others, you'll be expected to use the information displayed therein to guide your answer to the question. Familiarity with the underlying utility is the key to the correct answer.

Other questions involving exhibits may use charts or network diagrams to help document a workplace scenario that you'll be asked to troubleshoot or configure. Paying careful attention to such exhibits is the key to success— be prepared to toggle between the picture and the question as you work. Often, both are complex enough that you might not be able to remember all of either one!

Using Microsoft's Test Software Effectively

A well-known test-taking principle is to read over the entire test from start to finish first, but to answer only those questions that you feel abso- lutely sure of on the first pass. On subsequent passes, you can dive into more complex questions, knowing how many such questions you have to deal with.

Fortunately, Microsoft test software makes this approach easy to imple- ment. At the bottom of each question, you'll find a checkbox that permits you to mark that question for a later visit.

> *Note: Marking questions makes review easier, but you can return to any question by clicking the Forward and Back buttons repeatedly until you get to the question.*

As you read each question, if you answer only those you're sure of and mark for review those that you're not, you can keep going through a decreasing list of open questions as you knock the trickier ones off in order.

There's at least one potential benefit to reading the test over completely before answering the trickier questions: Sometimes, you find information in later questions that sheds more light on earlier ones. Other times, information you read in later questions might jog your memory about Windows NT facts, figures, or behavior that also will help with earlier questions. Either way, you'll come out ahead if you defer those questions about which you're not absolutely sure of the answer(s).

Keep working on the questions until you are absolutely sure of all your answers or until you know you'll run out of time. If there are still unanswered questions, you'll want to zip through them and guess. No answer guarantees no credit for a question, and a guess has at least a chance of being correct. This strategy only works because blank answers and incorrect answers are equally wrong.

 At the very end of your test period, you're better off guessing than leaving questions blank or unanswered.

Taking Testing Seriously

The most important advice we can give you about taking any Microsoft test is this: Read each question carefully! Some questions are deliberately ambiguous; some use double negatives; others use terminology in incredibly precise ways. We've taken numerous practice tests and real tests ourselves, and in nearly every test, we've missed at least one question because we didn't read it closely or carefully enough.

Here are some suggestions on how to deal with the tendency to jump to an answer too quickly:

➤ Make sure you read every word in the question. If you find yourself jumping ahead impatiently, go back and start over.

➤ As you read, try to restate the question in your own terms. If you can do this, you should be able to pick the correct answer(s) much more easily.

➤ When returning to a question after your initial read-through, reread every word again—otherwise, the mind falls quickly into a rut. Sometimes, seeing a question afresh after turning your attention elsewhere lets you see something you missed before, but the strong tendency is to see what you've seen before. Try to avoid that tendency at all costs.

➤ If you return to a question more than twice, try to articulate to yourself what you don't understand about the question, why the answers don't appear to make sense, or what appears to be missing. If you chew on the subject for a while, your subconscious might provide the details that are lacking, or you may notice a "trick" that will point to the right answer.

Above all, try to deal with each question by thinking through what you know about the NT utilities, characteristics, behaviors, facts, and figures involved. By reviewing what you know (and what you've written down on your information sheet), you'll often recall or understand things sufficiently to determine the answer to the question.

Question-Handling Strategies

Based on the tests we've taken, a couple of interesting trends in the answers have become apparent. For those questions that take only a single answer, usually two or three of the answers will be obviously incorrect, and two of the answers will be plausible. But, of course, only one can be correct. Unless the answer leaps out at you (and if it does, reread the question to look for a trick; sometimes those are the ones you're most likely to get wrong), begin the process of answering by eliminating those answers that are obviously wrong.

Things to look for in the "obviously wrong" category include spurious menu choices or utility names, nonexistent software options, and terminology you've never seen before. If you've done your homework for a test, no valid information should be completely new to you. In that case, unfamiliar or bizarre terminology probably indicates a totally bogus answer. As long as you're sure what's right, it's easy to eliminate what's wrong.

Numerous questions assume that the default behavior of a particular utility is in effect. It's essential, therefore, to understand that the default behavior for Windows NT security is to grant Full Control rights to the local group named Everyone when dealing with matters of access and rights. The same is true for many other aspects of the system. If you know the defaults and understand what they mean, this knowledge will help you cut through many Gordian knots.

Likewise, when dealing with questions that require multiple answers—such as one that asks what *must* be installed on Windows NT Workstation for Client Service for NetWare (CSNW) to work—it's vital to remember all aspects involved. In this example, you should remember that CSNW automatically installs NWLink as part of its own installation if that protocol isn't already present on the Windows NT Workstation in question. In English, this means that it's not necessary to install the protocol separately, because CSNW does it for you if NWLink is not already available. Certainly, NWLink is required for CSNW to work, but it's not necessary that it be installed before installing CSNW. This, too, qualifies as an example of why "careful reading" is so important.

As you work your way through the test, another counter that Microsoft thankfully provides will come in handy—the number of questions completed and questions outstanding. Budget your time by making sure that you've completed one-fourth of the questions one-quarter of the way through the test period (or between 13 and 17 questions in the first 22 or 23 minutes). Check again three-quarters of the way through (between 39 and 51 questions in the first 66 to 69 minutes).

If you're not through after 85 minutes, use the last 5 minutes to guess your way through the remaining questions. Remember, guesses are potentially more valuable than blank answers, because blanks are always wrong, but a guess might turn out to be right. If you haven't a clue with any of the remaining questions, pick answers at random, or choose all a's, b's, and so on. The important thing is to submit a test for scoring that has some answer for every question.

Mastering The Inner Game

In the final analysis, knowledge breeds confidence, and confidence breeds success. If you study the materials in this book carefully and review all of the Exam Prep questions at the end of each chapter, you should be aware of those areas where additional studying is required.

Next, follow up by reading some or all of the materials recommended in the "Need To Know More?" section at the end of each chapter. The idea is to become familiar enough with the concepts and situations that you find in the sample questions to be able to reason your way through similar situations on a real test. If you know the material, you have every right to be confident that you can pass the test.

Once you've worked your way through the book, take the practice test in Chapter 19. This will provide a reality check and will help you identify areas you need to study further. Make sure you follow up and review materials related to the questions you miss before scheduling a real test. Only when you've covered all the ground and feel comfortable with the whole scope of the practice test, should you take a real test.

 If you take our practice test and don't score at least 75 percent correct, you'll want to practice further. At a minimum, download the Personal Exam Prep (PEP) tests and the self-assessment tests from the Microsoft Training And Certification Web site's download page (its location appears in the next section). If you're more ambitious or better funded, you might want to purchase a practice test from one of the third-party vendors that offers them. We've had good luck with tests from Transcender Corporation and from Self Test Software (the vendors who supply the PEP tests). See the next section in this chapter for contact information.

Armed with the information in this book, and with the determination to augment your knowledge, you should be able to pass the certification exam. But if you don't work at it, you'll spend the test fee more than once before you finally do pass. If you prepare seriously, the execution should go flawlessly. Good luck!

Additional Resources

By far, the best source of information about Microsoft certification tests comes from Microsoft itself. Because its products and technologies—and the tests that go with them—change frequently, the best place to go for exam-related information is online.

If you haven't already visited the Microsoft Training And Certification pages, do so right now. As we're writing this chapter, the Training And Certification home page resides at www.microsoft.com/Train_Cert/ (see Figure 1.1).

Note: The Training And Certification home page might not be there by the time you read this, or it may have been replaced by something new and different, because things change regularly on the Microsoft site. Should this happen, please read the section titled "Coping With Change On The Web," later in this chapter.

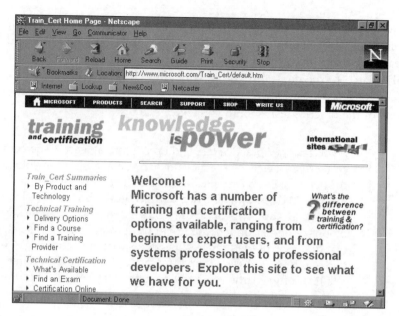

Figure 1.1 The Training And Certification home page should be your starting point for further investigation of the most current exam and preparation information.

The menu options in the left column of the home page point to the most important sources of information in the Training And Certification pages. Here's what to check out:

▶ **Train_Cert Summaries/By Product and Technology** Use this to jump to product-based summaries of all classroom education, training materials, study guides, and other information for specific products. Under the heading of Microsoft Windows/Windows NT, you'll find an entire page of information about Windows NT training and certification. This tells you a lot about your training and preparation options, and it mentions all the tests that relate to Windows NT.

▶ **Technical Certification/Find an Exam** This pulls up a search tool that lets you list all Microsoft exams, as well as locate all exams pertinent to any Microsoft certification (MCPS, MCSE, MCT, and so on), or those exams that cover a particular product. This tool is quite useful not only to examine the options, but also to obtain specific test preparation information, because each exam has its own associated preparation guide. For this test, be sure to grab the one for 70-073.

➤ **Site Tools/Downloads** Here, you'll find a list of the files and practice tests that Microsoft makes available to the public. These include several items worth downloading, especially the Certification Update, the Personal Exam Prep (PEP) tests, various assessment exams, and a general Exam Study Guide. Try to make time to peruse these materials before taking your first test.

Of course, these are just the high points of what's available in the Microsoft Training And Certification pages. As you browse through them—and we strongly recommend that you do—you'll probably find other things we didn't mention here that are every bit as interesting and compelling.

Coping With Change On The Web

Sooner or later, all the specifics we've shared with you about the Microsoft Training And Certification pages, and all the other Web-based resources we mention throughout the rest of this book, will go stale or be replaced by newer information. In some cases, the URLs you find here might lead you to their replacements; in other cases, the URLs will go nowhere, leaving you with the dread "404 File not found" error message.

When that happens, please don't give up! There's always a way to find what you want on the Web—if you're willing to invest some time and energy. To begin with, most large or complex Web sites—and Microsoft's qualifies on both counts—offer a search engine. Looking back at Figure 1.1, you'll see that a Search button appears along the top edge of the page. As long as you can get to the site itself (and we're pretty sure that it will stay at www.microsoft.com for a long while yet), you can use this tool to help you find what you need.

The more particular or focused you can make a search request, the more likely it is that the results will include information you can use. For instance, you can search the string "training and certification" to produce a lot of data about the subject in general, but if you're looking for the Preparation Guide for Exam 70-073, "Implementing and Supporting Microsoft Windows NT Workstation 4," you'll be more likely to get there quickly if you use a search string such as this:

```
"Exam 70-073" AND "preparation guide"
```

Likewise, if you want to find the Training and Certification downloads, try a search string such as this one:

```
"training and certification" AND "download page
```

Finally, don't be afraid to use general search tools such as www.search.com, www.altavista.com, or www.excite.com to search for related information. Even though Microsoft offers the best information about its certification exams online, there are plenty of third-party sources of information, training, and assistance in this area that do not have to follow a party line like Microsoft does. The bottom line is this: If you can't find something where the book says it lives, start looking around. If worst comes to worst, you can always email us! We just might have a clue.

Third-Party Test Providers

Transcender Corporation is located at 242 Louise Avenue, Nashville, TN, 37203-1812. You can reach the company by phone at (615) 726-8779, or by fax at (615) 320-6594. Trancender's URL is www.transcender.com; you can download an order form for the materials online, but it must be mailed or faxed to Transcender for purchase. We've found these practice tests, which cost between $89 and $179 if purchased individually (with discounts available for packages containing multiple tests), to be pricey but useful.

Self Test Software is located at 4651 Woodstock Road, Suite 203-384, Roswell, GA, 30075. The company can be reached by phone at (770) 641-9719 or (800) 200-6446, and by fax at (770) 641-1489. Visit the Web site at www.stsware.com; you can even order the wares online. STS's tests are cheaper than Transcender's—$69 when purchased individually; $59 each when two or more are purchased simultaneously—but they are otherwise quite comparable, which makes them a good value.

Windows NT Architecture

2

. . . .

Terms you'll need to understand:

√ Multitasking

√ Multithreaded

√ Multiprocessor

√ User mode

√ Kernel mode

√ Executive Services

√ Virtual Memory Manager (VMM)

√ Demand paging

√ Hardware Abstraction Layer (HAL)

√ File Allocation Table (FAT)

√ Virtual File Allocation Table (VFAT)

√ New Technology File System (NTFS)

√ CD-ROM File System (CDFS)

Techniques you'll need to master:

√ Understanding the Windows NT architecture

√ Knowing the differences between NT Workstation,
   NT Server, and Windows 95

Windows NT Workstation is the client product of the Microsoft Windows NT family of network operating systems. In this chapter, we introduce you to the major architectural underpinnings of NT. This is both a preparatory chapter that builds a framework for later discussions and an instructive chapter that gives you specific details you'll find on the certification exam. This is not a chapter (or a book, for that matter) to introduce you to NT. If you are not already familiar with the basics of NT and the Microsoft product line, then much of the material covered in this and subsequent chapters will be fairly difficult to grasp. This book is designed to aid you in passing the certification exams; it is not a primer or an administrative guide to the network operating system (NOS).

Basic Features

Windows NT Workstation is a graphical, secure, 32-bit network operating system. The most notable difference between this version and previous versions is the adoption of the Windows 95 look and feel. The real differences between NT Workstation and Windows 95 are detailed later in this chapter.

Each of these features is discussed in detail, at least in relation to the exam, in subsequent chapters:

> **Portable** NT can be installed on Intel 386, 486, Pentium; IBM/Motorola PowerPC; MIPS R4x00; and DEC Alpha AXP CPUs. The CPU-specific source files are all found on the distribution CD.

> **Multitasking** NT is a preemptive, multitasking OS that also supports cooperative multitasking for Win16 applications within a single Windows on Windows (WOW) instance.

> **Multithreaded** More than one thread from a single application can be executed simultaneously.

> **Multiprocessor** NT Workstation can be run on a dual-CPU system.

> **File Systems** NT supports VFAT (which is FAT-compatible), NTFS, and CDFS (read-only CD-ROM support).

> **Security** NT offers numerous security features, such as user authentication, access tokens, ACLs, auditing, memory protection, and so on. NT can be configured to meet the U.S. DOD Class C2 security specification.

➤ **Clients** NT can directly support all the Microsoft OSs as clients; in addition, it has limited support for OS/2, Macintosh, and Unix. Via IIS or PWS, NT can service any client that supports TCP/IP.

➤ **Applications** NT supports Win32, Win16, DOS, POSIX-1, and OS/2 1.x applications.

➤ **Storage** NT supports 4 GB of physical memory and 16 EB (Exabytes) of storage space. (1 EB = 1024 Terabytes = 1,048,596 GB = 1,073,741,824 MB.)

➤ **Networks** NT supports TCP/IP, NWLink (IPX/SPX), NetBEUI, AppleTalk, and DLC network protocols.

For these topics to make sense, we need to establish the base architecture of NT. The next sections are devoted to this. We cover such architecture components as NT's different modes, its memory organization, as well as the differences between the Windows NT Workstation, Windows NT Server, and Windows 95 operating systems.

User And Kernel Mode

Windows NT is a modular NOS. This means that NT is not a single, contiguous collection of programming code, but rather, it is a multifaceted entity built by combining individual components. Each significant system function is packed within a single module or component. No two modules share any code—they are completely "code isolated" from each other. This enables the Microsoft engineers to improve, exchange, or correct a single feature of NT without affecting the entire system or requiring lengthy system-wide reprogramming.

Figure 2.1 illustrates a high-level view of the larger components of NT. Within each of these sections are even smaller modules. However, this level of division adequately separates different activities and conglomerated related functions. The most significant division presented in this image is that of User mode and Kernel mode.

A mode is a programming and operational separation of components, functions, and services. Each mode contains only those features required to perform any and all operations delegated to that mode.

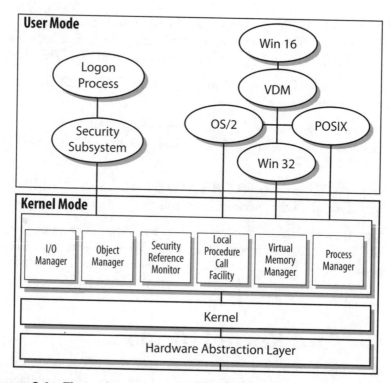

Figure 2.1   The major architectural divisions of NT.

User Mode

User applications and the environmental subsystems live or execute in the User mode. The User mode is the only mode within which a user can interact with the OS. This mode is nonprivileged—all processes operating within User mode must use the Executive Services (a component of the Kernel mode) to gain access to memory or hardware devices. The User mode contains two important subsystem types: environment and security.

Environment

The environmental subsystems host the virtual machines within which user applications are executed. The following are the three main native environmental subsystems:

➤ **Win32** Supports Windows 32-bit, Windows 16-bit, and DOS applications. Win32 also controls the NT user interface.

➤ **POSIX** Limited support for POSIX-1 applications.

➤ **OS/2** Limited support for OS/2 1.x applications.

These subsystems are discussed in Chapter 16.

Security

The security subsystem is responsible for the logon process. It works with the Executive service's Security Reference Monitor to validate users. Each time a logon attempt occurs, an authentication package is created and sent into the Kernel mode. The Security Reference Monitor compares its contents with its security accounts database (known as the SAM database). The Security Reference Monitor then builds and returns an access token if a valid user name and password are contained in the authentication package.

The logon-related security issues are discussed in Chapters 4, 7, and 8.

Kernel Mode

The Kernel mode is the inner core of the operating system. It is a privileged processor mode, meaning the components in this mode have execution priority over all User mode processes. A significant portion of the Kernel is maintained in memory and cannot be (or is not) swapped out to disk by the Virtual Memory Manager (VMM).

Through the Kernel mode, NT protects the hardware and all system-level components from user applications. Therefore, no hardware-direct calls can be made by a user application; instead, the application must make a request to the Kernel mode. This surrogate-like activity maintains a reliable computing environment and protects the system from poorly written applications.

The Kernel mode contains three important subsystems:

➤ Executive Services

➤ Kernel

➤ Hardware Abstraction Layer (HAL)

Executive Services

Executive Services (also known as the NT Executive) is the interface between the Kernel and the environmental subsystems of the User mode.

The NT Executive provides services through the following six modules:

➤ **Object Manager** Controls activities related to objects. These activities include use, naming, removing, tracking, and security of objects.

➤ **Security Reference Monitor** Handles logon procedures, user authentication, access validation, and the security subsystem in the User mode.

➤ **Process Monitor** Manages process activities, such as creation, deletion, and tracking.

➤ **Local Procedure Call Facility** Maintains communications, user applications, and environmental subsystems.

➤ **Virtual Memory Manager** Maintains and controls physical and virtual memory.

➤ **I/O Manager** Oversees all input and output. The I/O Manager acts like a proxy by intercepting an application's requests and directing commands to the appropriate hardware drivers.

Kernel

The central core of the NT operating system is called the Kernel. Its primary task is to manage all system activities (threads) while attempting to maintain optimal system performance through scheduling CPU allocation time for applications.

Hardware Abstraction Layer (HAL)

The Hardware Abstraction Layer (HAL) is the NT module where all hardware-specific components and configurations are stored. The collection of hardware-specific information in this module enables NT to be easily ported to different platforms. The HAL is the only module of NT that must be customized for new hardware.

Windows NT Memory Organization

The memory architecture of Windows NT is one of the central design elements that has established this NOS as robust, reliable, and scaleable. NT's memory organization is a single, contiguous block without any divisions. This type of memory is called "flat addressing" or "linear addressing."

Windows NT does not divide memory into conventional, upper, and extended sections; however, these settings can be defined for a subsystem virtual machine if required by a DOS or Win16 application.

NT's memory is managed by the Virtual Memory Manager (VMM) of the Executive Services. Each time an application is launched (more specifically, each time a new subsystem virtual machine is created), the VMM assigns it a 4 GB memory address space. Through a process of memory address mapping, the VMM maintains the relationship between the 4 GB assigned address space of each application and the actual memory present on the machine.

The total amount of memory used by NT is a combination of physical RAM and the size of the paging file. A paging file is a temporary storage file on a hard drive used by the VMM to hold little-used memory pages. The extra memory availed by this process is called "virtual memory." VMM manages physical RAM, virtual memory, and the address space of each application. The management process completely fools the application into perceiving that 4 GB of real, usable memory exists.

The process used by the VMM to manage virtual memory is called "demand paging." The address space of applications and the usable memory of a system are segmented into 4 K chunks. Unused or little-used (memory blocks that are accessed infrequently) blocks of memory are moved from physical RAM to the hard drive's paging file. When an application requests a segment of memory not in physical RAM, the VMM swaps a section of physical RAM with the requested section of paging file stored data. This page swapping occurs on demand.

 Because virtual memory relies on a hard drive to extend the physical RAM, the performance of the machine can be affected if too much paging takes place. Hard drive speeds are extremely slow when compared to that of RAM.

Details on setting paging file parameters and detecting high levels of page swapping are highlighted in Chapter 15.

Server And Workstation Differences

Windows NT Server and Windows NT Workstation are at the core of the same operating system because they have so many modules and code segments

Table 2.1   Differences between NT Server and NT Workstation.

Area	NT Workstation	NT Server
Simultaneous connections	10	Unlimited
Multiprocessor	2	4 (32 with OEM)
RAS sessions	1	256
Replication	Import	Import and export
Network services	None	DHCP server, DNS server, and WINS server
Internet services	Peer Web Services	Internet Information Server
Network server	No	Yes
Macintosh services	No	Yes
Disk fault tolerance	No	Yes (RAID 1, 5)
Domain logon validation	No	Yes

in common. However, there are still significant differences of which you need to be aware. These are listed in Table 2.1.

As you can see in this table, most of the differences relate to issues around supporting network functionality and features.

NT Workstation And Windows 95 Comparison

Even though NT Workstation shares the same look and feel with Windows 95, there are many significant differences between them. These differences are detailed in Table 2.2.

Table 2.2 The differences between Windows NT Workstation and Windows 95.		
Area	**NT Workstation**	**Windows 95**
Uses DOS and Win16 device drivers	No	Yes
Multiplatform	Yes	No
Multiprocessors	Yes	No
Win16 applications	Yes	Yes
DOS applications	Yes	Yes
POSIX and OS/2 applications	Yes	No
File systems	NTFS, VFAT	VFAT
Plug and play	No	Yes
Application/memory protection	Yes	No
Internet services	Peer Web Services	No
RAS	Inbound and outbound	Outbound only

From this table, you can see the wide variance in OS capabilities between NT Workstation and Windows 95.

Exam Prep Questions

Question 1

> Which of the following are features of NT Workstation? [Check all correct answers]
>
> ❑ a. Multiplatform support
>
> ❑ b. Wide range of security features
>
> ❑ c. Supports Macintosh and OS/2 clients
>
> ❑ d. Supports DNS and WINS servers
>
> ❑ e. Supports DLC and IPX/SPX protocols

Windows NT Workstation supports many platforms, has numerous security features, supports Mac and OS/2 clients, and supports DLC and IPX/SPX protocols. Therefore, answers a, b, c, and e are correct. NT Workstation does not support or host DNS or WINS servers—these are found only on NT Server. Therefore, answer d is incorrect.

Question 2

> In which mode do the application subsystems exist?
>
> ○ a. User
>
> ○ b. Kernel

The application subsystems exist in the User mode. Therefore, answer a is correct.

Question 3

> Windows NT can host 5 GB of storage space.
>
> ○ a. True
>
> ○ b. False

The correct answer is a. NT can support up to 16 EB of storage space, and 5 GB is less than that. However, the trick to this question is that 4 GB is the limitation of memory, and the use of that number may throw you off.

Question 4

Which of the following is not true about NT Workstation?

○ a. Supports up to two processors.

○ b. Supports the AppleTalk protocol.

○ c. Supports the FAT file system.

○ d. Supports the Sun Solaris platform.

○ e. Supports multithreading.

NT Workstation supports two processors, AppleTalk, FAT (through VFAT), and multithreading. Therefore, answers a, b, c, and e are incorrect. **NT Workstation does not support the Sun Solaris platform. Therefore, answer d is correct.**

Question 5

What components are found in the Kernel mode? [Check all correct answers]

❏ a. HAL

❏ b. Executive Services

❏ c. Security Reference Monitor

❏ d. Logon process

❏ e. I/O Manager

❏ f. User applications

The Kernel mode is host to the HAL, the Executive Services, the Security Reference Monitor, and the I/O Manager. Therefore, answers a, b, c, and e are correct. The logon process and user applications exist in the User mode. Therefore, answers d and f are incorrect.

Question 6

Which of the following statements are true for virtual memory?
[Check all correct answers]

❑ a. Managed by a component of the Executive Services.

❑ b. Created by using hard drive space.

❑ c. Accessed directly by applications.

❑ d. Combined with physical RAM to increase usable
      memory.

❑ e. Faster than physical RAM.

Virtual memory is managed by a component of the Executive Services, is created by using hard drive space, and is combined with physical RAM to increase usable memory. Therefore, answers a, b, and d are correct. Virtual memory is not accessed directly by applications and is slower than physical RAM. Therefore, answers c and e are incorrect.

Question 7

Which of the following two items do NT Workstation and NT Server
have in common? [Check two answers]

❑ a. Some replication support

❑ b. Unlimited simultaneous connections

❑ c. 256 RAS sessions

❑ d. Fault tolerance

❑ e. Multiprocessor support

NT Server and NT Workstation only share replication support (NT Workstation is import-only) and multiprocessor support (NT Workstation is 2, NT Server is 4 or up to 32 with OEM). **Therefore, answers a and e are correct.** NT Workstation is limited to 10 simultaneous connections, 1 RAS session, and has no fault tolerance. Therefore, answers b, c, and d are incorrect.

Question 8

What do Windows NT Workstation and Windows 95 have in common? [Check all correct answers]

❏ a. Plug and play

❏ b. Win16 and DOS application support

❏ c. VFAT

❏ d. Outbound RAS

NT Workstation and Windows 95 both support Win16 and DOS, VFAT, and outbound RAS. Therefore, answers b, c, and d are correct. NT Workstation does not support plug and play. Therefore, answer a is incorrect.

Question 9

A VMM managed page is how large?

○ a. 2 K

○ b. 4 K

○ c. 64 K

○ d. 4 GB

VMM pages are 4 K in size. Therefore, answer b is correct.

Question 10

The HAL is the only significant component of NT that varies between the supported hardware platforms.

○ a. True

○ b. False

Answer a is correct. The HAL is where all the platform-specific configuration is stored, and it is easily replaced with an alternative version for other platforms.

Need To Know More?

 Perkins, Charles, Matthew Strebe, and James Chellis: *MCSE: NT Workstation Study Guide*. Sybex Network Press, San Francisco, CA, 1997. ISBN 0-7821-1973-5. Chapter 1 discusses the overall architecture of Windows NT Workstation as well as a few more introductory details we did not mention (because they are not on the test).

 Search the TechNet CD (or its online version through www.microsoft.com) and the *Windows NT Workstation Resource Kit* CD using the keywords "mode," "Executive Services," "VMM," "HAL," "Windows 95 comparison," and "NT Server comparison."

Installing And Configuring Workstation

3

. . . .

Terms you'll need to understand:

√ Hardware Compatibility List (HCL)

√ NT Hardware Qualifier (NTHQ)

√ Dual boot

√ BOOT.INI

√ WINNT.EXE

√ WINNT32.EXE

√ FDISK

√ UNATTEND.TXT

√ Uniqueness Database File (UDF)

√ SYSDIFF

Techniques you'll need to master:

√ Understanding the different ways you can install Windows NT

√ Knowing how to perform an unattended installation

√ Performing an NT installation

√ Uninstalling Windows NT

The procedures involved in the installation of Windows NT Workstation are key elements found on the Workstation exam. In this chapter, we present all of the details you must know for the test, but we highly recommend you take the time to install NT Workstation once or twice on your own. Doing so will help you establish a solid understanding of the processes encountered during setup.

Preinstallation Requirements

The Windows NT operating system will only function properly if it is installed onto a computer comprised of compatible components. The list of these components is called the Hardware Compatibility List (HCL). In addition to listing supported devices, it also informs you if the driver for each device is:

➤ Included in the standard collection of distribution files

➤ Stored on the CD-ROM, but in an alternate specialized directory

➤ Only available directly from the vendor

A version of the HCL, dated August 9, 1996, is stored on the Workstation distribution CD-ROM in \SUPPORT\HCL.HLP. The latest version of the HCL is available on the Microsoft Web site (www. microsoft.com) for direct viewing or downloading. It can be found by performing a search for "HCL."

Fortunately, you don't need to memorize the HCL for the exam, but there are some important prerequisites you do need to remember:

Intel-based:

➤ 486 MHz (or faster) or Pentium-based system

➤ 12 MB of memory (RAM); 16 MB recommended

➤ 120 MB of available hard disk space

➤ CD-ROM drive or access to a CD-ROM over a computer network

➤ VGA or higher-resolution display adapter

➤ Microsoft Mouse or compatible pointing device

RISC-based:

➤ Alpha AXP, MIPS R4x00 or PowerPC processor

➤ 16 MB of memory; 24 MB recommended

➤ 150 MB of available hard disk space

➤ CD-ROM drive or access to a CD-ROM over a computer network

➤ VGA or higher-resolution display adapter

➤ Microsoft Mouse or compatible pointing device

Optional Hardware:

➤ Network adapter card

➤ Audio board/sound card

Microsoft has provided a useful tool called the NTHQ that helps determine if your computer meets the minimum requirements and if your components are on the HCL.

NT Hardware Qualifier Disk

The NT Hardware Qualifier (NTHQ) disk is a simple utility that inspects your computer and provides you with a detailed report of any suspected or definite incompatibility problems. NTHQ is found in the \SUPPORT\HQTOOL directory on the CD-ROM. It is installed onto a floppy and used to boot the computer.

 The NTHQ is only as good as the HCL it references, which is dated Aug. 9, 1996. Therefore, the CD-ROM version no longer has any useful applications. However, you still have to know this for the exam.

Installing Versus Upgrading

There are two possible methods of NT Workstation installation: complete and upgrade. In the following sections, we explain each of these installation options in detail.

Complete Installation Of Windows NT 4 Workstation

A complete installation of NT assumes that the computer is without a current OS or that any existing OS can be completely overwritten. Performing a complete install overwrites any existing version of NT, and a new Security ID will be assigned to that computer. This method is used for the initial installation, installing multiple OSs on different partitions, or starting over from scratch.

Upgrade Installation Of Windows NT 4 Workstation

An upgrade installation replaces all NT files, but it retains most of the Registry settings, application installation changes, and the SID. An upgrade can be performed on many OSs, including DOS, Windows 3.x, Windows 95, and Windows NT Workstation 3.51 and 4. However, little to nothing from DOS, Windows 3.x, and Windows 95 is migrated into NT 4 due to wide variance in architecture. Therefore, upgrading is only a realistic possibility for the NT level of Microsoft OSs. The upgrade installation is a common troubleshooting tool when less drastic measures have already been exhausted.

Booting Multiple OSs

Although it's a security risk on production machines, NT Workstation can be installed with other OSs on the same computer. NT Workstation can exist without problems on a computer with Windows 95, Windows For Workgroups, Windows 3.x, or DOS. For such a dual-boot to exist, it is recommended that you install the Microsoft non-NT OS first and then install NT onto a different partition. The resultant BOOT.INI file will contain the two standard lines for NT's normal and safe boot modes as well as a third entry for the alternate operating system—which is usually labeled MS-DOS, by default. You do have to keep in mind that non-NT OSs will not be able to read any data stored on NTFS volumes.

 It is important to install each OS onto a different partition because Microsoft's Windows OSs use similar naming conventions for directories. By installing each on a separate partition, the required files are not overwritten by the same-named files from another OS. Two examples of this are the \Windows default directory name and the \Program Files common application installation folder.

NT can also be installed in a multiboot configuration with other OSs, but the ease of installation and operation will vary. The only non-Microsoft OS mentioned on the certification exam is OS/2. It is shipped with its own version of a boot manager. When NT is installed onto an OS/2 machine, the OS/2 boot manager is disabled in favor of the NT boot manager. You can revert to the OS/2 boot manager by setting active the small OS/2 boot manager partition through Disk Administrator. If this change is made, the OS/2 boot manager will be displayed. If DOS or Windows is selected, the NT boot manager is then displayed.

To remove an alternate OS from the boot manager, simply edit the BOOT.INI file and delete the ARC name\path entry. These procedures are discussed in Chapters 17 and 18.

Planning Windows NT Workstation Installation

The actual installation of NT is not difficult. However, to ensure the smoothness of the operation, several issues must be resolved beforehand.

The WINNT Installation File And Distribution Directories

The installation of Windows NT Workstation is initiated through the execution of the WINNT.EXE utility, which is a 16-bit application that will function under DOS, Windows 3.x, Windows 95, and Windows NT. There is also a 32-bit version, WINNT32.EXE, for exclusive use within NT for better performance.

This utility has many switches and parameters for controlling or altering the installation procedure. These parameters, shown in Table 3.1, are important to know for the exam.

Table 3.1 WINNT.EXE and WINNT32.EXE switches and parameters.	
Parameter	**Description**
/B	Installs Windows NT Workstation without using the boot floppies.
/C	Skips the check for available space on the installation boot floppies.
/F	Copies the files from the boot floppies without verifying the copies.
/I:*inf_file*	Specifies the file name for the setup information file. The default is DOSNET.INF.
/O	Creates boot floppies and starts the installation.
/OX	Creates boot floppy disks to use in floppy-based installations. Does not start the installation.
/R	Specifies optional directory to be installed.
/RX	Specifies optional directory to be copied.

(continued)

Table 3.1	WINNT.EXE and WINNT32.EXE switches and parameters (continued).
Parameter	**Description**
/S:*sourcepath*	Specifies the source of the Windows NT setup files. This must be a fully qualified path in the form drive_letter:\path or \\server_name\share\path. The current directory is the default source for the installation files.
/T:*drive*	Specifies the drive in which to place the temporary setup files.
/U:*answer_file*	Specifies an unattended installation and lists the optional script file.
/UDF:*id*, [*UDF_file*]	Specifies the identifier that is to be used to apply sections of the UDF_file in place of the same section in the answer_file. If no UDF is specified, the Setup program will prompt the user to insert a disk that contains a file called $UNIQUE$.UDF. If a UDF is specified, Setup will look for the identifier in that file.

There are four OS-specific directories on the NT Workstation distribution CD-ROM. These directories correspond to the four CPU types supported by NT. Be sure to launch the WINNT utility from the appropriate directory for your platform type.

➤ \alpha—DEC Alpha AXP

➤ \i386—Intel CPUs

➤ \mips—MIPS R4x00

➤ \ppc—IBM/Motorola PowerPC

If you do not have the three NT boot and setup disks, you can create them by launching WINNT or WINNT32 with the /O or /OX parameter. The floppies must be preformatted. The /O parameter starts the install once the floppies are created, whereas the /OS parameter will not start the install. The floppies are built in reverse order, starting with 3, moving to 2, and then 1.

Selecting An Installation Method

NT Workstation can be installed via several methods:

➤ From an HCL-compatible CD-ROM with boot floppy disks

➤ From a CD-ROM in an existing OS without boot floppies

➤ From a CD-ROM in an existing OS without boot floppies

➤ From a network share

Each of these methods is discussed in the following sections.

From A HCL-Compatible CD-ROM Drive With Boot Floppies

If the CD-ROM is HCL-compatible, the three NT boot floppies can be used to install NT. No OS is required to be present on the computer. Using the boot floppies is effectively launching WINNT.EXE without any parameters.

From An CD-ROM In An Existing OS Without Boot Floppies

If an OS is present on the computer, boot floppies can be avoided by launching WINNT.EXE with the /B option. This instructs the Setup utility to copy the files otherwise found on the boot floppies to a hard drive so they can be launched when the machine next reboots.

If an OS is present and the CD-ROM is not HCL compatible, the distribution directory for the appropriate platform can be copied to the hard drive. Then, the WINNT utility can be launched from the hard drive with the /B option.

From A Network Share

If an OS is present on the computer and it has network access, the NT distribution files can be accessed from a network share. The Setup utility can be launched from the share, provided that the NIC and the network's protocols are supported by NT. Once again, the /B option can be used to avoid the floppies. The share can be the CD-ROM itself or a copy of the distribution directory on a server's hard drive. We recommend the latter for its performance (speed) benefits.

If the NIC or protocols are not supported by NT, the entire distribution directory can be copied to the local drive. Then, WINNT can be launched locally with the /B option.

If your computer does not have an OS, a client boot/install disk can be built from an NT Server's Client Administrator utility. This disk will bootstrap the computer to the network with a DOS OS, giving the machine just enough network capabilities to copy the distribution files to a local drive.

NT does *not* support a network installation for RISC platforms.

Partitioning The Hard Drive

If multiple OSs are to be used on the same machine, partitioning the hard drive is best performed using the DOS utility FDISK. Otherwise, the Setup utility will enable you to modify your partitions before selecting the destination partition for the NOS. When changing partitions, you should keep in mind that removing a partition destroys the data it contains.

Details To Collect

The installation process will prompt you for numerous pieces of information; it's a good idea to have the following information at hand before starting:

➤ **Computer name** The name of the computer. This should comply with a naming convention used by your organization.

➤ **Domain or Workgroup name** The name of the domain or workgroup in which this computer will participate.

➤ **Device configuration settings** The configuration settings for each device in your computer, especially NICs and devices that require third-party drivers.

➤ **Partitions** The number, order, and size of existing or desired partitions.

➤ **Name of the NT directory** The name of the main NT system directory; the default is \WINNT.

➤ **Protocols** Which protocol(s) you want to use, as well as any settings related to the selected protocols (see Chapters 9, 10, and 11).

➤ **Licensing** Who the product licenses to. Enter the name and organization.

➤ **Administrator password** This is the initial password for the Administrator account.

Automated Windows NT Workstation Installation

Even though the installation of NT is often fairly simple, it can take over an hour to complete, especially if the CD-ROM or network transfer speed is poor. Microsoft has provided two ways to speed and automate the install process.

Unattended Install

An "unattended (or automated) install" can be performed by using special script files that contain all of the details normally provided by a human operator. The first file, UNATTEND.TXT, can be used to install or upgrade to NT Workstation 4 on multiple machines with similar configurations. An example of this file can be found in each of the platform-specific subdirectories. Here is the Intel sample file:

```
; Microsoft Windows NT Workstation Version 4.0 and
; Windows NT Server Version 4.0
; (c) 1994 - 1996 Microsoft Corporation. All rights reserved.
;
; Sample Unattended Setup Answer File
;
; This file contains information about how to automate the
; installation or upgrade of Windows NT Workstation and Windows
; NT Server so the Setup program runs without requiring user
; input.
;
; For information on how to use this file, read the appropriate
; sections of the Windows NT 4.0 Resource Kit.

[Unattended]
OemPreinstall = no
ConfirmHardware = no
NtUpgrade = no
Win31Upgrade = no
TargetPath = WINNT
OverwriteOemFilesOnUpgrade = no

[UserData]
FullName = Your User Name
OrgName = Your Organization Name
ComputerName = COMPUTER_NAME
```

```
[GuiUnattended]
TimeZone = (GMT-08:00) Pacific Time (US & Canada); Tijuana

[Display]
ConfigureAtLogon = 0
BitsPerPel = 16
XResolution = 640
YResolution = 480
VRefresh = 70
AutoConfirm = 1

[Network]
Attend = yes
DetectAdapters = ""
InstallProtocols = ProtocolsSection
JoinDomain = Domain_To_Join

[ProtocolsSection]
TC = TCParameters

[TCParameters]
DHCP = yes
```

You can modify this file to match your needs manually. Or, you can use the SETUPMGR.EXE utility (located in the \support\deptools*platform type* directory) to create this file. The Setup Manager uses a three-tabbed (General, Networking, and Advanced) GUI interface to simplify the process of creating the UNATTEND.TXT file. Knowing that this utility exists is enough for the Workstation exam, but you might want to use it once just to familiarize yourself with it.

To use the UNATTEND.TXT file to automate an installation, you need to use specific parameters on the WINNT Setup utility, as follows:

```
WINNT /S:d:\i386 /U:c:\unattend.txt
```

Note that /S is required to define the source of the distribution files when /U is used.

A second script file can be used in conjunction with the UNATTEND.TXT file to specify different computer-specific details without having to create a unique UNATTEND.TXT for each machine. This is called a Uniqueness Database File (UDF). A UDF is created by hand using a text editor. It begins with a section that defines IDs for each computer and what sections of UNATTEND.TXT need modification for this specific computer. The remainder of the UDF simply defines the changes for each machine, based on the ID of that machine and the section of the install to which the modification corresponds. The details used in the text portion of the install (see the section entitled "Text Portion" later in this chapter) are only specified in the UNATTEND.TXT file, not in the UDF. The sections can be the following:

➤ **[OEM_Ads]** Defines the banner, logo, and background bitmap to be displayed during GUI mode setup.

➤ **[DisplayDrivers]** Specifies display drivers.

➤ **[Display]** Specifies video display settings.

➤ **[GuiUnattended]** Defines the behavior of the Setup program during GUI mode setup.

➤ **[UserData]** Specifies information associated with each user or computer.

➤ **[Network]** Specifies network settings, such as protocols and adapters. If this section is not present, support for networking will not be installed.

➤ **[Modem]** Identifies whether or not a modem should be installed. It is used by RAS to install a modem if **DeviceType = Modem** is in the list of RAS parameters.

If the sample UNATTEND.TXT file was used, a possible UDF file could look like this:

```
[UniqueIds]
id1 = UserData,GuiUnattended
id2 = UserData
id3 = UserData,GuiUnattended,Display
[id1:usedata]
FullName = "Bob Smith"
OrgName = "LivePeople Inc."
ComputerName = Sales_02
[id1:GuiUnattended]
TimeZone = "(GMT-06:00) Central Time (US & Canada)"
[id2:usedata]
FullName = "Mary Jones"
OrgName = "LivePeople Inc."
ComputerName = Sales_05
[id3:usedata]
FullName = "Rebecca Doe"
```

```
OrgName = "LivePeople Inc."
ComputerName = Sales_01
[id3:GuiUnattended]
TimeZone = "(GMT-06:00) Central Time (US & Canada)"
[id3:Display]
XResolution = 1024
YResolution = 768
```

To use a UDF file to automate installation, apply the following syntax on each defined machine, but alter the ID value to match that of the computer:

```
WINNT /S:d:\i386 /U:c:\unattend.txt /UDF:ID1,udfsales.txt
```

SYSDIFF Utility

Another method for customizing NT's installation process is to use the SYSDIFF utility. SYSDIFF is used to record the differences between a normal (or default) installation of NT Workstation and an installation of NT that has been customized and has had additional applications added. Thus, with this data, the setup of other machines with the same (or nearly the same) requirements of hardware and software is greatly simplified.

The SYSDIFF program can perform five functions:

➤ **Snap** A snapshot of NT, including the Registry and file system, is taken and recorded to a file.

➤ **Diff** Records another snapshot of NT that only stores the changes made since the original snapshot. This is the difference file.

➤ **Apply** Applies the difference file to another installation of NT.

➤ **Inf** Creates an INF file and installation data files from a difference file. These items can be stored with a network share copy of the NT distribution files to automate the process of initial setup of NT and application of the difference file to the new install (used with **/I:INF_FILE**).

➤ **Dump** Creates a directory or contents list of the changes to be found in the difference file.

The command-line parameters and syntax of SYSDIFF are

```
sysdiff /snap [/log:log_file] snapshot_file
sysdiff /diff [/c:title] [/log:log_file] snapshot_file
difference_file
sysdiff /apply /m [/log:log_file] difference_file
```

```
sysdiff /inf /m [/u] difference_file oem_root
sysdiff /dump difference_file dump_file
```

where:

➤ **/log:log_file** records the activity of the utility.

➤ **snapshot_file** is the recording of the initial state of the NT installation.

➤ **/c:*title*** defines a title for the difference package.

➤ **difference_file** is the recording of the difference between the current state of the NT installation and the snapshot_file.

➤ **/m** forces file changes in the per-user profile structure to be mapped to the Default User profile structure, rather than to the profile structure of the user logged on when the difference file was created.

➤ **/u** specifies that the INF file should be generated as a Unicode text file instead of the default system ANSI codepage.

➤ **oem_root** is the destination of the INF and data files for custom installation.

➤ **dump_file** defines the name for the dump file.

These two methods of automating or customizing the NT installation procedure are present in force on the Workstation exam.

Actual Installation Step-By-Step

Once you have started the installation, whether by using the three boot floppies or by launching WINNT(32) /B, it proceeds in the following order.

Text Portion

The installation process begins in a blue background with a white text-based environment. When the text portion completes, your computer will reboot to the GUI portion of the install.

Initial Selection Screen

The first menu presented by Setup includes the following choices:

➤ **F1** Learn more about NT Workstation before continuing with Setup

➤ **ENTER** Set up NT

➤ **R** Repair damage to an existing installation of NT (as described in Chapter 18)

➤ **F3** Exit Setup

Hardware Detection

NT attempts to identify the storage devices and controller cards present on your system. It will display a list of what it finds. If the list is incomplete or wrong, pressing "S" will enable you to select from a list of supported devices or to install a vendor-provided driver.

Next, NT Workstation displays what it has found for other devices: computer type, display, keyboard, language, and pointing device. You are given the opportunity to change these settings or continue.

File Systems And Partitions

The next section displays a list of existing partitions and unused space on your hard drives. If the correct partition is present, it can be selected as the destination for NT. If not, new partitions can be created and existing ones deleted. Once the destination partition is selected, NT prompts you for a file system type to be used to format the partition. You have the choices of leaving it "as is" (for preexisting partitions only), or selecting FAT or NTFS. You also have the choice of converting preexisting FAT partitions to NTFS; all existing data will be maintained.

Windows Main Directory

Setup will detect if an existing version of NT Workstation is present on the destination partition. If one is found, you'll be prompted to upgrade or overwrite it (the current main directory name will be used). If no other version exists, you are prompted for the main directory name for NT. The default is \WINNT.

System Examination

Setup prompts for a cursory or an exhaustive hard disk examination. The former will take a few seconds, whereas the latter will take much longer (depending on the partition size). Once the examination is complete, Setup performs file copies and then reboots your computer.

GUI Portion

The remainder of the setup process occurs in a basic Windows graphical environment. You can use a mouse or keyboard commands to move around and respond to queries.

Option Selection
A menu appears with the following selections:

➤ **Typical** Installs those features Microsoft deems the most common.

➤ **Portable** Optimizes the installation for a mobile computer or one not always connected to the network.

➤ **Compact** Installs the minimum necessary features.

➤ **Custom** Installs only manually selected features.

Next, enter your name and the name of your organization.

Computer Name
You can define the computer name for this machine—it can be up to 15 characters long—as well as the Administrator account password.

Emergency Repair Disk
You can instruct the Setup utility to create or bypass an ERD once installation is complete.

Components
You can choose the noncritical components of NT Workstation for installation by selecting the most common option or displaying a list that allows you to choose.

Network Configuration
You can select whether the computer is attached directly to a network, through remote access, or not at all. Next, the Network Interface Card (NIC) is installed. By selecting Detect, you cause NT Workstation to attempt to discover through hardware calls the nature of the NIC. If found, you need to verify the make and model. If not found, you can select from a list or install drivers from the vendor.

If you do not have an adapter already installed, select Microsoft, MS Loopback Adapter. This is a software device that fools NT into thinking a real NIC exists. Once you physically install a NIC, you can install the correct drivers and remove this facade.

Protocols
You select the protocols to be used on the network. The default options are TCP/IP, NWLink, and NetBEUI. Additional protocols, such as DLC and

AppleTalk, can be installed at this point. Once the protocols are selected, you'll need to define and set the relevant parameters for each protocol.

Workgroup/Domain

NT Workstation can be a member of a workgroup or a domain, but not both at the same time. At this point, choose the appropriate membership type and then define that group's name—WORKGROUP and DOMAIN are default values for these. If you select DOMAIN, you need to provide the name of an Administrator account and its password so that a computer account can be created for the NT Workstation. This is not required if an account with the same computer name has already been created through the Server Manager on a domain controller.

Final Settings

The last two option screens allow you to define the time zone, set the time, and select the display settings. Once the computer reboots, NT installation is complete.

Uninstalling Windows NT Workstation

If you need to remove NT Workstation from your computer, you'll have to do it manually. Workstation does not have a specific uninstall utility. However, the following steps can be used to remove it:

1. Back up all important files from any NTFS partitions.

2. Remove NTFS partitions.

3. Change the bootstrap routine.

4. Delete the following Windows NT Workstation directories and files: \winnt, \program files, NTLDR, BOOT.INI, NTDETECT.COM, PAGEFILE.SYS, and BOOTSECT.DOS

A primary NTFS partition can be deleted by DOS FDISK, but not logical drives in an extended partition. That requires using the three boot diskettes to return to the destination partition section, deleting all existing partitions, and then exiting setup.

Changing the bootstrap routine involves using the command **SYS C:** from a DOS disk to remove the NT boot manager.

Exam Prep Questions

Question 1

> Which of the following are provided by the HCL? [Check all correct answers]
>
> ❑ a. A list of Windows NT Workstation supported hardware
>
> ❑ b. A list of tested but nonfunctioning hardware
>
> ❑ c. Contact information for each vendor
>
> ❑ d. Where the driver is located on the CD-ROM

The HCL only provides a list of the supported hardware and where the driver for that device is located. Therefore, only answers a and d are correct. The HCL does not list unsupported hardware or vendor contact information. Therefore, answers b and c are incorrect.

Question 2

> What does the **/OX** parameter do when it is used on WINNT32.EXE?
>
> ○ a. Defines an alternate drive for the temp files.
>
> ○ b. Creates the three setup disks and starts the installation.
>
> ○ c. Creates the three setup disks.
>
> ○ d. Starts the install without using the disks.

The "/OX" parameter creates the setup disks without starting the installation. Therefore, answer c is correct. The /T command specifies an alternate temp drive; /O creates the disks and starts the installation; and /B starts the install without disks. Therefore, answers a, b, and d are incorrect.

Question 3

> Which of the following items can be part of an automated or custom installation of NT Workstation? [Check all correct answers]
>
> ❑ a. Setup Manager
>
> ❑ b. UNATTEND.TXT
>
> ❑ c. Uniqueness Database File
>
> ❑ d. WINNT.EXE or WINNT32.EXE

All of these items can or are involved in an automated or customized installation of NT. Therefore, answers a, b, c, and d are correct.

Question 4

> Which of the following are optional hardware requirements for Windows NT? [Check all correct answers]
>
> ❑   a. Mouse
>
> ❑   b. Audio card
>
> ❑   c. Network card
>
> ❑   d. SCSI storage devices

NT's optional hardware requirements are an audio card and a network card. **Therefore, answers b and c are correct.** A mouse is specified as a requirement. Therefore, answer a is incorrect. SCSI storage devices are preferred over IDE, but this is neither mandated nor listed as optional. Therefore, answer d is incorrect.

Question 5

> What methods or choices of installation are possible with NT Workstation 4? [Check all correct answers]
>
> ❑   a. Network share
>
> ❑   b. Local, non-HCL CD-ROM
>
> ❑   c. All-floppy installation
>
> ❑   d. System image transfer
>
> ❑   e. CD-ROM and floppy combo

Windows NT can be installed from a network share, from a non-HCL CD-ROM (if an OS is present), or with a CD-ROM and floppy combo. **Therefore, answers a, b, and e are correct.** NT is not available in an all-floppy install—that would take over 120 disks. Therefore, answer c is incorrect. A system image transfer is a process used in the OS/2 world; the closest NT equivalent is the SYSDIFF utility, but it still requires the normal installation before its special difference file is applied to the computer. Therefore, answer d is incorrect.

Question 6

> NT Workstation can exist in a multiboot environment with what other OSs on a Pentium computer? [Check all correct answers]
>
> ❑ a. Windows 95
> ❑ b. DOS
> ❑ c. Macintosh System 7.51
> ❑ d. OS/2
> ❑ e. Windows NT 3.51

NT can exist with any other Intel-supporting OS, such as Windows 95, DOS, OS/2, and NT 3.51. Therefore, answers a, b, d, and e are correct. NT cannot exist with Mac OS 7.51. Therefore, answer c is incorrect. The trick to this question is knowing that the Mac OS is not supported on the Intel platform.

Question 7

> The NT Hardware Qualifier disk is used to inspect your computer for compatible hardware before installation of NT Workstation.
>
> ○ a. True
> ○ b. False

Answer a, true, is correct. The NTHQ should be used prior to installing NT.

Question 8

> When an upgrade is performed, which of the following occurs? [Check all correct answers]
>
> ❑ a. The Registry is left mostly intact.
> ❑ b. The SID is changed.
> ❑ c. Installed applications are removed.
> ❑ d. Defective drivers are overwritten.

The upgrade method of installation leaves the Registry mostly intact and overwrites the original distributed files on the hard drive. Therefore, answers a and d are correct. The upgrade install does not change the SID or uninstall applications. Therefore, answers b and c are incorrect.

Question 9

> Which of the following SYSDIFF command lines will enable you to automatically install NT Workstation and a custom set of applications with a single execution of WINNT?
>
> ○ a. sysdiff /dump difference_file dump_file
> ○ b. sysdiff /apply /m [/log:log_file] difference_file
> ○ c. sysdiff /inf /m [/u] difference_file oem_root
> ○ d. sysdiff /snap [/log:log_file] snapshot_file

The command "sysdiff /inf /m [/u] difference_file oem_root" will enable NT and custom applications to be automatically installed with a single command. Therefore, answer c is correct. Answer a creates a contents list of the difference file; answer b applies a difference file to an installation of NT; and answer d creates the initial snapshot of NT. Therefore, answers a, b, and d are incorrect.

Question 10

> Which WINNT command-line parameters are required when using a Uniqueness Database File? [Check all correct answers]
>
> ❑ a. /B
> ❑ b. /T
> ❑ c. /U
> ❑ d. /C
> ❑ e. /S

The required command-line parameters are "/S" and "/U." "/U" initiates an unattended installation that is modified by a UDF. "/S" defines the distribution file location and is required when "/U" is used. Therefore, answers c and e are correct. /B performs a "floppy-less" install; /T defines an alternate drive for temp files; and /C skips the boot floppy space check. Therefore, answers a, b, and d are incorrect.

Need To Know More?

 Boyce, Jim, et al.: *Windows NT Workstation 4.0 Advanced Technical Reference*. Que, Indianapolis, IN, 1996. ISBN 0-7897-0863-9. This book has very limited coverage of NT installation; therefore, we do not recommend it as a reference for this topic.

 Perkins, Charles, Matthew Strebe, and James Chellis: *MCSE: NT Workstation Study Guide*. Sybex Network Press, San Francisco, CA, 1997. ISBN 0-7821-1973-5. Chapter 3 discusses Windows NT Workstation installation.

 Search the TechNet CD (or its online version through www.microsoft.com) and the *Windows NT Workstation Resource Kit* CD using the keywords "INSTALL," "WINNT," "NTHQ," "UNATTEND.TXT," "Uniqueness Database File," and "SYSDIFF."

4

Users, Groups, And Policies

. . . .

Terms you'll need to understand:

√   Domain Model

√   User accounts

√   User rights and permissions

√   Groups

√   Policies

√   Profiles

√   Auditing

Techniques you'll need to master:

√   Familiarization with NT's User Manager For Domains

√   Understanding the group concept

√   Setting up and maintaining user accounts

√   Setting up user rights and permissions

√   Establishing system policies and user profiles

√   Auditing events on your NT system

The main impetus behind setting up a network is to share resources among users. Windows NT makes managing such resources fairly intuitive. In this chapter, we examine what you need to know for the resource management section of the Microsoft certification exam. We begin with a discussion of how to manage user accounts, which is where you assign rights to individual users. From there, we move on to groups and security policies.

Users And User Accounts

For most networks, user management on a per-user basis is frustrating. To relieve this administrative burden, Windows NT Workstation 4 comes equipped with an administrative tool for managing users. This tool is the User Manager For Domain, which is accessed from Start|Programs| Adminstrative Tools (Common)|User Manager for Domains. This is essentially the same tool as the one found on Windows NT Server, with a few variances. You cannot manage user accounts or global groups from within User Manager; however, you can add and remove them from local groups. User Manager is not used to establish trust relationships or manage other domains—these functions are handled by the Server version of User Manager For Domains.

User Manager is where local administrators create and manage user and group accounts. After you have familiarized yourself with this tool, the User Manager will be your primary access control tool for users and groups.

To ease management, the group administration philosophy is the trick for managing users. Rather than managing users one by one, it's easier to place individual users into groups and assign rights to the groups rather than the users. Once a user is a member of a group, he or she inherits the access rights and restrictions assigned to that group.

To simplify matters further, Microsoft had the foresight to provide built-in local groups for user management. Please note that you cannot delete or rename the built-in groups. It is a good idea to make use of these groups for administering user rights and restrictions. In addition, these built-in groups have certain users assigned to them by default. You may add or remove users from these groups as needed. Group concepts, as well as NT's built-in local groups, are discussed throughout this chapter.

Working With The User Manager

The User Manager is the primary tool for controlling users' rights. Here are the various functions and tasks of User Manager:

➤ Produce, change, duplicate, and remove local group accounts

➤ Produce, change, duplicate, and remove local user accounts

➤ Enable account policies (this function establishes defaults for pass-word requirements, account lockouts, disconnect status, and so on)

➤ Create user rights and audit policies

Creating New Users And Groups

To create a new user (see Figure 4.1) or group account in User Manager, perform the following steps:

1. Open User Manager and then click the User menu.

2. Select New User or New Local Group, as desired.

3. Complete the New User dialog box by filling in the User Name, Full Name (optional), Description (optional), Password, and Confirm Password fields.

4. Select the appropriate buttons from the four checkboxes at the bottom of the New User dialog box as needed. The options are:

➤ User Must Change Password At Next Logon

➤ User Cannot Change Password

➤ Password Never Expires

➤ Account Disabled

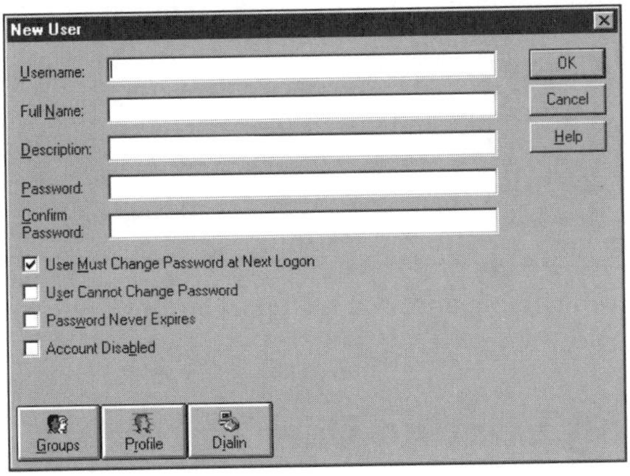

Figure 4.1   The New User dialog box.

In addition to these checkboxes, there are three option buttons at the bottom of the dialog box (as opposed to six on the NT Server version). These buttons govern many of the user's capabilities, as described in the following list:

➤ **Groups** This button enables you to add users to and remove users from a certain group or groups.

➤ **Profiles** This button enables you to define the path to the user profiles for individual users, to logon scripts, and to a user's home directory.

➤ **Dialin** This is where you establish the right for users to dial in to the network, as well as establish callback security if desired.

Default Accounts

There are two default user accounts: Administrator and Guest. The Administrator account:

➤ Needs a password that is impossible to guess to be protected.

➤ Has full, unrestricted system access.

➤ Cannot be disabled or locked out.

➤ Cannot be deleted.

➤ Can be renamed.

The Guest account:

➤ Does not save user preferences or configuration changes.

➤ Has a default blank password.

➤ Can be disabled and locked out.

➤ Cannot be deleted.

➤ Can be renamed.

It is important to rename and assign a password for these two accounts to maximize security.

Modifying Existing User Accounts

A common action for network administrators is setting up accounts for users. Often, new users take the place of existing users, and it is easier to rename an account for an employee who is taking the place of another than to create a new account. To do this, simply select User|Rename from the User Manager. Be sure to instruct the new employee to change the account's password at first logon because the old employee's password will be retained along with all other settings.

However, the easiest method is not always the best method. Microsoft recommends that you create a copy of the old account for the new user instead of renaming it. NT recognizes users by their SID (Security Identification), not their user name. Everything the previous user did will now be associated with the new user. By making a copy of the old account, you duplicate everything except the user name, real name, and password. Also, the checkboxes for User Must Change Password At Next Logon and Account Disabled are deselected. Fill these in and you've got a new account with a new SID, but with the same privileges. The old account can now be disabled instead of deleted—this makes it available for possible future security auditing.

It is (unfortunately) common to accidentally delete a user's account. The only way to remedy this is to start anew and create a user account with the same name, rights, and restrictions. This is not as bad as it sounds because you can create a template for departments or groups. Then, from the User menu, you can copy the template, type in the new user's information, and add additional rights or restrictions as needed. If an account is deleted, its SID is destroyed and any new account—even with the same name and settings—is considered a different account by NT.

If you change the access rights for a user, that user must log off and then log back on for the new rights to take effect. This is because the access token for a user is created at logon and is not updated until the next time he or she logs on.

Managing Local Groups

Managing users would be difficult if it weren't for group administration. The group concept is to assign access rights only to groups and then control access by adding and deleting users from the various groups as needed. By taking this approach, you rarely have to adjust access rights for individual users to a resource. The user accounts by themselves have almost no rights assigned; all of these rights are inherited from the groups in which they are placed.

A good method for approaching user security in NT is to create groups for each resource on the network so that each resource has a group that manages access for that particular resource. After establishing this setup of resource groups, you'll spend most of your time managing the groups and their members, not the resources.

Windows NT has two types of groups: local and global. Local groups only are available on the local domain; global groups are available across domain lines. This distinction is very important to understand. Another important difference is that local groups can contain both users and groups, whereas global groups can only contain users. No local or global groups can be members of another global group. Global groups must be created and managed on an NT server with the User Manager For Domains. Local groups are managed from the computer hosting the group, but global groups from the domain can be added as members.

As previously mentioned, NT Workstation comes with some built-in local groups that have default users and access privileges assigned. Table 4.1 describes these groups, indicates whether they are local or global, and lists the default users assigned.

 When a user belongs to multiple groups in a domain, the most restrictive rights take precedence. For example, if a user has Full Control of one resource, and No Access to another, that user has No Access privileges. By the way, no access means NO ACCESS. Chapter 7, "File And Directory Security," goes into more detail about NTFS and share access, as well as how multiple access settings resolve.

Table 4.1   NT Workstation's built-in local groups.

Group Name	Default Users	Description
Administrators	Administrator, Domain Admins	Members can administer the computer.
Backup Operators	None	Members can bypass file security to back up files.
Guests	Guest, Domain Guests	Users are granted minimal access to the computer.
Power Users	None	Members can manage directories and printers.
Replicators	None	Supports file replication in a domain.
Users	Domain Users	Ordinary users.

Security Policies

NT has three security policies that are managed through the User Manager:

➤ Account

➤ User Rights

➤ Auditing

There are also system policies that control a user's environment, such as customization controls, Control Panel applets, network settings, logon access, and so on. System polices—whether they apply to a user, a computer, or a group—are managed with the System Policy Editor, which only ships with NT Server. System policies are not covered on the Workstation exam.

Account Policy

The account policy governs passwords for user accounts and the lockout feature. Settings made to the account policy will apply to all users on the Workstation. Users who are currently logged in will not be affected by the new settings until they log out and then log on again. Figure 4.2 shows the dialog box used to set the account policy.

The settings of the account policy are described in Table 4.2.

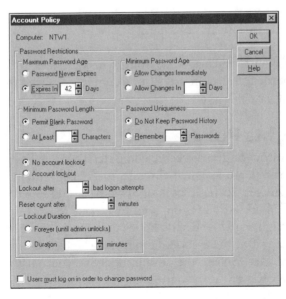

Figure 4.2   The Account Policy dialog box.

Table 4.2	NT Workstation account policy settings.		
Policy	**Action**	**Settings**	**Default**
Maximum password age	When password change is required	1 to 999 days or never	42 days
Minimum password age	When password change is prevented	1 to 999 days, or immediately	Immediately
Minimum password length	Minimum length	1 to 14, or blank	Permit blank
Password uniqueness	Forces password uniqueness	1 to 24 history list, or none	No history
Account lockout	Enables failed log-account lockout	Selected or not	No lockout
Lockout after	Number of attempts before lockout	1 to 999	Blank
Reset count after	Time until auto-matic reset of counter	1 to 99,999 minutes	Blank
Lockout Duration	Length of lockout	1 to 99,999 minutes, or forever	Blank
Users must log on in order to change password	Requires users to log on to change password	Selected or not	Not selected

These settings must be managed carefully to maximize security while mini-mizing the burden placed on users (for example, requiring frequent pass-word changing).

User Rights Policy

User rights restrict or grant specific computer-based abilities to a user or group. User rights are assigned through the Policies menu of the User Manager. There are 10 basic user rights and an additional 17 advanced rights on NT Workstation (as opposed to 11 and 16, respectively, on NT Server). Through the User Rights Policy dialog box, you can view any of these rights, as well as the users and groups to which each right is currently granted. Note that to view the advanced rights, you must check "Show Advanced User Rights" at the bottom of the dialog box.

The basic user rights, their purposes, and their members (in parentheses) are shown in Table 4.3.

Table 4.3 NT Workstation user rights.		
User Right	**Description**	**Default Groups**
Access this computer from workstation	Allows remote access to shared resources on this network	Administrators, Everyone, Power Users
Backup files and directories	Allows backups	Administrators, Backup Operators
Change system time	Allows clock changing	Administrators, Power Users
Force shutdown from remote system	Allows remote system shutdown	Administrators, Power Users
Load and unload device drivers	Allows drivers to be changed	Administrators
Log on locally	Allows the workstation to be used locally	Administrators, Backup Operators, Everyone, Guests, Power Users, Users
Manage and audit Security log	Allows security policy changes	Administrators
Restore files and directories	Allows restoration	Administrators, Backup Operators
Shut down the system	Allows system shutdown	Administrators, Backup Operators, Everyone, Power Users, Users
Take ownership of files or other objects	Allows users to gain authority over system objects	Administrators, Backup Operators, Everyone, Guests, Power Users, Users

The advanced rights are associated with software development and are not generally used for Workstation administration. Do not use the advanced user rights unless you are certain about their functions and effect on the workstation. The advanced rights are not on the Workstation exam.

Auditing Policy

On a computer running Windows NT, the administrator has the option to audit access to resources such as directories, printers, and shares. The audit informs the administrator if someone attempts to access secured resources or just how often a particular resource is accessed. The information gathered by NT's auditing system can be brought to bear against performance problems, security risks, and expansion planning.

The auditing system is designed to watch every event occurrence on your entire network. To simplify the act of fine-tuning the areas you want to audit, there are three levels of switches with which you'll need to work. The master switch is the Audit These Events radio button located on the Audit Policy dialog box (see Figure 4.3). This dialog box is accessed through the User Manager's Policies pull-down menu.

This master switch turns on and off NT's entire audit system. By default, this switch is set to Do Not Audit.

The second level of switches becomes available when you set the master switch. There are seven event types listed in the Audit Policy dialog box. Each event type can be audited by tracking its success or failure. Here are the seven event types and descriptions of the events they control:

➤ **Logon And Logoff** Tracks logons, logoffs, and network connections.

➤ **File And Object Access** Tracks access to files, directories, and other NTFS objects, including printers.

➤ **Use Of User Rights** Tracks when users make use of user rights.

➤ **User And Group Management** Tracks changes in the accounts of users and groups (password changes, account deletions, group memberships, renaming, and so forth).

➤ **Security Policy Changes** Tracks changes of user rights, audit policies, and trusts.

➤ **Restart, Shutdown, And System** Tracks server shutdown and restarts; also logs events affecting system security.

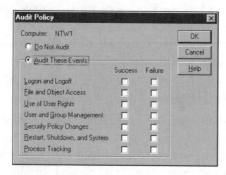

Figure 4.3 The Audit Policy dialog box.

➤ **Process Tracking** Tracks program activation, program termination, and other object/process access.

The third level of audit switches is on the object level. This level of control only applies to File And Object Access events. These switches reside within the properties of each NTFS object, such as file, directory, and printer. Figures 4.4 through 4.6 show the audit switch screens for file, directory, and print access. Note the differences in the tracking events among the object types. Both the file and directory objects have Read, Write, Execute, Delete, Change Permissions, and Take Ownership; but the printer object has Print, Full Control, Delete, Change Permissions, and Take Ownership.

A second, important difference to notice is on the directory object. The directory object allows you to change the files and/or subdirectories within the current directory to the same audit settings. Although this is convenient, you should use it with caution because any current audit settings on these objects will be cleared and replaced with the new settings.

To get to these dialog boxes, right-click over the object, select Properties from the pop-up menu, select the Security tab, and then click the Auditing button. Remember, object auditing is only available to NTFS objects, not FAT objects.

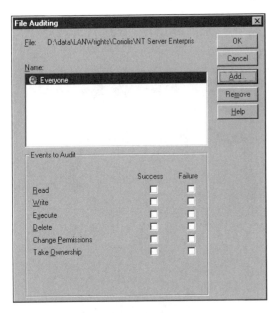

Figure 4.4 The File Auditing dialog box.

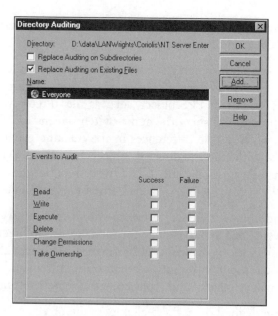

Figure 4.5   The Directory Auditing dialog box.

Note: By default, the object–level audit switches are all blank, with no users or groups present in the Name field. We added the Everyone group before taking these images so that the Events list at the bottom of the dialog boxes would become readable instead of almost invisible gray.

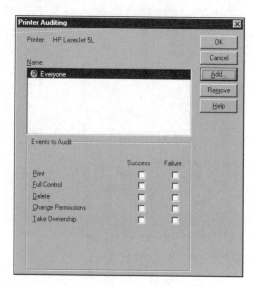

Figure 4.6   The Printer Auditing dialog box.

The object-level audit dialog boxes allow you to set the same success/failure event tracking for all users and groups listed in the Names field. You cannot track success for one group and failure for another.

Again, here are the steps required to audit:

1. Turn on the master Audit These Events switch.

2. Select one or more of the event types to track success or failure.

3. If you choose the File And Object Access option, you must also edit the auditing settings for each NTFS object.

Auditing system events demands large amounts of computing overhead, especially if the event monitored, such as file access, occurs often. It is not recommended to audit any event or object more than is absolutely necessary to track a problem or test equipment. Otherwise, your system will experience overall performance degradation.

The information gathered by NT's auditing system is stored in the Security log. You can view this log using the Event Viewer. The Event Viewer lists detailed information about each tracked event. Some of the data recorded includes user logon identification, the computer used, time, date, and the action or event that instigated an audit.

When numerous objects or events are audited, the Security log can grow large quite quickly. You need to monitor the size of this log and possibly implement a size restriction and/or automated new file creation to prevent data loss and maximize the usefulness of the gathered data.

Exam Prep Questions

Question 1

> You suspect that an Account group member is accessing a direc-
> tory that the user should be prevented from reaching. This might
> mean that you've set up the group memberships incorrectly. You
> aren't sure who it is, but you do know what directory is being
> accessed. What feature of NT will let you track who gains access
> to this directory?
>
> ○ a. NTFS file activity logging
>
> ○ b. Event auditing
>
> ○ c. Event Viewer
>
> ○ d. Account lockout

The NTFS file activity logging is a fault tolerance feature used to ensure
the integrity of stored data. It cannot be used to track access. Therefore,
answer a is incorrect. **Event auditing will track the activity around any
object within NT. Therefore, answer b is correct.** The Event Viewer is used
to review the Security log created by the auditing system, but it is not the
feature that does the actual tracking. Therefore, answer c is incorrect.
Account lockout is the feature used to prevent compromised accounts from
being used. Therefore, answer d is incorrect.

Question 2

> Which of the following are valid activities for User Manager on NT
> Workstation? [Check all correct answers]
>
> ❑ a. Create global groups
>
> ❑ b. Manage local users
>
> ❑ c. Add global groups to local groups
>
> ❑ d. Create domain users
>
> ❑ e. Manage local groups

The User Manager is able to manage local users, add global groups to local groups, and manage local groups. Therefore, answers b, c, and e are correct. Only the Server version, not the NT version, is able to create global groups and domain users. Therefore, answers a and d are incorrect.

Question 3

Mary is leaving the company and David is her replacement. What is the best way to give David the same access to all of the resources previously used by Mary?

- ○ a. Create an account in Server Manager for David using Mary's account as a template; then delete Mary's account.
- ○ b. Let David use Mary's account by giving him the password.
- ○ c. Rename Mary's account in Server Manager and tell David to change the account password when he logs on for the first time.
- ○ d. Create an account for David in the User Manager using Mary's account as a template; then disable Mary's account.

User accounts are created, maintained, and deleted through the User Manager, not the Server Manager. Therefore, answers a and c are incorrect. Just passing an account from one user to the next is a poor security policy. Therefore, answer b is incorrect. **It is preferable to copy an existing account to establish a replacement rather than just renaming the existing account. Therefore, answer d is correct. Also, copying an account makes a duplicate of all the security settings.** Keep in mind that when you see the phrase "the best way" in a question, multiple answers might be reasonable resolutions to the problem at hand, but only one is "the best way."

Question 4

Which of the following built-in groups, other than Administrators, have the default right to log on locally to Windows NT Workstation?

- ○ a. Power Users, Users, and Guests only
- ○ b. Users only
- ○ c. Backup Operators, Power Users, and Users only
- ○ d. Backup Operators, Power Users, Users, Guests, and Everyone

The default groups that can log on locally to NT Workstation are Backup Operators, Power Users, Users, Guests, and Everyone. Therefore, answer d is correct. All the other answers—a, b, and c—do not list all of the correct default groups and are therefore incorrect.

Question 5

You want to track the activity around a new high-speed color laser printer so that you can use the tracking information to restrict and grant privileged and priority access. Which of the following are required steps for implementing printer auditing? [Check all correct answers]

❑ a. Set the auditing switches on the printer object to track the successful print events for the Everyone group.

❑ b. Grant the Everyone group the auditing right through the User Rights policy.

❑ c. Set the Audit policy to Audit These Events through the User Manager for Domains.

❑ d. Set the audit switch of File and Object Access to Success under Audit These Events.

❑ e. Set the priority of the printer to 99 (maximum) under the Scheduling tab on the printer's Properties dialog box.

Setting the auditing switches on the object is required in order to enable printer tracking. Therefore, answer a is correct. There is not an auditing user right. Therefore, answer b is incorrect. Setting the master auditing switch to Audit These Events is required in order to track printer access. Therefore, answer c is correct. Setting the event type switch of File And Object Access to Success is required in order to track printer usage. Therefore, answer d is correct. Setting a printer's priority has nothing to do with tracking access. Therefore, answer e is incorrect. Thus, the correct answers are a, c, and d.

Question 6

> An important new custom application is conflicting with an exist-
> ing utility. The conflict seems to cause both programs to termi-
> nate prematurely. Which audit event type should be tracked to
> record some information about the conflict and which programs
> are affected?
>
> ○ a. File And Object Access
>
> ○ b. Security Policy Changes
>
> ○ c. Restart, Shutdown, And System
>
> ○ d. Process Tracking
>
> ○ e. Application Activity

File And Object Access is for tracking NTFS objects such as files and
printers. Therefore, answer a is incorrect. Security Policy Changes tracks
modifications to security and policies. Therefore, answer b is incorrect.
Restart, Shutdown, And System tracks system restarts. Therefore, answer c
is incorrect. **Process Tracking tracks threads and processes (for example,
applications). Therefore, answer d is correct.** Application Activity is not a
valid selection. Therefore, answer e is incorrect.

Question 7

> Which of the following settings cannot be managed through the
> Account Policy dialog box? [Check all correct answers]
>
> ❑ a. Password length
>
> ❑ b. Password history
>
> ❑ c. User Must Change Password At Next Logon
>
> ❑ d. User Must Logon To Change Password
>
> ❑ e. Password age
>
> ❑ f. User Cannot Change Password

Password length, history, and age, as well as User Must Logon To Change Password are all set by using the Account Policy dialog box. Therefore, answers a, b, d, and e are incorrect. **User Must Change Password At Next Logon and User Cannot Change Password are settings of the user account through the Properties dialog box of each account; therefore, answers c and f are correct.**

Question 8

> Which of the following is the best application to use in order to create a new shared directory on a domain server from your Windows NT workstation?
>
> ○ a. User Manager
>
> ○ b. Server Manager
>
> ○ c. Windows NT Explorer
>
> ○ d. Network Client Administrator

Server Manager allows users to create new shares on remote computers. Therefore, answer b is correct. The "trick" in this question is knowing that, although you can use Windows NT Explorer to manage share locally, you cannot manage shares remotely from it. You must use Server Manager to do this.

Question 9

> When you create a copy of an existing user account, what pieces of information are reset or left blank? [Check all correct answers]
>
> ❑ a. User Must Change Password At Next Logon
>
> ❑ b. User Name
>
> ❑ c. Account Disabled
>
> ❑ d. Password Never Expires
>
> ❑ e. Profile settings
>
> ❑ f. Password
>
> ❑ g. Group memberships

The fields that are reset or left blank when a user account is copied are User Must Change Password At Next Logon, user name, Account Disabled, and Password. Therefore, answers a, b, c, and f are correct. The Password Never Expires, profile settings, and group membership options remain as they were set in the original account. Therefore, answers d, e, and g are incorrect.

Question 10

Which characteristic do the default Administrator and Guest accounts share?

○ a. Both give Full Access to the network

○ b. Both can have blank passwords

○ c. Both cannot be deleted

○ d. Both can be locked out

Only the Administrator account has Full Access to the network. Therefore, answer a is incorrect. Only the Guest account can be set to a blank password. Therefore, answer b is incorrect. **Neither account can be deleted. Therefore, answer c is correct.** Only the Guest account can be locked out. Therefore, answer d is incorrect.

Need To Know More?

 Boyce, Jim, et al.: *Windows NT Workstation 4.0 Advanced Technical Reference.* Que, Indianapolis, IN, 1996. ISBN 0-7897-0863-9. Chapter 32 discusses the administration of user accounts. However, this reference should be used with caution because Workstation and Server details seem to be overlapped and confused.

 Perkins, Charles, Matthew Strebe, and James Chellis: *MCSE: NT Workstation Study Guide.* Sybex NetworkPress, San Francisco, CA, 1997. ISBN 0-7821-1973-5. Chapter 3 has a detailed account of users, groups, and policies.

 The *Windows NT Server Resource Kit* contains a lot of useful information about shares and share permissions. You can search the TechNet (either online or CD version) or *Resource Kit* CD versions using keywords such as "users," "groups," and "policies."

 Search the TechNet CD (or its online version through www.microsoft.com) using the keywords "user management," "security policy," and "groups."

Configuring Windows NT Workstation

5

Terms you'll need to understand:

√   Control Panel applets

√   User profiles

√   Logon scripts

√   Registry

√   REGEDIT

√   REGEDT32

√   Windows NT Diagnostics (WINMSD)

Techniques you'll need to master:

√   Understanding and using Control Panel applets

√   Installing and configuring hardware

√   Implementing and maintaining user profiles and logon scripts

√   Working with the Windows NT Registry

√   Understanding and using Windows NT Diagnostics (WINMSD)

Although users, groups, and policies are essential for a network to function, there are still many issues and elements regarding system configuration that must be addressed before optimum use of NT Workstation can be achieved. A broad range of configuration issues exist; however, most of these issues you won't see on the exam. In this chapter, we cover nearly all of the configuration interfaces so that you'll have a complete picture of what can and cannot be done within the NT Workstation environment.

Control Panel Applets

Most system alterations are controlled through the numerous applets found in the Control Panel. Each of these applications has a specific purpose and modifies the Registry behind the scenes. We'll talk about the Registry later in this chapter, in the section titled "Working With The Windows NT Registry."

Some of the Control Panel applets are present only if their corresponding services or devices have been installed. In other cases, the applets are present even if you don't use them.

The two basic divisions or types of control applets are system and user. The system applets, or controls, modify hardware or software settings for the entire computer. In other words, when a system control is used, all users experience the change. The user controls only modify how the environment of a specific user operates, not the entire computer. System controls are only accessible by Administrators, whereas the user controls are available to standard users (unless a system profile prevents this). This dichotomy is usually fairly easy to recognize; however, there are some applets, such as the Display applet, that have both system- and user-level option tabs. In the following sections, we separate the system controls from the user controls and list all the important applets (that means those included on the exam) located in the Control Panel.

We think visual familiarity with the Control Panel applets is a key to passing the Workstation exam. Even though we include some images of the controls, we recommend you spend time on an NT Workstation working through this text while viewing the applets online to get a full grasp of what's involved.

System Configuration Controls

The system-level controls are those applets that modify the operation of hardware or software for the entire computer.

The System Applet

The System applet is used to alter environmental variables, pagefile parameters, and startup options. This applet has six control tabs:

- ➤ **General** Lists the OS version, registration detail, and basic computer configuration (see Figure 5.1).

- ➤ **Performance** Sets the performance boost for foreground apps (2 = max) and the virtual memory pagefile (see Figure 5.2). (Chapter 15 discusses the Performance tab in more detail.)

- ➤ **Environment** Displays and modifies the environmental variable settings (see Figure 5.3).

- ➤ **Startup/Shutdown** The top portion of this tab modifies the BOOT.INI file by setting the default startup selection and timeout; the bottom portion defines the action to take when a STOP error occurs, such as create a memory dump file and/or reboot the system (see Figure 5.4). (Chapter 18 discusses the Startup/Shutdown tab in detail.)

- ➤ **Hardware Profiles** Multiple hardware configurations can be configured through this tab, thus allowing a portable computer to interact with PC cards (also called PCMCIA) or a docking station. The top

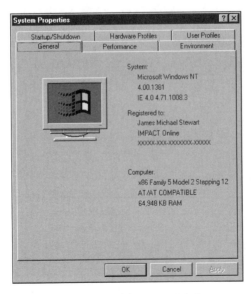

Figure 5.1   The General tab of the System applet.

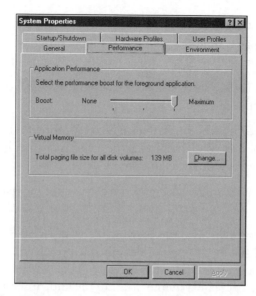

Figure 5.2 The Performance tab of the System applet.

profile is the default, and a timeout can be set for the selection menu that appears during bootup. The most common use for hardware profiles is a notebook that is sometimes detached from a network.

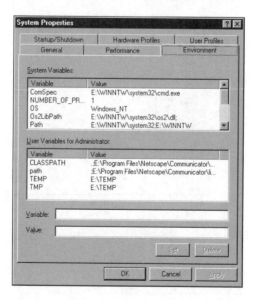

Figure 5.3 The Environment tab of the System applet.

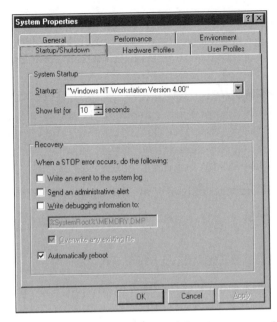

Figure 5.4   The Startup/Shutdown tab of the System applet.

➤ **User Profiles** User profiles can be copied and deleted from this tab (see Figure 5.5). Also, profiles can be modified to be roaming or local through the Change Type button.

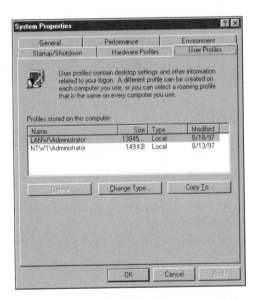

Figure 5.5   The User Profiles tab of the System applet.

The Date/Time Applet

This simple, but useful applet sets the system time and date on the Date & Time tab, and it defines the time zone on the Time Zone tab.

The Services Applet

Through the Services applet, you can obtain the status of available services and alter when and if the services load. To modify the startup method of a service, double-click the item in the Services list, then choose from the following three choices for Startup Type:

➤ **Automatic** The service loads if possible.

➤ **Manual** The service is started only when it is needed by other processes.

➤ **Disabled** The service will not be started.

By default, services run under the System account. However, certain network services, such as the Directory Replication service, require a network logon. In such cases, you can define the user account to be used by the service.

Additionally, hardware profiles can be modified through the HW Profiles button for each service.

The Ports Applet

Through this applet, you can set the operational parameters of the communications ports. The settings include baud rate, data bits, stop bits, and flow control, as well as advanced settings of COM port number, base I/O address, IRQ, and FIFO serial buffer setting.

The Telephony Applet

The Telephony applet is the primary area where a dialing location can be defined and modified. A dialing location simply sets the area code, long-distance dialing requirements, credit card calls, whether to disable call waiting, and tone or pulse dialing. All these options are listed on the My Locations tab. The other tab, Telephony Drivers, lists the TAPI or communication drivers installed on the machine. This is usually not the place where new drivers for communication devices are installed.

Uninterruptible Power Supplies Applet

Uninterruptible Power Supplies, or UPSs, are invaluable devices for production computers. A UPS is a power supply that can be used by a computer for a short time after normal power is terminated. The UPS applet enables the integration of UPS features with NT through a serial port using an RS-232 cable. Depending on the type of UPS, you need to configure the applet to properly interpret signals from the device. The most important item to get correct is the voltage type for each signal—it's either positive or negative. The wrong voltage definition can cause your system to turn itself off prematurely or to fail to shut down before electricity is terminated. Other details to define are battery life, recharge time, and warning timeouts.

Another issue in regard to UPSs occurs during bootup. By default, NT polls the serial ports for mice. If a UPS is present, this signal can be interpreted by the UPS as a terminate power command; thus, the machine will lose power and fail to boot. However, the /NOSERIALMICE=[COM*x* | COM*x,y,z*...] BOOT.INI parameter can be used to disable serial mouse detection of one or more specified COM ports.

Configuring And Installing Hardware

Unlike Windows 95, from which NT received its current look and feel, the Control Panel lacks an Add New Hardware applet. This is mainly due to NT's lack of support for the plug-and-play architecture. However, two methods are available for installing and configuring new hardware:

➤ Use one of the device type-specific applets (defined later in this section)

➤ Use the manufacturer-supplied installation/setup utility

If neither of these methods is available to you, the device cannot be installed into NT. Generally, the install process involves powering down the system, installing the device, booting to install the driver, and then rebooting. Removing a device follows a reverse path: remove the driver, shut down, remove the device, and then reboot.

Configuring a hardware device under NT is tricky. As we've stated already, NT does not support plug-and-play. This means the hardware device does not have the capability to directly modify the configuration settings as stored in the device's BIOS. Usually, you must boot to DOS (even if it means booting with a floppy), use a DOS-based configuration tool to alter the settings on the card, boot to NT and modify the settings of the driver to match that of the device, and then reboot.

There are numerous hardware-related Control Panel applets. We've already talked about UPSs earlier in this chapter, and the Modems applet is discussed in Chapter 13. The remaining applets are discussed in the following sections.

Network Applet

Network adapter drivers are installed, modified, and removed through the Network applet on the Adapters tab. The other features of the Network applet are discussed in Chapters 9, 10, and 11.

SCSI Applet

The SCSI Adapters applet is where the installation, modification, and removal of SCSI devices and controllers occur. However, many IDE controllers, especially those built into the motherboard, will appear in this applet. The Devices tab lists all the SCSI adapters installed on the system and the devices connected to each daisy chain. Details for any of these devices can be obtained through the Properties button. The Drivers tab allows the installation and removal of SCSI drivers. CD-ROMs, although often thought of as multimedia devices, are installed through the SCSI Adapters applet instead of the Multimedia applet.

Tape Devices Applet

The Tape Devices applet is where backup devices are installed. The Detect button will search for known devices and install drivers for any devices located. If your device is not detected, it can be manually installed on the Drivers tab.

Multimedia Applet

The Multimedia applet is used to configure audio, MIDI, and video settings for NT. On its Devices tab, new drivers for audio and multimedia cards or features can be installed and removed.

Display Applet

The Display applet is where video display drivers are installed for VGA cards and the parameters for your display are set (this all occurs on the Settings tab). The other tabs of the Display applet are user controls.

Keyboards And Mouse Applets

Two applets, namely Keyboard and Mouse, are used to install drivers for these input devices, as well as configure their operational parameters.

PC Card Applet

This applet is only functional on those computers with a PC card (also referred to as PCMCIA) interface. Through this applet, drivers can be installed for these add-on cards.

> *Note: NT does not respond favorably to the insertion and removal of PC cards; changing of PC cards should be done only when NT is shut down to avoid problems. This is another symptom of the lack of plug-and-play support.*

Devices Applet

The Devices applet is where all the drivers installed onto NT are listed with their respective Status and Startup parameters. The Startup parameters can be set to boot, system, automatic, manual, or disabled. Additionally, hardware profiles can be modified through the HW Profiles button for each device driver.

Application Control

Most software applications are installed through their own setup utility. However, NT offers an interface to launch applications with special Control Panel tie-ins. Also, on the Install/Uninstall tab is a list of applications known by NT that can be uninstalled. The Windows NT Setup tab offers the ability to install or remove NT-specific components.

User Configuration Controls

The user controls are those portions of the Control Panel applets that any and all users (unless denied or restricted by a system policy) can access to fine-tune their computing environment. These user-control applets include the following applets:

➤ Display

➤ Keyboard

➤ Mouse

➤ Regional Settings

➤ Sounds

Display

The Display applet in the Control Panel has four tabs for user-specific control. The Background tab controls desktop wallpaper and the default pattern. The Screen Saver tab controls screen savers and password protection. The Appearance tab controls the color and font scheme used by windows and dialog boxes. The Plus! tab controls default icon images and special visual effects.

Keyboard And Mouse

Users generally have access privileges to change the operational parameters of the keyboard and mouse using the Control Panel Keyboard and Mouse applets. These controls include typing speed, language support, multiple key mappings, pointer schemes, and motion speeds.

Regional Settings

The Regional Settings applet is where settings for language, time zone, number appearance, currency type, time and date display methods, and input locals (a language scheme) appear.

Sounds

The Sounds applet is where sounds are associated with events (for example, a warning buzzer that is played each time a system error occurs.) All sound/event associations are unique to each individual and can be saved into a single scheme for transference to another user or machine.

User Profiles

A user profile is a stored collection of elements that define a user's desktop and computing environment. Through a profile, users can customize their desktops to meet their computing needs. Settings such as screen savers, network connections, customized desktops, mouse settings, and program groups are specified with a user profile. Profiles can be created for both users and groups. User profiles are located in the \%winntroot%\Profiles\<*username*>\Desktop directory.

User profiles protect your network resources from your users and your users from themselves. Establishing user profiles can help you when network users remove or relocate program items and groups. By forcing users to maintain settings with user profiles, you produce a consistent user interface that is not modifiable, reducing your support costs as well as the users' frustration levels.

You can force a user to use a certain profile by creating a mandatory user profile that cannot be changed or saved by the user. This is produced by establishing a profile (local or roaming) for a user, changing the name of the NTUSER.DAT file to NTUSER.MAN, and entering the profile UNC path into User Profile Path, located in the User Environment Profile screen for each user.

Incidentally, in the event of a PDC failure, the user will not receive the mandatory profile at logon. When this happens, Windows NT accesses the user's last locally cached profile or the default profile assigned to the user's workstation. The locally cached profile is used if the user has logged on to the domain successfully in the past. The default profile is used if the user has never logged on to the domain successfully.

Use the following steps to create a roaming profile:

1. Copy the user's profile from the workstation to a shared network path.

2. Open the Control Panel and double-click System.

3. Select the user's profile entry, select Copy To, and type in the full UNC path name to the server where the profile will reside.

4. In the User Profile dialog box, enter the full UNC path name for the profile in the User Profile path field.

You also can set the user's home directory settings in the user's profile. To do this for an existing account that currently has a local home directory, you must perform the following steps:

1. Select the Connect option in the User Environment Profile dialog box in the User Manager.

2. Select a shared driver letter and then enter the full UNC path name of the user's new home directory.

   The full UNC path name contains the server name on which the home directory resides (the domain name is not required). The variable %HOMEPATH% contains the user's home directory UNC path name only after the new home directory has been established.

If you have users who change settings constantly and/or inappropriately, it's a good idea to establish profiles and force users to stick to these settings.

Logon Scripts

When you consider all the user configuration utilities and capabilities that come with NT Workstation, it seems strange to include logon scripts. However, to maintain backward compatibility, you must provide for the use of logon scripts—for several reasons. First, because user profiles only work with NT-based computers, DOS-based clients require logon scripts to provide consistent network connections. Also, if you still have an old LAN Manager server on your network, logon scripts preserve backward compatibility to those servers for all clients.

In addition, you can specify a user's network connections or network printer connections without developing a sophisticated user profile plan. In the event that you only have defined personal profiles but you want to define persistent network connections, logon scripts can do that, too. Finally, if you don't want to spend an extensive amount of time developing a complex and coherent user profile strategy, logon scripts are a quick and easy alternative.

Using logon scripts is beneficial in custom-building a user's environment without managing all aspects of it. For backup purposes, you should replicate logon scripts from the PDC to all BDCs on the network. That way, should the PDC go down, the BDCs maintain a copy of the logon scripts and make them available to users at logon. Logon scripts do not need to be exported to every workstation. Always place files that are to be exported into subdirectories of the \%winntroot%\System32\Repl\Export directory. Files that are located in the root \%winntroot%\System32\Repl\Import directory will not be replicated. The default export directory for logon scripts on the PDC is \%winntroot%\System32\Repl\Export\Scripts.

Working With The Windows NT Registry

The Registry is a hierarchical database of information about the system hardware, installed software, system settings, and user settings. This database replaces INI, CONFIG.SYS, and AUTOEXEC.BAT files where this information was stored in previous versions of Windows. The Registry is made up of several files, but it isn't necessary to edit any of these files individually. To the end-user, the Registry appears as one seamless database. Fortunately, most information that is contained in the Registry is set through the user interface, primarily with the applets found in the Control Panel.

For items that are not controlled through the user interface, Windows NT provides two editing utilities: REGEDT32.EXE and REGEDIT.EXE. These utilities are not available on the Start menu—they must be launched from the Run command or a command prompt.

The Registry is organized in a hierarchical structure, much like the directory structure of a hard drive. This hierarchy consists of subtrees, hives, keys, values, and data. Table 5.1 lists the hives and presents a summary of the information located in them.

The Registry is not an exhaustive record of an NT system configuration. Instead, it only contains those values that are different from the system defaults. In other words, the data in the Registry is the exception. When the NT system makes a system call and no Registry setting says otherwise, it assumes the intuitive defaults. Unfortunately, this makes editing the Registry a real nightmare, because the default values are generally known only to the OS.

HKEY_LOCAL_MACHINE

From an administrative point of view, the HKEY_LOCAL_MACHINE key contains the most useful information about the local system. This subtree has five direct hives: Hardware, SAM, Security, Software, and System. Table 5.2 lists the general information contained in each of these hives.

Table 5.1   The six main hives of the NT Registry.

Hive	Description
HKEY_CLASSES_ROOT	Establishes OLE file associations (retained for backward compatibility).
HKEY_CURRENT_USER	Displays user profile information for the user currently logged in.
HKEY_LOCAL_MACHINE	Manages hardware and software configuration, installed drivers, and security.
HKEY_USERS	Provides user profile information for all users.
HKEY_CURRENT_CONFIG	Displays the currently used hardware profile (a subset of HKEY_LOCAL_MACHINE).
HKEY_DYN_DATA	Provides temporary storage for the state of dynamic events and performance information.

Table 5.2	The five subkeys of the HKEY_LOCAL_MACHINE hive of the NT Registry.
Subkey	**Description**
Hardware	Shows devices attached to the system and their current state.
SAM	Displays the Security Account Manager, which includes local user, group account, and domain values. This information is not available for direct editing using the Registry Editor.
Security	Shows security information used locally by the security subsystem.
Software	Displays the software settings that apply to all local users.
System	Shows boot information and associated device drivers.

REGEDIT Vs. REGEDT32

The only real difference between these two Registry editing tools—besides the Explorer-type interface of REGEDIT and the File Manager-type interface of REGEDT32—is in their power to search or modify security settings. REGEDIT can be used to search for keys, values, and data throughout the entire Registry at once, whereas REGEDT32 can only search for keys. However, REGEDT32 can be used to alter any security settings.

Windows NT Diagnostics (WINMSD)

The Windows NT Diagnostics (or WINMSD) utility gives you a shallow insight into the current configuration of the NT software and the hardware on which it is operating. This tool is similar to both the MSD utility for DOS and the Device Manager for Windows 95. WINMSD can only be used to view system information—it cannot make any modifications to installed software or devices. However, users can get a quick view of system information and configurations through WINMSD.

Exam Prep Questions

Question 1

> What Control Panel applet should be used to create a roaming profile for a user?
>
> ○ a. System
> ○ b. Network
> ○ c. Regional Settings
> ○ d. User Manager

The User Profile tab, located in the System applet, is where roaming profiles are established. Therefore, answer a is correct. The Network applet is not involved in the creation of user profiles. Therefore, answer b is incorrect. The Regional Settings applet makes changes that are stored in a user profile, but roaming profiles are not managed through this tool. Therefore, answer c is incorrect. The User Manager is not a Control Panel applet, and it is only able to establish the path of a profile. It is not used to create profiles. Therefore, answer d is incorrect.

Question 2

> After the successful installation of NT Workstation, you need to remove an old Network Interface Card and install a new high-speed interface. Where should you attempt to remove the old drivers and install the new drivers?
>
> ○ a. Drivers
> ○ b. SCSI
> ○ c. Network
> ○ d. System

The Drivers applet is where drivers can be started and stopped; however, they cannot be installed or removed through this interface. Therefore, answer a is incorrect. The SCSI applet is used to install and remove SCSI device drivers. Therefore, answer b is incorrect. **The Adapters tab in the Network applet is used to install and remove NIC drivers. Therefore, answer c is correct.** The System applet is not involved in the operation or installation of NICs. Therefore, answer d is incorrect.

Question 3

After you have installed a new application, the instructions state that you must manually modify the PATH statement so that the software will function properly. How can this be accomplished?

○ a. Edit the PATH.BAT file.

○ b. Modify the PATH variable on the Environment tab of the System applet

○ c. Edit the CONFIG.NT file.

○ d. Edit the PATH value in the Registry located in the \HKEY_LOCAL_MACHINE\CurrentControlSet\System\ key.

There is no such thing as a PATH.BAT file. Therefore, answer a is incorrect. **The Environment tab of the System applet is the proper place to modify the PATH variable. Therefore, answer b is correct.** The CONFIG.NT file is not editable by users. Therefore, answer c is incorrect. The Registry key listed for this PATH value is fictitious. Therefore, answer d is incorrect.

Question 4

How can you change the timeout value for the boot menu? [Check all correct answers]

❑ a. Edit the BOOT.INI file.

❑ b. Set the TimeOut variable on the Environment tab of the System applet.

❑ c. Set the timeout on the Startup/Shutdown tab of the System applet

❑ d. Through the BootMenu key in the Registry.

Editing the BOOT.INI file is one method of changing the timeout value of the boot menu. Therefore, answer a is correct. There is not a TimeOut variable that relates to the boot menu to be found on the Environment tab of the System applet. Therefore, answer b is incorrect. **The Startup/Shutdown tab of the System applet has a timeout control for the boot menu. Therefore, answer c is correct.** There is not a BootMenu key in the Registry. Therefore, answer d is incorrect.

Question 5

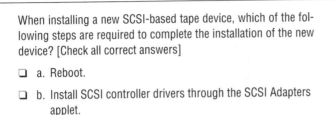

When installing a new SCSI-based tape device, which of the following steps are required to complete the installation of the new device? [Check all correct answers]

❑ a. Reboot.

❑ b. Install SCSI controller drivers through the SCSI Adapters applet.

❑ c. Use the Add New Hardware applet.

❑ d. Detect the tape device through the Tape Devices applet.

Rebooting, the SCSI Adapters applet, and the Tape Devices applet are all required steps for installing a new SCSI-based tape device. Therefore, answers a, b, and d are correct. There is not an Add New Hardware applet in NT. Therefore, answer c is incorrect.

Question 6

How can you use your NT Workstation-based notebook computer at the office on a LAN as well as at home over a modem, without launching the network services while not connected to the network?

○ a. Create two local user profiles.

○ b. Create two computer system policies.

○ c. Create two hardware profiles.

○ d. Create two user accounts.

Two user profiles will not prevent the network services from launching when not physically connected to the network. Therefore, answer a is incorrect. Two computer system polices will not prevent the network services from launching either. Therefore, answer b is incorrect. **Two hardware profiles will allow the non-network profile to be selected when not physically connected to the network. Therefore, answer c is correct.** Two user accounts will not offer the desired effect. Therefore, answer d is incorrect.

Question 7

You recently purchased a UPS to protect your computer from power failures and spikes. You have taken the precaution of adding the **/NOSERIALMICE** parameter to your BOOT.INI file. After charging the UPS and attaching it to the correct serial port, you boot your NT Workstation computer. You test your configuration by unplugging the UPS from the wall. After five minutes, the UPS battery is drained, cutting off power to your computer. NT did not gracefully shut down, even though you heard the repeated beeps from the UPS device. What is a possible explanation of this?

○ a. The UPS drivers were not installed through the Devices applet.

○ b. The voltages were reversed in the UPS applet.

○ c. NT is not compatible with UPS devices.

○ d. The UPS variables were not defined in the System applet on the Environment tab.

The Devices applet is not used to install drivers; also, a UPS requires no additional drivers for operation. Therefore, answer a is incorrect. **If the voltages defining the communications from a UPS are reversed, the computer will fail to understand its signals. Therefore, answer b is correct.** NT is UPS-compatible. Therefore, answer c is incorrect. There are no UPS variables to be defined through the System applet. Therefore, answer d is incorrect.

Question 8

Where would drivers for a MIDI device be installed under NT?

○ a. Drivers applet

○ b. System applet

○ c. SCSI applet

○ d. Multimedia applet

The Drivers and System applets cannot be used to install drivers. Therefore, answers a and b are incorrect. The SCSI applet is not used to install MIDI device drivers. Therefore, answer c is incorrect. **The Multimedia applet is used to install MIDI device drivers. Therefore, answer d is correct.**

Question 9

> Which Registry editing tool can be used to change the security settings on individual Registry keys?
>
> ○ a. REGEDIT
>
> ○ b. REGEDT32

REGEDT32 is the Registry editing tool that can modify the ACLs on Registry keys. Therefore, answer b is correct.

Question 10

> Users whose profiles are defined by the NTUSER.MAN file can be changed to their personal preferences, and these changes will be stored for their next computing session.
>
> ○ a. True
>
> ○ b. False

False, answer b is correct. Profiles defined by NTUSER.MAN are mandatory profiles. Any changes a user makes are not stored.

Need To Know More?

Perkins, Charles, Matthew Strebe, and James Chellis: *MCSE: NT Workstation Study Guide.* Sybex Network Press, San Francisco, CA, 1997. ISBN 0-7821-1973-5. Chapter 4 discusses most of these Control Panel and configuration issues.

Search the TechNet CD (or its online version through www.microsoft.com) and the *Windows NT Workstation Resource Kit* CD using the keywords "Control Panel," "profile," and the name of each Control Panel applet discussed in this chapter.

Windows NT File Systems And Structures

6

Terms you'll need to understand:

√ File Allocation Table (FAT)

√ New Technology File System (NTFS)

√ High Performance File System (HPFS)

√ Compact Disk File System (CDFS)

√ 8.3 file names

√ Long file names (LFNs)

√ Virtual FAT (VFAT)

√ FAT32

√ CONVERT.EXE

Techniques you'll need to master:

√ Selecting a file system for NT

√ Using CONVERT.EXE to convert FAT to NTFS

√ Using Disk Administrator to establish a disk structure

Windows NT supports two primary file systems to save and retrieve data from storage systems of all kinds (primarily hard disks): File Allocation Table (FAT) and New Technology File System (NTFS). In this chapter, we review these file systems and explore the key aspects of their features, functions, and behavior that you're likely to encounter on the Workstation exam. We also examine a couple of other special-purpose file systems that work with Windows NT so that you're familiar with Microsoft Windows NT file systems' alphabet soup. Then, we conclude with some sample file-system-related test questions and some good places to go looking for more information on this fascinating subject.

FAT Comes In Many Flavors

FAT stands for File Allocation Table and refers to a linear table structure used to represent information about files. The information represented includes file names, file attributes, and other directory entries that locate where files (or segments of files) are stored in the FAT environment.

Original FAT

FAT is the file system originally used with DOS. The file allocation table from which FAT draws its name stores directory information in a simple table structure that must be searched from beginning to end, one entry at a time, when users access directories or the files that reside within them.

Although FAT is both primitive and simple, its implementations abound: A variety of versions for DOS, Windows 3.x, Windows NT, many flavors of Unix, and Macintosh are available. Numerous other, more exotic operating systems also support FAT file structures. For this reason, Microsoft recommends using FAT-formatted volumes with Windows NT Workstation (or Server) whenever many different types of clients must exchange data through a single file system.

One of the most important characteristics of original FAT is its use of so-called 8.3 (pronounced "eight-dot-three") file names, where the name of a file can be up to eight characters long, all extensions must be preceded by a period, and file extensions can be no more than three characters long. The latter specification has led to the proliferation of many common three-character file extensions, such as .TXT for text files, .DOC for word processing files, .XLS for Excel spreadsheet files, and more. For many users, this is a defining characteristic for DOS, but it's really a requirement of the FAT file system.

Because the size of files and partitions that FAT can manage has grown with each new version of DOS, FAT uses two kinds of pointers in its allocation tables. Partitions smaller than 50 MB use 12-bit pointers, whereas larger partitions require the use of 16-bit pointers. That's why sometimes you'll see FAT volumes labeled as either "FAT12" (the volume's FAT uses 12-bit pointers) or "FAT16" (the volume's FAT uses 16-bit pointers). As shown in Figure 6.1, a FAT12 or FAT16 label appears in disk partition management utilities like the FDISK command that ships with most versions of DOS. Table 6.1 shows the features and capabilities of the FAT file system. For versions of DOS from 3.0 to 6.22, all FAT drivers are 16-bit only (but this does not affect whether a volume is called FAT12 or FAT16—that's purely a size of the FAT volume itself).

In addition to ordinary FAT, there are two other flavors of FAT in use in the most modern Microsoft operating systems (Windows 95 and Windows NT, to be precise): Virtual FAT (VFAT) and the FAT32 File System. We'll cover those in the sections that follow.

Virtual FAT (VFAT)

The Virtual FAT (VFAT) file system was first introduced with Windows for Workgroups 3.11 to process file I/O in protected mode. With the introduction of Windows 95, VFAT added support for long file names (LFNs). Nevertheless, VFAT remains backward compatible with original FAT, which means that it supports access using 8.3 file names as well as LFNs and, in fact, maintains an equivalence mechanism that maps 8.3 names into LFNs, and vice versa.

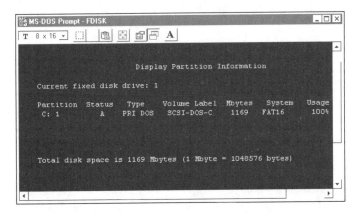

Figure 6.1   The DOS FDISK utility indicates whether a FAT volume is FAT12 or FAT16.

Table 6.1   Vital statistics for the FAT file system.

Feature	Capability/Maximum
Maximum volume size	2 GB
Maximum file size	2 GB
Maximum files in root directory	512
Maximum files in non-root directory	65,535
File-level security	No
Long file name support	No
Self-repairing	No
Transaction logging capabilities	No
File-level compression	No
File-level security	No
Dual file fork support (Macintosh)	No
POSIX support	No

VFAT is the version of FAT that the original releases of Windows 95, Windows NT 3.51, and Windows NT 4 currently support. When using VFAT file systems, it's absolutely essential to use file management utilities that understand VFAT in general and LFNs in particular. That's because earlier DOS file management utilities will happily reorganize what appears to them as an original FAT structure and will often lose or damage any LFN information contained in the FAT table maintained by VFAT (or FAT32 for that matter). Therefore, when working with VFAT volumes, you must be certain to use file management utilities that can understand and preserve VFAT file structures.

In the initial release of Windows 95, the 32-bit VFAT file system is the primary file system. VFAT can use either 32-bit protected-mode drivers or 16-bit real-mode drivers. Actual allocation on disk is still 12 or 16 bit (depending on the size of the volume), so VFAT on the disk uses the same structure as earlier implementations of FAT. VFAT handles all hard drive requests and uses 32-bit code for all file access to hard drive volumes. Table 6.2 shows the features and capabilities of the VFAT file system.

As Table 6.2 illustrates, the primary differences between VFAT and FAT are an increase in maximum volume and file sizes, an increase in non-root directory container size, and the addition of long file name support to 8.3 file names. VFAT also supports both 16- and 32-bit calls, whereas original FAT supports only 16-bit calls.

Table 6.2 Vital statistics for the VFAT file system.	
Feature	**Capability/Maximum**
Maximum volume size	4 GB
Maximum file size	4 GB
Maximum files in root directory	512
Maximum files in non-root directory	No limit
File-level security	No
Long file name support	Yes
Self-repairing	No
Transaction logging capabilities	No
File-level compression	No
File-level security	No
Dual file fork support (Macintosh)	No
POSIX support	No

The FAT32 File System

FAT32 is the 32-bit successor to VFAT that was introduced with Microsoft Windows 95 OEM Service Release 2, in September, 1996. You will sometimes see this release, called Windows 95 OSR2 in Microsoft publications. FAT32 is a completely native 32-bit file system (much like NTFS), and it supports numerous updates and enhancements compared to other FAT implementations.

Most important, FAT32 uses disk space more efficiently than other FAT implementations. FAT32 can use smaller disk clusters than earlier implementations, which were limited to a maximum of 65,635 clusters per volume (so as drives got bigger, cluster sizes had to increase as well). This means that even for drives up to 8 GB in size, FAT32 can use 4 K clusters. This results in a 10 to 15 percent savings in storage allocation and more efficient disk space usage compared to FAT16 drives.

The details about FAT32 are not covered on any of the NT 4 exams. This information is provided to offer you a contrasting view of FAT in comparison with NTFS. You can skip this section without detriment to your exam preparation.

FAT32 can also relocate the root directory and use a backup copy of FAT, rather than the default copy. FAT32 supports an expanded boot record to include copies of critical data structures, making FAT32 drives less susceptible to failures owing to FAT corruption than earlier implementations. FAT32 even represents the root directory as an ordinary cluster chain, which means that the directory can be located anywhere on a drive. Also, the prior limitation of 512 entries on a root directory no longer applies (as it does to earlier FAT implementations). Planned implementations of FAT32 may even support dynamic resizing of FAT32 partitions, but this is not supported in Windows 95 OSR2. Table 6.3 shows the features and capabilities of FAT32.

> *Note: The asterisk (*) under the self-repairing column denotes that the FAT32 self-repairing characteristics, although useful, fall short of NTFS's broader set of self-repair capabilities.*

Windows 95 OSR2 is the only current Microsoft operating system that supports FAT32. This means that not even Windows NT 4, with the latest service pack applied supports this file system. If you create a multiboot configuration on a machine with Windows 95 OSR2 and Windows NT installed, NT will not be able to access any files that reside in a FAT32 partition. Windows 95 OSR2 can, however, access the VFAT partitions that Windows NT creates.

The same proviso about using VFAT utilities on VFAT volumes applies to FAT32 volumes. Because earlier FAT utilities (including both FAT and VFAT, where FAT32 is concerned) can damage or lose critical disk information, *never* use anything but FAT32 file management utilities on FAT32 volumes.

Table 6.3   Vital statistics for the FAT32 file system.

Feature	Capability/Maximum
Maximum volume size	4 TB
Maximum file size	4 TB
Maximum files in root directory	No limit
Maximum files in non-root directory	No limit
File-level security	No
Long file name support	Yes
Self-repairing	Yes*
Transaction logging capabilities	No
File-level compression	No
File-level security	No
Dual file fork support (Macintosh)	No
POSIX support	No

In addition to increasing FAT's storage capacity (to a whopping 4 TB maximum for files and volumes), FAT32 makes some much-needed improvements to the root directory structure for FAT. Previous implementations required that all information in a FAT root directory fit into a single disk cluster. For all intents and purposes, this limited the number of files in the root to a maximum of 512 entries.

The introduction of LFNs further limited what the root directory could hold. Because the maximum length of an LFN is 256, a single full-length LFN can consume 25 entries in a FAT (one for the 8.3 name, 24 more for the LFN itself). This reduces the number of entries possible in a VFAT root directory to 21. Microsoft recommends that LFNs be avoided in FAT root directories unless FAT32 is in use.

Then, too, full file specifications, which require both path names and file names (whether LFNs or 8.3 names), are limited to a total of 260 characters. FAT32 does away with the problems that LFNs in root directories can pose, but it does nothing to increase the 260-character limit on full file specifications. For that reason, Microsoft recommends that even LFNs not be allowed to exceed 75 to 80 characters in length in order to leave plenty of room for path designations (up to 180 to 185 characters).

Finally, FAT32 delivers several improvements to FAT's fault tolerance. For one thing, FAT32 boot records now capture important file system data (such as partition table information). For another, FAT mirroring can be disabled in FAT32 so that another copy of the FAT can be used to drive file lookup and access. That's why Table 6.3 includes a "Yes" under the Self-repairing category.

New Technology File System (NTFS)

In keeping with the "New Technology" part of its name, NTFS incorporates significant improvements and changes to the file system native to Windows NT. From a user's point of view, files remain organized into directories (often called "folders" in the Windows environment). But unlike with FAT, there is no special treatment for root directories, nor limitations set by underlying hardware (such as the capability to access only a maximum number of disk sectors or clusters, as is the case with FAT). Likewise, there are no special indexing structures on an NTFS volume, like the file allocation table that gives FAT its name.

NTFS was designed to provide the following characteristics:

> **Reliability** Desirable on high-end or shared systems, such as file servers, reliability is a key element of NTFS design and behavior.

> **Added functionality** NTFS is designed to be extensible and incorporates advanced fault tolerance, emulates other file systems easily, supports a powerful security model, handles multiple data streams, and permits the addition of user-defined attributes to files.

> **POSIX support** Because the U.S. government requires minimal POSIX compliance in all systems it buys, NTFS provides them. Basic POSIX file system capabilities include optional use of case-sensitive file names, an additional timestamp for time of last file access, and an aliasing mechanism called "hard links" that lets two or more file names (potentially in different directories) point to the same file.

> **Flexibility** NTFS supports a highly flexible clustering model, with cluster sizes from 512 bytes to 64 K, based on a multiple of the hardware's built-in disk allocation factor. NTFS also supports LFNs and the Unicode character set, as well as maintains 8.3 file names for all files for backward compatibility with FAT.

NTFS Advantages

NTFS is constructed to handle large collections of data particularly well (see Table 6.4 for the details), and it also works well for volumes of 400 MB

Table 6.4 Vital statistics for the NTFS file system.	
Feature	**Capability/Maximum**
Maximum volume size	16 EB
Maximum file size	16 EB
Maximum files in root directory	No limit
Maximum files in non-root directory	No limit
File-level security	Yes
Long file name support	Yes
Self-repairing	Yes
Transaction logging capabilities	Yes
File-level compression	Yes
File-level security	Yes
Dual file fork support (Macintosh)	Yes
POSIX support	Yes

or greater. Because the directory structure for NTFS is based on a highly efficient data structure called a "B-tree," search time for files under NTFS does not degrade as the number of files to be searched increases (as it does for FAT-based systems).

NTFS also has been designed with sufficient recoverability so that users should never need to employ any kind of disk repair utility on an NTFS partition. Among other things, NTFS maintains a Recycle Bin so that users ordinarily can retrieve their own deleted files without having to run an Undelete utility of any kind. But NTFS also supports a variety of file system integrity mechanisms, including automatic transaction logging, which permits all file system writes to be replayed from a special System log. Should an NT system fail for some reason, all data up to the last completed file system write can be re-created by restoring from a good system backup, and then replaying the transaction log captured since that backup was made.

NTFS also supports Windows NT's native object-level security and treats all volumes, directories, and files as individual objects. Every time users request a file system object, they will be subjected to a security check that matches their right to access the requested object against a list of permissions for that object. Requests from users with sufficient rights will be granted; requests from users with insufficient rights will be denied. This security applies whether users are logged in to an NT machine locally or they make their requests across a network. Table 6.4 shows the features and capabilities of the NTFS file system.

The vital statistics for NTFS show it as the powerhouse it is. In addition to a staggering capacity of 16 EB for volumes or files (an Exabyte is 2^{64}, or approximately 16 GBs' worth of Gigabytes!), NTFS offers built-in compression that can be applied to individual files, entire directories, or complete volumes (and selectively removed or applied thereafter).

NTFS offers file-level security, which means that access to volumes, directories, and files can be controlled by an individual's account and the groups to which that account belongs. LFNs are customary with NTFS, but NTFS can map to 8.3 names to maintain support for FAT-based users. In addition to maintaining multiple copies of file system information, Windows NT offers multiple mechanisms to repair and restore an NTFS volume, should problems arise. Likewise, NTFS's transaction logging helps minimize the potential for data loss.

Finally, NTFS supports a much richer file structure, which means it's easy to graft support for other file systems onto an NTFS foundation. Microsoft exploits this capability to provide native support for the Macintosh Hierarchical Filing System (HFS) in NTFS, when Windows NT's Services For Macintosh are installed. Likewise, third parties have built native implementations of Sun's Network Filing System (NFS) that run on top of NTFS (NFS is a popular distributed file system on Unix networks).

Differences Between FAT And NTFS

Where file system overhead is concerned, FAT is more compact and less complex than NTFS. Most FAT volumes impose an overhead of less than 1 MB for the file allocation table structures that represent the directory entries for all files stored in the volume. Because of this low overhead, it is possible to format small hard disks and floppy disks with FAT. NTFS, on the other hand, has a larger overhead than FAT, partly because each directory entry requires 2 K (this has the advantage, however, of enabling NTFS to store files of 1,500 bytes or less entirely within their directory entries).

NTFS cannot be used to format floppy disks, and it shouldn't be used to format partitions smaller than 50 MB. Its relatively high overhead means that for small partitions, directory structures would consume as much as 25 percent of the available storage space.

Microsoft recommends always using FAT for partitions of 50 MB or smaller, and NTFS for partitions of 400 MB or larger. In the "gray area" between 50 and 400 MB, other factors come into play. Chief among these is file-level security: If this is important, NTFS is the way to go. If security is not an issue, FAT may offer what you want (but performance degrades as the size increases).

In relation to file size, FAT partitions can be up to 2 GB, VFAT up to 4 GB, and FAT32 up to 4 TB; however, FAT partitions work best when they are 200 MB or less, because of the way the FAT itself is organized. NTFS partitions can be as much as 16 EB; however, they currently are restricted to 2 TB by hardware and other system constraints.

FAT partitions may be used by Windows 95, Windows NT, MS-DOS, and Windows for Workgroups, not to mention other operating systems with added FAT support (for example, both Unix and Macintosh can accommodate such add-ons). With a few notable exceptions, only Windows NT can directly access NTFS partitions. NTFS information is readable across the network by many operating systems (including DOS, Windows 3.x and 95, as well as other operating systems), partly because of its backward compatibility with FAT and because of its capability to host other file systems. Also, a recently released utility called NTFSDOS makes it possible to read NTFS data on a PC booted into DOS.

Local security is not an option when you are using FAT partitions (see the next section for more details). NTFS partitions, on the other hand, allow both files and directories to be locally secured. Another difference is that FAT partitions are required for Windows NT to dual boot with other operating systems; likewise, one FAT partition of at least 2 MB is required to install and operate Windows NT on RISC-based systems.

A Matter Of Conversion

Windows NT includes a utility named CONVERT.EXE that converts FAT volumes to NTFS equivalents, but there is no utility to perform a conversion from an NTFS volume to a FAT version. To do this, you would have to create a FAT partition, copy the files from an NTFS partition to that FAT partition, and then delete the NTFS originals. Remember that when files are copied from NTFS to FAT, they lose all their NTFS security attributes (FAT lacks the ability to associate and store security attributes with the files under its care). When installing Windows NT across a network, files are copied to a FAT partition, and the install program automatically invokes the CONVERT.EXE utility just before the install switches from character mode to the GUI interface (which occurs about halfway through the Windows NT installation process).

What About HPFS?

HPFS stands for High Performance File System. Originally introduced with OS/2 1.2 and LAN Manager, HPFS was the first PC-compatible file system that supported LFNs. Like FAT, HPFS maintains a directory structure, but it adds automatic sorting of the directory and includes support for special attributes to better accommodate multiple naming conventions and file-level security.

With the introduction of Windows NT 4, NT no longer supports HPFS directly. Also, HPFS file security is not directly compatible with NTFS security. However, a special conversion utility, ACLCONV.EXE, is available from Microsoft. This utility converts HPFS volumes (from LAN Manager, LAN Server, or Windows NT 3.51 or earlier NT versions) to an NTFS equivalent. The utility's README file also explains how HPFS security is mapped into an NTFS near-equivalent.

Anytime you see HPFS mentioned in a question with regard to Windows NT 4, be prepared for a possibility of a trick question. Remember, HPFS is no longer supported in Windows NT 4!

CDFS

Both Windows 95 and Windows NT 3.51 and higher number versions (including 4) support a special read-only file system called the Compact Disk File System (CDFS) to permit easy access to CDs in these operating systems. One interesting enhancement that CDFS confers is the capability to boot a PC directly from the CD that contains the Windows NT distribution media.

Windows NT Volume Structures

Windows NT Workstation does not have native support for fault tolerant volume structures—such as disk mirroring, disk duplexing, or disk striping with parity—which are supported by Windows NT Server. However, NT Workstation does support extendible volumes and stripe sets. In the following sections, these structures and the Disk Administrator utility are examined.

Disk Administrator

The manipulation of disk volumes is primarily handled through the Disk Administrator utility (see Figure 6.2). Without the fault tolerance features

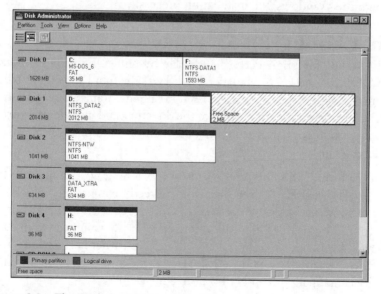

Figure 6.2   The Disk Administrator utility.

found on NT Server, the Workstation version of this utility is not as versatile. However, familiarity with its layout, menus, and use will enable you to understand numerous exam questions.

Take time to familiarize yourself with the layout of Disk Administrator's menus, the locations of commands, and the resulting dialog boxes. If you are visually inclined, you may be able to work with the tool for a short time and then be able to "see" it in your mind's eye. Those of you unable to visualize the utility must memorize its menus. Table 6.5 is a chart that will help you with that task. (Note: We omitted the Help menu.)

 One important command is Commit Changes Now. This command instructs Windows NT to make your requested changes to the affected storage devices. In other words, partitions and drives will not be created or changed in Disk Administrator until this menu option is chosen.

Obviously, there are many commands in the five menus found in Disk Administrator. Some of these commands are discussed in further detail in this chapter. If a menu selection is not discussed further in this text, it's safe to assume you need know little (if anything) about it.

Disk Structure 101

Hopefully, you are already familiar with storage devices and the terminology used to describe their configuration and operation. Be sure you're equipped with the bare minimum of such information—a short refresher follows.

Table 6.5 Disk administrator's menus and options.			
Partition	**Tools**	**View**	**Options**
Create	Format	Volumes	Toolbar
Create Extended	Assign Drive Letter	Disk Configuration	Status Bar
Delete	Eject	Refresh	Legend
Create Volume Set	Properties		Colors and Patterns
Extend Volume Set			Disk Display
Create Stripe Set			Region Display
Mark Active			Customize Toolbar
Configuration			
Commit Changes Now			
Exit			

Partitions

Hard drives are subdivided into partitions. A partition can contain one or more file systems, each of which enables an NOS or OS to store and retrieve files. Even though NT only supports FAT and NTFS natively, partitions that support other file systems can reside on a machine that runs Windows NT (even if NT cannot access them). For instance, it's possible that a drive on a dual-boot machine running Windows 95 OEM release 2 (OSR2) and Windows NT 4 could contain a FAT32 partition; in that case, only Windows 95 could access that partition.

In general, a hard drive can contain between 1 and 32 separate partitions. Therefore, a single physical hard drive can appear as multiple logical drives. Hard drives should be partitioned to maximize their usage by the underlying NOS and its applications. If you attempt to change a partition, any information stored in that space on disk will be destroyed. If there is free unpartitioned space on a drive, you may create new partitions without damaging existing partitions. Likewise, deleting any one partition does not affect other partitions on a drive.

The NTFS file system supports a variety of partition schemes. A single drive may contain up to four primary partitions, or one to three primary partitions and a single extended partition. An extended partition can be subdivided further into multiple logical drives. The total number of primary partitions plus logical drives, however, cannot exceed 32 on any one physical hard drive under NT's control.

Volumes

A volume is an organizational structure imposed on one or more partitions that support file storage. If you select one or more partitions on a physical drive and format them with a specific file system, the resulting disk structure is a volume. Under Windows NT, volumes can span multiple partitions on one or more physical drives.

A volume set is a volume comprised of 2 to 32 partitions. A volume set may be extended at any time by adding another partition to the set without damaging existing stored data. However, a volume set and its data must be destroyed to reduce the size of a volume. All the partitions in a volume set must use the same file system, and the entire volume set is assigned a single drive letter. A volume provides no fault tolerance for its data. If any one of the partitions or drives within a volume set fails, all of the data is lost.

The best way to remember the impact of losing a volume set element is the phrase "You lose one, you lose them all." This also means that the only way to recover the data in a damaged volume set is to restore the data from a backup.

Drive Letters

Nearly every volume on a Windows NT machine has an associated drive letter; in fact, Windows NT cannot access a volume unless it has an associated drive letter. Drive letters simplify the identification of an exact physical drive, partition, and volume for any referenced folder or file. NT can assign drive letters to storage devices using the letters C through Z (A and B are reserved for floppy disk drives). Because this only covers 24 potential drives, and Windows NT supports as many as 32, the assumption is that some volumes will span multiple physical drives (which all share a single drive letter).

NT automatically assigns the next available drive letter to each new volume created. You can reassign dynamically or shuffle drive letters using the Assign Drive Letter option on the Tools menu in Disk Administrator.

Another exception to association of volumes with drive letters applies to volumes formatted with file systems not supported by Windows NT. These volumes generally are not assigned drive letters because NT cannot access them.

Master Boot Record

The Master Boot Record (MBR) is a BIOS bootstrap routine used by low-level hardware-based system code stored in read-only memory (ROM) to initiate the boot sequence on a PC. This, in turn, calls a bootstrap loader, which commences loading the machine's designated operating system. The MBR directs the hardware to a so-called "active partition" whence the designated operating system may be loaded.

Only a primary partition can be made active by using the Mark Active command on Disk Administrator's Partition menu. The boot partition is where the MBR and boot loader reside; for Windows NT, the system partition is where the Windows NT system files reside.

Disk Striping

Disk striping stores data across multiple physical storage devices. In a stripe set, multiple partitions of equal size on separate devices are combined into a single logical device. When data is stored to a stripe set, it is written in 64K chunks—"stripes"—across the drives, starting at the drive on the left with data block 1, then on the middle drive with data block 2, and so on (see Figure 6.3 for an example of a stripe set).

Disk striping is fast, especially when the individual storage devices are attached to separate disk controllers. You only need two devices to create a stripe set, and such a stripe set can include as many as 32 devices. Disk striping can be implemented using either FAT or NTFS.

Note that disk striping without parity provides no fault tolerance. Should any one of the drives in a stripe set without parity fail, all of the data on all disks is lost (once again, it's "Lose one, lose them all!"). If any of the drive controllers fails, none of the data is accessible until that drive controller is repaired.

The boot and system partitions cannot be part of a disk stripe set.

Special Boot Considerations

The BOOT.INI file, which lives on the system partition, uses Advanced RISC Computing (ARC) name syntax to map the path to the system files (stored on the boot partition). This path designation starts by identifying

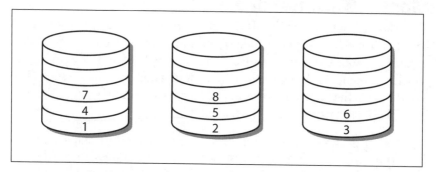

Figure 6.3   A stripe set.

the hard disk controller and finishes with the name of the folder that contains the Windows NT system files.

Here are some examples of BOOT.INI entries:

```
multi(1)disk(0)rdisk(1)partition(2)\WINNT="Windows
NT Workstation Version 4.00"

scsi(0)disk(0)rdisk(0)partition(1)\WINNT="Windows
NT Workstation Version 4.00"
```

Should a boot or system partition fail, these entries might need to be changed, especially if the order, number, or configuration of your drives and partitions changes, or if the Windows NT system files must be accessed from an alternate location.

BOOT.INI lives in the boot partition, usually on drive C, on your Windows NT machine. BOOT.INI is a text file, which means you can edit it with any text editor. BOOT.INI attributes are set as a system, hidden, and read-only file; therefore, you must turn off these attribute settings before you can edit the file and then reset them once your changes are complete. Here's an example of a BOOT.INI file:

```
[boot loader]
timeout=10
default=scsi(0)disk(0)rdisk(0)partition(1)\WINNT
[operating systems]
scsi(0)disk(0)rdisk(0)partition(1)\WINNT="Windows NT
Workstation Version 4.00"
scsi(0)disk(0)rdisk(0)partition(1)\WINNT="Windows NT
Workstation Version 4.00 [VGA mode]" /basevideo /sos
C:\="MS-DOS 6.22"
```

To edit the BOOT.INI file properly—and there are specific test questions on this topic—you must know the following about ARC names:

➤ To change the BOOT.INI file to point to the proper location, you must edit both the **default=** line and the main NOS line (which is **scsi(0)disk(0)rdisk(0)partition-(1)\WINNT="Windows NT Workstation Version 4.00"** in the preceding example). Both ARC names must match exactly.

➤ The first four elements of an ARC name are always lowercase in the BOOT.INI file. We use uppercase in this discussion to set them off from normal text.

➤ The first element in an ARC name, either SCSI or MULTI, is the controller type. SCSI indicates that a SCSI disk controller is being used that does not support BIOS translation. If SCSI appears, it also means that a driver file named NTBOOTDD.SYS must appear in the system partition to handle BIOS translation for the controller. MULTI indicates the drive controller is of a type that supports BIOS translation, including IDE and SCSI (among others).

➤ The number immediately following SCSI or MULTI identifies the position of the controller within the system, numbered ordinally. Thus, the first controller is numbered (0), the second is (1), and the third is (2).

➤ The second element in an ARC name, DISK, designates the device number for a SCSI controller with no BIOS translation capabilities. DISK will appear in an ARC name. But, if SCSI is the first element in the name, the number that follows DISK identifies the storage device, numbered ordinally. Thus, the first device also is numbered (0), the second is (1), and so on. If MULTI appears first in an ARC name, DISK is ignored and will always be set to (0).

➤ The third element, RDISK, designates the device number for a BIOS translating SCSI controller or for any other controller. RDISK always appears in any ARC name. But, only if MULTI is its first element does the number following RDISK identify the storage device, numbered ordinally. Again, the first device is numbered (0), the second (1), and so on. If SCSI appears first in an ARC name, RDISK is ignored and is always set to (0).

➤ The fourth element in an ARC name identifies a disk partition. PARTITION indicates the partition where system files reside, numbered cardinally. Unlike the other terms, the first partition is (1), the second is (2), the third is (3), and so on.

➤ The fifth element in an ARC name is the name of the folder where the system files reside. "\WINNT" indicates that the folder (or directory) on the specified partition named WINNT is where system information may be found. Whatever the directory is named, this element must reflect that exact name.

➤ The data following the folder name provides the information that appears in the Windows NT Boot menu. The equals sign and the quotes that enclose the text string must follow the folder name without any additional spaces outside the quotes.

➤ After the Boot menu name, additional command-line parameter switches may be added to control how Windows NT boots. These switches include /SOS and /BASEVIDEO. /SOS causes Windows NT to display the named drivers on screen as they are loaded during system boot. /BASEVIDEO puts Windows NT into VGA mode, which is useful when trouble-shooting video configuration problems.

One important item to remember for the exam is that Microsoft reversed what you might expect the terms "boot partition" and "system partition" to mean. As it happens, boot files are stored on the system partition, where the default WINNT directory resides. System files are stored on the boot partition—that is, the active partition where BOOT.INI and NTLDR reside. When a question requests the ARC name of a partition that contains boot files, remember that these files reside on the system partition, and vice versa. We can only guess at Microsoft's thinking—that system files are for low-level hardware initiation of the boot process, and therefore reside on the boot partition, and boot files supply bootup intelligence for Windows NT itself, and therefore, reside on the system partition. Just remember that it's the opposite of common sense, and you'll do just fine!

Exam Prep Questions

Question 1

> Using free, unpartitioned space on a SCSI drive, you create a new
> partition. You highlight the free space, select Create from the Par-
> tition menu, and then specify the size of the partition and click OK.
> Now, the new drive appears in the Disk Administrator display. What
> should you do next in your endeavor to create a new place to
> store data?
>
> ○ a. Assign a drive letter
>
> ○ b. Select Configuration|Save
>
> ○ c. Format
>
> ○ d. Commit Changes Now

It is not possible to assign a drive letter to a partition unless it is formatted.
Therefore, answer a is incorrect. The Configuration|Save command stores
the current configuration status as stored in the Registry to an Emergency
Repair Disk, and is not a step in creating a usable volume. Therefore,
answer b is incorrect. Formatting a partition to create a volume is a required
step, but this cannot be performed until the partition creation changes are
committed. Therefore, answer c is also incorrect. **You must use the Commit Changes Now command to save the partition creation changes as the
next step, then you can proceed to format the partition and assign it a drive
letter.** Therefore, answer d is correct.

Question 2

> You have two IDE hard drives on a single drive controller in your
> Windows NT Workstation computer. There is only one partition
> on each of the two drives. The first drive's partition is formatted
> with FAT, and the second drive's partition is formatted with NTFS.
> The boot files are located on the second drive. What is the ARC
> name for the system partition?
>
> ○ a. multi(0)disk(1)rdisk(0)partition(1)
>
> ○ b. multi(0)disk(0)rdisk(1)partition(1)
>
> ○ c. multi(1)disk(0)rdisk(1)partition(1)
>
> ○ d. multi(0)disk(0)rdisk(1)partition(0)
>
> ○ e. multi(1)disk(0)rdisk(0)partition(1)

Answer a displays an improperly formatted ARC name—when MULTI is used the DISK(0) number must be zero. Therefore, answer a is incorrect. **Answer b indicates the first partition of the second hard drive on the first MULTI type drive controller; this is the location of the system partition for this question. Therefore, answer b is correct.** Answer c points to a second drive controller that doesn't exist for this example. Therefore, answer c is incorrect. Answer d uses an incorrect number for the partition element— this number can never be zero; the first partition is defined by using the number one. Therefore, answer d is wrong. Answer e indicates a second drive controller that doesn't exist and the first drive on that controller. The system partition for this example is on the first and only existing controller and on the second hard drive. Therefore, answer e is incorrect.

Question 3

You establish a direct access file transfer area for users on your network. The range of clients requiring access to this area includes PCs running DOS, Windows 3.1x, Windows 95, and Windows NT, Macintoshes, and Unix. You create a 50 MB partition on your Windows NT Workstation. You do not want to impose any access restrictions on the volume, but instead, are leaving the policing of the area up to the users. What file format type should you use?

○ a. FAT

○ b. NTFS

○ c. HPFS

○ d. VFAT

FAT cannot be used because it is not directly supported by NT; it is supported only through backward compatibility of VFAT. Therefore, answer a is incorrect. NTFS isn't required due to the requirement for broad cross-platform access and the size of the partition. Therefore, answer b is incorrect. HPFS is not supported in Windows NT 4, so answer c is incorrect. **VFAT is the file system that should be used, because it works well with small volumes, does not impose security restrictions, and is backward compatible with the widely supported FAT, as well as supported by NT. Therefore, answer d is correct.**

Question 4

You want to install Windows NT Workstation onto your system. You create two 500 MB partitions—one for the NOS and applications, and the other for personal data and confidential documents. How would you format these volumes?

○ a. Format both with VFAT.

○ b. Format both with NTFS.

○ c. Format the NOS partition with VFAT and the data partition with NTFS.

○ d. Format the NOS partition with NTFS and the data partition with VFAT.

The correct answer is b, "Format both with NTFS," because file-level security is just as important for NT's own files as it is for user files that must be kept confidential (that is, secure). Answer a, "Format both with VFAT," provides no file-level security, whereas answers c and d omit file-level security for the data and NOS partitions, respectively.

Question 5

Which of the following ARC names indicates the third partition of the fourth SCSI drive on the second controller that has its BIOS disabled?

○ a. multi(1)disk(3)rdisk(0)partition(3)

○ b. multi(1)disk(0)rdisk(3)partition(3)

○ c. scsi(1)disk(3)rdisk(0)partition(3)

○ d. scsi(1)disk(3)rdisk(0)partition(4)

Answer a indicates a BIOS-enabled controller. Therefore, answer a is incorrect. Answer b also indicates a BIOS-enabled controller. Therefore, answer b is incorrect. Answer c indicates the third partition on the fourth drive on a non-BIOS SCSI controller. Therefore, answer c is correct. Answer d indicates the fourth partition. Therefore, answer d is incorrect.

Question 6

> Your NT Workstation has been designated as the file storage area for your small peer-to-peer workgroup. To accommodate the additional files, an 8 GB SCSI hard drive has been installed into your system. You must set up a FAT partition to maximize access for non-NT clients. If most of the files your organization works with are large, what is the best configuration for this new drive?
>
>
>
> ○ a. A single 8 GB VFAT partition
>
> ○ b. Two 4 GB VFAT partitions
>
> ○ c. Four 2 GB VFAT partitions
>
> ○ d. Sixteen 500 MB VFAT partitions

The only wrong configuration is answer a, because VFAT is limited to a maximum partition size of 4 GB. **Two 4 GB partitions is the best choice, because you know the files in question are extremely large. Therefore, answer b is correct. If there were a lot of small files, four 2 GB partitions would be beneficial.** Therefore, answer c is incorrect. Sixteen 500 MB partitions, while theoretically possible, would require searching too many partitions to locate individual files (and the partitions might be too small for "extremely large" files as well). Therefore, answer d is incorrect.

Question 7

> You want to upgrade from Windows NT Workstation 3.51 to 4. Your main data directory, H, is an HPFS volume. After NT Workstation 4 is installed, you can use the CONVERT.EXE utility to convert H from HPFS to NTFS.
>
> ○ a. True
>
> ○ b. False

The correct answer is b, "False." Because Windows NT 4 no longer supports HPFS, you'll have to obtain the ACLCONV.EXE utility from Microsoft to convert the HPFS partition into NTFS. The Windows NT 4 utility CONVERT.EXE can only transform FAT partitions into NTFS partitions. However, because NT 3.51's convert utility works with HPFS, it might be even better to convert HPFS to NTFS before installing the upgrade to NT 4.

Question 8

Which of the following characteristics are true of VFAT but not
true of FAT? [Check all correct answers]

❑ a. Maximum volume size of 4 GB

❑ b. Support for file sizes of 2 GB

❑ c. No file-level security

❑ d. Is self-repairing

❑ e. Support for LFNs

VFAT supports volumes up to 4 GB, FAT only 2 GB. Therefore, answer a
is correct. Both VFAT and FAT can support 2 GB sized files; in fact, VFAT
can support up to 4 GB. Therefore, answer b is incorrect. Neither VFAT or
FAT have file-level security. Therefore, answer c is incorrect. Neither VFAT
or FAT are self-repairing. Therefore, answer d is incorrect. Only VFAT
supports LFNs; FAT is limited to 8.3. Therefore, answer e is correct.

Question 9

What files should be placed on a boot disk in order to boot to the
duplicate drive of a disk duplex from a floppy in the event of a
failure of the original drive? Assume the drive controller is SCSI
that does not support BIOS translation. [Check all correct answers]

❑ a. NTDETECT.COM

❑ b. BOOT.INI

❑ c. NTLDR

❑ d. WINA20.386

❑ e. NTBOOTDD.SYS

NTDETECT.COM is required on the boot floppy. Therefore, answer a
is correct. BOOT.INI is required on the boot floppy. Therefore, answer b
is also correct. NTLDR is required on the boot floppy. Therefore, answer
c is also correct. WINA20.386 is a Windows device driver that is not needed
on the boot floppy. Therefore, answer d is incorrect. NTBOOTDD.SYS is
the driver for SCSI translation required for non-BIOS controllers. Therefore, answer e is also correct.

Question 10

On your Windows NT Workstation, you have partitions from six drives linked together in a stripe set. One of these drives fails due to a power spike. How can you restore your system to proper working order?

○ a. No restoration is necessary; NT will automatically rebuild the lost data on the fly.

○ b. Replace the failed drive and use the Reconstruct command from Disk Administrator.

○ c. Rebuild the volume with a new drive and restore all data from a backup.

○ d. Use the three setup disks and the ERD to perform a system repair.

NT Workstation does not have any fault tolerant features; the solution described in answer a would occur only with disk striping with parity, which is not available on NT Workstation. Therefore, answer a is incorrect. Answer b describes the activity involved in restoring a strip set with parity, a feature not available on NT Workstation. Therefore, answer b is incorrect. **Rebuilding the volume and restoring from backup is the only method available to NT Workstation to restore failed sets. Therefore, answer c is correct.** The ERD repair process will not restore the failed drive to operational status; this is a useless solution attempt for this particular problem. Therefore, answer d is incorrect.

Need To Know More?

Boyce, Jim, et al.: *Windows NT Workstation 4.0 Advanced Technical Reference.* Que, Indianapolis, IN, 1996. ISBN 0-7897-0863-9. This book has scattered references to the topics discussed in this chapter, with some conglomeration in Chapters 10 and 11.

Perkins, Charles, Matthew Strebe, and James Chellis: *MCSE: NT Workstation Study Guide.* Sybex Network Press, San Francisco, CA, 1997. ISBN 0-7821-1973-5. Chapter 5 focuses on NT file systems, volume structures, and the use of Disk Administrator.

Search the TechNet CD (or its online version through www.microsoft.com) and the *Windows NT Workstation Resource Kit* CD using the keywords "FAT," "VFAT," "FAT32," and "NTFS." KnowledgeBase article Q100108 "Overview of FAT, HPFS, and NTFS File Systems" is particularly informative.

File And Directory Security

Terms you'll need to understand:

- √ File Allocation Table (FAT)
- √ New Technology File System (NTFS)
- √ Security Accounts Manager (SAM)
- √ Objects
- √ Access control list (ACL)
- √ Permissions
- √ NTBACKUP
- √ Share
- √ No Access
- √ Read
- √ Change
- √ Full Control
- √ Add
- √ Add and Read
- √ List
- √ Auditing
- √ Transaction logging

Techniques you'll need to master:

- √ Selecting a file system for NT
- √ Securing system resources
- √ Establishing access permissions
- √ Creating shares and implementing share permissions
- √ Understanding the difference between copying and moving files
- √ Setting up auditing to monitor network activity

The purpose of security is to regulate access to data and protect that data from destruction. This is accomplished through many activities—ranging from limiting physical access to computers to allowing certain users the ability to work with important files. Backup methods can be used to protect data from being destroyed due to hardware problems, viruses, or malicious file commands. However, protecting data from copyright violations, unauthorized disclosure, and malicious alteration requires complete control of files, applications, and users.

How much and what type of restrictions are placed on your network must be determined by your organization's security policy. The NT Workstation exam demands a solid, working understanding of access rights, permissions, and user access. In this chapter, we discuss these topics thoroughly.

Basics Of Security

Before we launch into a detailed discussion of the security features of NT that focus on the protection of data files, we need to establish the context where file security occurs.

Logon And User Identification

The first step in understanding NT security must start where every user starts—at logon. By pressing Ctrl+Alt+Del at the initial NT splash screen, you initiate the WINLOGON utility. This utility displays the Logon dialog box and sends the inputted data to the security manager. The security manager (part of the Executive Services in the Kernel) verifies the name and password, creates an access token, and launches the user's shell (usually NT Explorer). The verification process is the act of comparing the user name and password with the data stored in the Security Accounts Manager (SAM). This database also contains the list of access privileges for each user. From this list, the access token is built. Once this process is complete, the user is able to use the computer for productive work.

The access token created by the security manager is the collection of identifiers and permissions unique to each individual. The NOS uses this access token to verify authority to access and manipulate every object and resource. The access token is built by combining the individual settings of a user with those of each group to which he or she belongs.

The access token is created when a user logs in, and it is not changed until that user logs out and then logs in again. This means that any changes to a user account or a group to which that user belongs will not affect those users currently logged in—the changes will only affect them the next time they log in.

The access token not only defines what objects and resources a user can interact with, but it also is attached to every process launched by that user. WINLOGON uses the access token it creates to launch the shell for a user. The shell inherits the same access privileges as the user, based on the access token. Every process launched or initiated by the user can only have the level of access authority granted by the user's access token, or less. (In fact, every single process has an access token assigned to it.) Under NT, it is not possible for a user to launch a process or access an object that requires a higher level of access than that defined by his or her current access token.

Objects

The ultimate purpose of security is to control who has access to what. The WINLOGON process determines the "who," and objects are the "what." Within the world of Windows NT, everything is an object. An object has a type, a collection of services, and a set of attributes.

The type of an object defines what services and attributes are valid. Object types within NT include files, directories, symbolic links, printers, processes, threads, ports, devices, and even windows. (See Figure 7.1.)

Directory
List
Read
Add
Change
Delete
File Name
Data
Access Control List

Figure 7.1   A Windows NT object.

The services of an object are the activities that can be performed on, with, or by the object. For example, a directory object has services of List, Read, Change, Delete, and so on; a printer object has services of Print, Manage, Delete, and so on.

The attributes of an object include the name of the object, the actual data, and the access control list.

Access Control List

An access control list (or ACL) is the attribute of each object that defines which users and groups have what level of services for that object (see Figure 7.2). An ACL is merely comprised of a list of services (Read, Write, Delete) and the associated users and groups who can perform each action (Mary, Bob, Sales group, Marketing group).

 When a user attempts to use an object, that user's access token is compared to the ACL of the object. You can think of the access token as a key ring with multiple keys, each related to a group membership or specific permission setting for that user. You can also think of the ACL as a linked group of padlocks for each object, and each lock will open only for a specific user or group key and then only allow the specified level of access.

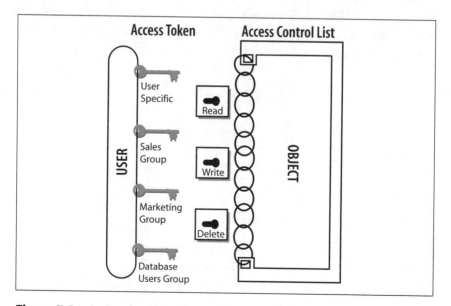

Figure 7.2 A visualization of a user's access token and an object's access control list.

You can set the ACLs on an object in two ways. First, you can use the GUI dialog boxes and your mouse to point and click to make any and all ACL changes you desire. Go check it out for yourself—right-click over an object, select Properties, the Securities tab, and then click the Permissions button. The second method is to use the CACLS command. This command can display or modify the ACL of files. Here's the syntax:

```
cacls filename [/t] [/e] [/c] [/g user:r|c|f] [/r user [...]]
[/p user:n|r|c|f [...]] [/d user [...]]
```

The parameters are as follows:

➤ *filename* Displays ACLs of specified file(s)

➤ /t Changes ACLs of specified files in the current directory and all subdirectories

➤ /e Edits the ACLs instead of replacing them

➤ /c Continues changing ACLs, ignoring errors

➤ /g *user:*r|c|f Grants specified user access rights of Read, Change, or Full Control

➤ /r *user* Revokes specified user's access rights

➤ /p *user:*n|r|c|f Replaces specified user's access rights of None, Read, Change, or Full Control

Checking Permissions

When a user attempts to access an object, the security system performs a permissions check to determine if that user has proper authority to access the object and which services he or she can interact with. Using the key-and-lock analogy, the security system tries the keys on the user's key ring (access token) in each of the object's locks (ACL). If a match is found, the user can proceed with the intended activity.

This analogy doesn't quite explain every aspect of the permissions check, but it does give you a good mental image of what goes on. One important facet of the permissions check that the lock-and-key analogy fails to communicate is No Access. Any user or group can be assigned No Access for an object. If such an assignment is made, a user cannot gain any access whatsoever.

Putting the lock-and-key analogy aside, when a user requests access to an object's service, the security system performs the following authority check:

1. Checks for any specified No Access for the user or any groups the user is a member of. If No Access is found, the user is denied access.

2. Checks for any specific granting of access based on the service requested for the user and any groups. If access is found, the user is granted access.

3. If neither a specific No Access or service permission is found, the default of No Access is used, and thus, the user is denied access.

As you can see, a specific No Access is like a trump card—it overrides any other settings, including specific granting of access. Plus, if no specific permission is given (that is, no key is present in the access token), the user cannot gain entry.

Note: No Access under NT prevents a user from using any of the six file operations, but a user is still able to see the name of the object as stored in the Master Browser object list.

NTFS Security

The NT File System (NTFS) has a standard set of access permissions for files and directories. Through these permissions, every single file and directory within the file system namespace can be controlled through the use of access tokens and ACLs. Six specific operations can occur on a file or directory:

➤ R Read. The object's data contents can be viewed.

➤ W Write. The object's data contents can be changed.

➤ X Execute. The object can be executed (in relation to directories, this means the directory can be opened).

➤ D Delete. The object can be deleted.

➤ P Change Permissions. The object's access permissions can be altered.

➤ O Take Ownership. The ownership of the object can be changed.

Note: Ownership can only be taken; it cannot be given. However, you must have the Take Ownership permission or the user right in order to do so. As the owner of an object, you have Full Control permission over that object.

These six operations are combined into the standard permissions sets for files and directories. The standard permissions for files are:

➤ **Read (RX)** The file can be read and/or executed.

➤ **Change (RWXD)** Includes Read (RX), plus Modify and Delete.

➤ **Full Control (RWXDPO)** Includes Change (RWXD), plus Change Permissions and Take Ownership.

➤ **No Access ()** Absolutely no access.

The standard permissions for directories are (the first pair of parentheses refers to the directory itself, and the second refers to the contents of the directory, but not the contents in any subdirectories):

➤ **List (RX)(not specified)** Users can view the names of the contents of this directory; no content-specific settings are specified.

➤ **Read (RX)(RX)** Users can read and traverse the directory as well as read and execute the contents.

➤ **Add (WX)(not specified)** Users can add files to the directory but cannot read or change the contents of the directory.

➤ **Add and Read (RWX)(RX)** Users can add files to and read files from the directory, but they cannot change them.

➤ **Change (RWXD)(RWXD)** Users can add, read, execute, modify, and delete the directory and its contents.

➤ **Full Control (RWXDPO)(RWXDPO)** Users have full control over the directory and its contents.

➤ **No Access ()()** Absolutely no access is granted to the directory and its contents.

In addition to these sets of standard file and directory permissions, special access can be defined on a directory or file basis. Special access consists of one or more of the six file/directory object operations (RWXDPO). Special access can be set for files and for directories—but directories have two levels of settings: one for the directory itself and another for the contents of that directory.

Other object types have their own unique set of operations and permissions. For example, print objects have a Print operator but do not have a Read operator. For each object type, the NTFS permissions might be slightly different to accommodate the functionality of that object. For the printer's permission discussion, please see Chapter 14.

Shares And Permissions

NT uses two types of permission settings to control object access—local and remote. Local access includes the NTFS permissions just discussed, and remote access is controlled by shares.

A share is a network resource that allows remote users to gain access to an object. The share is an object in itself that points to the resource object. The share knows how to translate data from the user (or more specifically an application employed by the user) to interact with the resource over the network. Shares enable a local resource to be used anywhere on the network.

Shares have their own set of permission levels (notice these are the same as the standard file permissions):

➤ **No Access** Absolutely no access

➤ **Read (RX)** Read and execute

➤ **Change (RWXD)** Read, write, execute, delete

➤ **Full Control (RWXDPO)** Full control

For users who belong to more than one group with permission settings to the same share, these permissions are cumulative, except the No Access permission. When the No Access permission is assigned, all other permissions become obsolete. In other words, the broadest permission always will apply, unless No Access appears anywhere. When that happens, No Access always "wins."

These permissions grant or restrict a users interaction with the share itself. If a user has access, the NTFS permissions on the object itself determine what services the user can access. When a share is used to access a resource, the combination of the share restrictions and NTFS restrictions will result in granting only the most restrictive permissions common to both the share and the object itself. You can think of a share as a door and the services of an object as boxes. The share will only allow object services to pass though its gateway if they are the same or less restrictive than the permissions on the share itself. As you can see in Figure 7.3, the "boxes" of NTFS permissions will only fit through the "doors" of a share if they are smaller than the opening.

Permissions on a share only apply to users attempting to access a resource through that share (that is, over the network). Local users are not affected by the share restrictions because they have direct access to the resource. Therefore, local users are only restricted by the NTFS permissions on an object, whereas remote or network users are restricted by both the share permissions and the NTFS object permissions.

 An extremely important item to remember about shares is that the initial default settings of all newly created shares is Full Control to the Everyone group. You'll need to remember this for the test. Also, this can cause some interesting problems if you don't reduce the access range for premium shares.

Mapping Shares

Mapping shares (or mapping a drive) is the process of defining a local drive letter that points to a network resource, such as a share. This can be accomplished many ways, but only two are mentioned on the test:

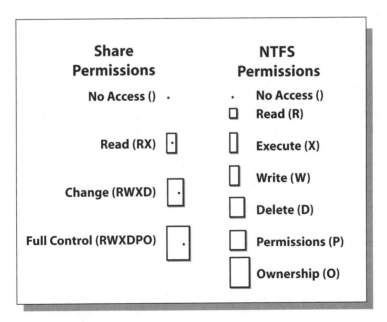

Figure 7.3 A visualization of share permissions in relation to NTFS object permissions.

➤ The Map Network Drive command of NT Explorer or Network Neighborhood can be used to define the assigned drive letter, the share to map to (selectable from a browse list), the user to connect as, and whether or not to maintain the mapping permanently.

➤ A command line using the UNC name of the share. Here's an example:

```
NET USE <driveletter> \\server\sharename <password>
/USER:<username> /PERSISTENT:YES|NO
```

Default Shares

Windows NT creates special default shares of each of the system's storage volumes each time the computer is booted. These shares are used by the system to support network activity and administer internal operations. These default shares—also called "system shares" or "hidden shares"—are not listed in standard browser lists of share resources. The common default shares are:

➤ **ADMIN$** Points to the Windows NT root directory (that is, C:\WINNT)

➤ **IPC$** A share used by InterProcess Communications

➤ **PRINT$** Points to the printer driver directory

➤ **C$, D$, E$, ...** A share for each hard drive volume, pointing to the root directory

Default shares all have a trailing "$" (dollar sign) as part of their name. Default shares can be temporarily disabled, but they cannot be deleted. NT will re-enable all default shares during the next boot. You can map a drive letter to a default or hidden share by providing an Administrator name and password in the map drive dialog box.

You can create your own hidden shares simply by adding a dollar sign to the end of your share name. On NT Server, the server manager can be used to display all shares—normal and hidden—but NT Workstation does not offer a similar function. The only indicator of hidden shares on NT Workstation is the small "sharing hand" icon added to the drive or directory within My Computer or NT Explorer. Hidden shares can be modified in the same way as standard shares through the Sharing Properties tab.

Permission Combinations

Each time a user attempts to access an object, there are many hurdles his security settings must pass in order to reach the object. It is possible for a single user to belong to more than one named group in Windows NT. Access to resources may be assigned to groups or individual users. This makes it possible for a single user or group to be assigned different levels of access for any particular resource. The specified settings of the user account and each group membership must be examined for both the share and the object itself. Here are some items to keep in mind when deciphering permission combinations:

➤ No Access on the share or the object prevents all access, even if Full Control is granted by another group membership.

➤ The permissions from all groups of which a user is a member are cumulative. This applies both to shares and objects.

➤ The most restrictive set of common permissions between a share and an object are used.

Managing Shared Resources

The customary method for sharing files, directories, and resources on Windows NT is by creating what is called a "share." The process is simple. Use the following steps to share a resource or directory:

1. Select the directory or resource you want to share in NT Explorer or through the My Computer icon.

2. Right-click the directory or resource and select Sharing from the drop-down menu (the default is Not Shared).

3. Click the Share As button. When you do this, a dialog box pops up, and NT displays a default share name (this is usually the first eight characters of the selected directory name). You can change the share name if you desire. It is important to note, however, that share names that are greater than eight characters long cannot be accessed from DOS-based clients.

You also can limit access to the share to a maximum number of users on the Sharing tab. It's a good idea to limit the number of users in order to prevent users from overloading a slow computer or to ensure that other server processes can run unimpeded. Select the Maximum Allowed option if you do not want to impose this limitation. To set the number of allowed users, select the Allow button. A number then appears in the Users box. You can use the up and down arrows to set this number, or you can type a number directly in the Users box.

 Subdirectories inherit the permissions of the parent directories as their default share permissions.

After creating the share, you can assign permission to the share. To do this, select the Permissions button or click the Security tab. Note that the default setting for newly created shares is Full Control for the Everyone group. You have four levels of security available for the purpose of restricting access to server shares: No Access, Read, Change, and Full Control.

 You must always set explicit directory permissions on new shares. The default permissions grant Full Control to the Everyone group.

Securing FAT And NTFS Resources

FAT partitions cannot support local security. However, FAT partitions can use share permissions, which may be imposed when directories are shared on a network. This does not prevent someone who is logged on locally from accessing files located on a particular machine, but it can protect even FAT-based files from unauthorized network access.

For security purposes, NTFS is the wiser choice. NTFS partitions can lock out or limit access both for remote and local users. All files and directories on an NTFS partition can be locked using NTFS security. This means that the only people who can access protected files are the users who have been granted explicit access to them.

Directory shares and NTFS security are controlled by security properties associated with a directory to be shared, or with any NTFS file system object (which can be either a directory or an individual file). By selecting the Properties entry in the File menu, or by right-clicking a file name and selecting the Properties entry in the resulting pop-up menu, users can examine the Sharing (for directories only) and Security (for files and directories) tabs.

The default for the system group Everyone is Full Control for both shares and secured resources. Only a network administrator, the owner, or a user who has been granted the special Change permission can reset the access levels on an NTFS or shared resource.

Moving NTFS Secured Files

Higher-level folders usually share NTFS permissions with the files and folders they contain. For example, if you create a folder within a folder in which administrators have Full Control permission and backup operators have Read Only permission, the new folder will inherit those same permissions. The same goes for files that are copied from another folder or moved from a different NTFS partition.

If you move a folder or a file into another folder on the same NTFS partition, security attributes are not inherited from the new container object. For example, if you move a file from a folder with Read permission for the Everyone group to a folder on the same partition with Full Control permission for the Everyone group, the moved file retains its original Read permission. That's because an NTFS move operation within the same partition changes only the object's location pointer, not any of the object's other attributes (including security information).

These three important rules will help you decide if permissions will be inherited or retained when performing move or copy operations on NTFS objects:

➤ If you move or copy files within the same NTFS partition, they will *retain* their original permissions.

➤ Other operations, such as file creation, file copy, and moves from one NTFS partition to another, will *inherit* the parent folder's permissions.

➤ All NTFS permissions are lost when files are moved or copied from NTFS to a FAT partition.

Windows NT Backup

Backing up critical data is a very important task for any network administrator. Windows NT 4 ships with a program called NTBACKUP.EXE, for backup functions. Although this program is automatically installed with NT, you must install drivers for your tape backup (performed through the Tape Devices applet) and have a good understanding of how the backup process works to be able to successfully back up and restore important data. In this section, we explain the aspects of NTBACKUP that you need to know to pass the Workstation exam.

NTBACKUP Facts

NTBACKUP's advantages include the following:

➤ The program is free; you do not have to purchase any third-party backup utility.

➤ Because NTBACKUP is a native NT program, the chances of the server running into stability problems are slim to none.

➤ NTBACKUP can back up from the two supported files systems— FAT and NTFS. It also can restore just as easily to either file system.

NTBACKUP also has the following disadvantages:

➤ The only acceptable media that NTBACKUP supports is a tape drive; you cannot back up to another hard drive, floppy, or even across the network to a network drive.

➤ There is no built-in scheduler program included with NT backup; to accomplish an unattended backup, you must write a batch file (see the section titled "Scheduling Backups," later in this chapter).

➤ You cannot back up a remote Registry. This task must be done locally. You can, however, back up files both locally and remotely.

➤ NTBACKUP only does a file-by-file backup and not a disk-image backup.

Who Has The Right?

Just like everything else in NT, a user must have the right to perform back-ups and restorations. All users with Read permission can back up any file and folder. This right must be granted to the user by selecting User Rights from the Policies menu in the User Manager. To restore files and folders, a user must have the Restore Files And Directories right, which is also granted in the User Manager. By default, only members of the Backup Operator and Administrator groups have these rights.

Backup Types

Table 7.1 lists the different backup types in NTBACKUP.

Performing Backups

Performing backups with NTBACKUP is simple and straightforward. Drives, folders, and individual files are selected through an Explorer-like

Table 7.1	Vital statistics about NTBACKUP's backup types.	
Type Of Backup	**Backs Up**	**Marked?**
Daily copy	Files and folders that have changed during that day	No
Copy	All selected files and folders	No
Differential	Selected files and folders if they have changed since the last backup	No
Incremental	Selected files and folders if they have changed since the last backup	Yes
Normal	All selected files and folders	Yes

interface. Files to be protected are marked with an X; those that are not to be backed up have an empty checkbox.

Once you have selected which items to back up, you can select different NTBACKUP options from the Backup Information dialog box. Table 7.2 describes each option, along with the tape name.

After you select the options and type a meaningful description of the backup in the description box, you need to choose the backup type to be performed (refer back to Table 7.1).

The last set of options to set is the log information. If you want to create a backup log, simply put a path in the log file line of the Backup Information dialog box. The default is BACKUP.LOG in the \systemroot folder. The three options under Log Information are shown in Table 7.3.

Table 7.2	Vital statistics about NTBACKUP's tape options.
Option	**Description**
Operation: Append	Adds new backup set after the last backup set on the tape.
Operation: Replace	Overwrites all data on the tape.
Verify After Backup	Confirms that files/folders were backed up.
Backup Registry	This option is available only if you have selected at least one other file. You *cannot* back up only the Registry.
Restrict Access To Owner/Administrator	Limits access to users with the correct permissions. When backing up the Registry, you should always choose this option.
Hardware Compression	If your tape drive supports data compression, select this option.

Table 7.3 Vital statistics about Log Information options.

Option	Description
Full Detail	Logs all backup information, including the names of all of the files and folders backed up and skipped.
Summary Only	Logs only the major backup operations, such as loading and unloading the tape and starting backup.
Do Not Log	No log is created.

Scheduling Backups

There isn't a scheduler inside the NTBACKUP program, but you can write a batch file to start the NT backup process. The syntax follows:

```
NTBACKUP.EXE BACKUP [pathname[options]]
```

Table 7.4 shows the options or switches you can use with this command line process.

Table 7.4 Vital statistics about NTBACKUP options.

Option/Switch	Description
/a	This is not available for a blank tape. This appends the backup set to any existing backup set.
/b	Backs up the local Registry.
/d *text or description*	Allows for a backup description.
/e	Logs exceptions; similar to a summary log.
/l *file name*	Assigns a log file name.
/r	Limits the rights of the backup operation to Administrators, Backup Operators or Owners.
/t{normal|copy |incremental |differential|daily}	Allows you to specify which type of backup to perform.
/v	Confirmation of backup.
/hc: {on|off}	Enables or disables hardware compression (if your tape drive will support it). The default is off.
Cmd /c net use x:	Connects to a remote share. Use this to connect to a remote machine.
Cmd /c net use x: /delete	Disconnects from remote shares.

The exact details of how to schedule an NTBACKUP operation are not covered on the Workstation exam, but the fact that NTBACKUP can be scheduled through batch files and the Scheduler service /**AT** command are.

Once you have a batch file with the NTBACKUP link included, you can use AT.EXE to schedule the batch file to run at a specific time (see Table 7.5 for **AT** command options). AT.EXE schedules commands to be run by the Scheduling service in Windows NT. The scheduling service must be running on the machine that will run the scheduled task. The syntax for the **AT** command is as follows:

```
AT [\\computername] [id] [/delete] time [interactive]
[/every: date[,...]| next; date[,...] "command"
```

Restoring With NTBACKUP

Restoring data with the NTBACKUP program is quite simple. You can restore data to the same system or a completely different system, which is a great advantage. (Note: Remember that a Registry cannot be backed up or restored remotely.) The restore process is the reverse of the backup process, with a few different options. (These options are detailed in Table 7.6.)

> *Note: Restoring files to an NTFS partition will ensure that the ACLs of each file and folder remain intact. However, restoring files to a FAT partition will result in files and folders with no security restrictions.*

Table 7.5   Vital statistics about AT.EXE options.

Option	Description
\\computer name	Specifies a remote machine.
id	Assigns an ID number to a scheduled command.
/delete	Cancels a scheduled command. If this is omitted, all the scheduled commands are omitted.
time	Expresses time in hour:minute mode; runs from 00:00 through 23:59.
/interactive	Allows the user to see network activity in realtime.
/every: date[,...]	Specifies the days for the command to run.
/next:date[,....]	Specifies the next day of the month the command is to run.
"command"	Specifies the actual command to be run (for example, NTBACKUP).

Table 7.6	Vital statistics about restoration options and their descriptions.

Option	Description
Restore Local Registry	If you backed up the Registry, this option will restore the local Registry.
Restore File Permissions	Restores NTFS permissions. If this is not selected, the files and folders will follow the general rule of inheriting the new parent directory permissions.
Verify After Restore	Does a check of the tape against the files on the hard drive.

Other NT Security Issues

Two other important aspects of NT security that are briefly covered on the Workstation exam are auditing and transaction logging. In the next two sections, we give you an overview of these issues.

Auditing

On a computer running Windows NT, the administrator has the option to audit access to resources such as directories, printers, and shares. The audit will inform the administrator if someone attempts to access secured resources or just how often a particular resource is accessed. The information gathered by NT's auditing system can be brought to bear against performance problems, security risks, and expansion planning.

The auditing system is designed to watch every event occurrence on your entire network. To simplify the act of fine-tuning the areas you want to audit, there are three levels of switches with which you'll need to work. The master switch is the Audit These Events radio button located on the Audit Policy dialog box (see Figure 7.4). This dialog box is accessed through the User Manager's Policies pull-down menu. This master switch turns on or off NT's entire audit system. By default, this switch is set to Do Not Audit.

The second level of switches becomes available when you set the master switch. Seven event types are listed in the Audit Policy dialog box. Each of these event types can be audited by tracking their success and/or failure. Here are the seven event types and descriptions of the events they control:

➤ **Logon And Logoff** Tracks logons, logoffs, and network connections.

➤ **File And Object Access** Tracks access to files, directories, and other NTFS objects. This includes printers.

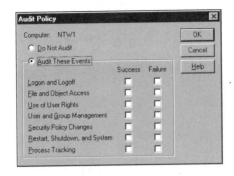

Figure 7.4   The Audit Policy dialog box.

➤ **Use Of User Rights** Tracks when users make use of user rights.

➤ **User And Group Management** Tracks changes in the accounts of users and groups (password changes, account deletions, group memberships, renaming, and so forth).

➤ **Security Policy Changes** Tracks changes of user rights, audit policies, and trusts.

➤ **Restart, Shutdown, And System** Tracks server shutdowns and restarts and also logs events affecting system security.

➤ **Process Tracking** Tracks program activation, program termination, and other object/process access.

The third level of audit switches is on the object level. This level of control only applies to File And Object Access events. These switches reside within the properties of each NTFS-based object, such as files, directories, and printers. Figures 7.5 through 7.7 show the Audit switch screens for file, directory, and print access. Note the differences in the tracking events among the object types: Both the file and directory have Read, Write, Execute, Delete, Change Permissions, and Take Ownership, but the printer object has Print, Full Control, Delete, Change Permissions, and Take Ownership.

A second, important difference to notice is on the directory object. The directory object allows you to change the files and/or subdirectories within the current directory to the same audit settings. Although this is convenient, you should use it with caution, because any current audit settings on these objects will be cleared and replaced with the new settings.

To get to these dialog boxes, right-click over the object, select Properties from the pop-up menu, select the Security tab, and then click the Auditing button. Remember, object auditing is only available to NTFS objects, not FAT objects.

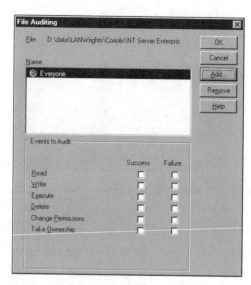

Figure 7.5   The File Auditing dialog box.

Note: By default, the object-level audit switches are all blank with no users or groups present in the Name field. We added the Everyone group before taking these images so the Events list at the bottom of these dialog boxes would become readable instead of their default near-invisible gray.

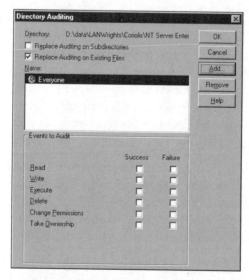

Figure 7.6   The Directory Auditing dialog box.

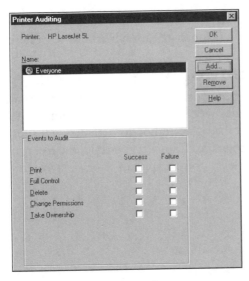

Figure 7.7   The Printer Auditing dialog box.

The object-level audit dialog boxes allow you to set the same success/failure event tracking for all users and groups listed in the Names field. You cannot track success for one group and failure for another.

Let's repeat the steps required to audit:

1. Turn on the master Audit These Events switch.

2. Select one or more of the event types to track success or failure.

3. If you choose the File And Object Access option, you must also edit the auditing settings for each NTFS object.

The activity of auditing system events demands large amounts of computing overhead, especially if the event monitored, such as file access, occurs often. It is not recommended to audit any event or object more than is absolutely necessary to track a problem or test equipment. Otherwise, your system will experience overall performance degradation.

The information gathered by NT's auditing system is stored in the Security log. You can view this log using the Event Viewer. The Event Viewer lists detailed information about each tracked event. Some of the data recorded includes the user logon identification, the computer used, the time, the date, and the action or event that instigated an audit.

When numerous objects or events are audited, the Security log can grow large quite quickly. You need to monitor the size of this log and possibly implement a size restriction and/or an automated new file creation to prevent data loss and maximize the usefulness of the gathered data.

Transaction Logging

NT automatically records a log of all activities performed on NTFS volumes. This includes writes, modifications, renaming, deletions, attribute changes, index alterations, and hot-fix activities. This log of NTFS transactions is a fault tolerance feature that enables the reconstruction or repealing of disk activities in the event of an error, data loss, or system error.

Exam Prep Questions

Question 1

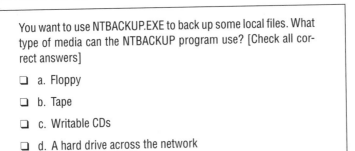

You want to use NTBACKUP.EXE to back up some local files. What type of media can the NTBACKUP program use? [Check all correct answers]

- ❏ a. Floppy
- ❏ b. Tape
- ❏ c. Writable CDs
- ❏ d. A hard drive across the network

The only backup media type that NTBACKUP.EXE supports is a tape drive. Therefore, answer b is the only correct choice. NTBACKUP does not support floppy, writable CDs, or network drive backups. Therefore, answers a, c, and d are incorrect.

Question 2

You suspect that an Account group member is accessing a directory that the user should be prevented from reaching. This might mean that you've set up the group memberships incorrectly. You aren't sure who it is, but you do know what directory is being accessed. What feature of NT will let you track who gains access to this directory?

- ○ a. NTFS file activity logging
- ○ b. Event auditing
- ○ c. Event Viewer
- ○ d. Account lockout

The NTFS file activity logging is a fault tolerance feature used to ensure the integrity of stored data. It cannot be used to track access. Therefore, answer a is incorrect. **Event auditing will track the activity around any object within NT. Therefore, answer b is correct.** The Event Viewer is used to review the Security log created by the auditing system, but it is not the feature that does the actual tracking. Therefore, answer c is incorrect. Account lockout is the feature used to prevent compromised accounts from being used. Therefore, answer d is incorrect.

Question 3

User JimBob is a member of the Accounting, Managers, and Print Operators groups. For a share named SalesFeb, these groups have the following share permissions:

- Accounting: Change
- Managers: Read
- Print Operators: Full Control

In addition, JimBob's NTFS permission for the SalesFeb directory and its contents is Read. What is JimBob able to do with files from the SalesFeb directory when he accesses them through the share?

- ○ a. Nothing, he has no access.
- ○ b. Read and execute.
- ○ c. Read, write, execute, and delete.
- ○ d. Read, write, execute, delete, change permissions, and take ownership.

To calculate share and NTFS permissions combined, take the most permissive of each kind and then the least permissive of the remaining share and NTFS permissions. If No Access appears anywhere, the resulting permission will always be No Access. Of the three share permissions that pertain to SalesFeb by virtue of JimBob's group memberships, Full Control is the most permissive, so that becomes his share permission. His NTFS permission is Read. **The less permissive of Read and Full Control is Read, so Bob's effective permission to SalesFeb is Read. Therefore, only answer b is correct, because Read access includes both read and execute.**

Question 4

> JimBob remains a member of the Accounting, Managers, and Print Operators groups, but he has been added to the Dangerous group by an annoyed boss. For the SalesFeb share, these groups have the following share permissions:
>
> - Accounting: Change
> - Managers: Read
> - Print Operators: Full Control
> - Dangerous: No Access
>
> In addition, JimBob's NTFS permission for the SalesFeb directory and its contents is Read. What is JimBob able to do with files from the SalesFeb directory when he accesses them through the share?
>
> ○ a. Nothing, he has no access.
> ○ b. Read and execute.
> ○ c. Read, write, execute, and delete.
> ○ d. Read, write, execute, delete, change permissions, and take ownership.

Because No Access always takes precedence over everything, JimBob has no access to SalesFeb and its contents due to his membership in the Dangerous group. Therefore, answer a is correct. Remember, No Access always wins.

Question 5

> Which of the following are attributes of an object? [Check all correct answers]
>
> ❑ a. Data
> ❑ b. ACL
> ❑ c. Services
> ❑ d. Name

The data of an object is an attribute. The ACL of an object is an attribute. The name of an object is an attribute. Thus, answers a, b, and d are correct. The services of an object are services, not attributes. Therefore, answer c is incorrect.

Question 6

> Where should you check to see if NTBACKUP ran successfully?
>
> ○ a. User Manager
>
> ○ b. Server Manager
>
> ○ c. Backup log
>
> ○ d. Registry

The User Manager is where most administration takes place for NT—such as adding users and changing their passwords. Backup is not affected directly by User Manager. Therefore, answer a is incorrect. (You do, however, assign backup rights in User Manager.) Server Manager is not a utility found on NT Workstation, but even on NT Server this utility does not offer details about successful backups. Therefore, answer b is incorrect. **To find out whether a backup was successful, you must check the Backup log in NTBACKUP. Therefore, answer c is correct.** You wouldn't look there for successful backup information in the Registry. Therefore, answer d is incorrect.

Question 7

> Which of the following is not a directory or file standard permission?
>
> ○ a. Read
>
> ○ b. List
>
> ○ c. Create Directory
>
> ○ d. Change
>
> ○ e. Add

Read is both a directory and a file permission. Therefore, answer a is incorrect. List is a directory permission. Therefore, answer b is incorrect. **Create Directory is not a permission. Therefore, answer c is correct.** Change is both a directory and file permission. Therefore, answer d is incorrect. Add is a directory permission. Therefore, answer e is incorrect.

Question 8

You want to track the activity around a new high-speed color laser printer so you can use the tracking information to restrict and grant privileged and priority access. Which of the following are required steps to implement printer auditing? [Check all correct answers]

❑ a. Set the auditing switches on the printer object to track the successful print events for the Everyone group.

❑ b. Grant the Everyone group the auditing right through the User Rights policy.

❑ c. Set the Audit policy to Audit These Events through the User Manager.

❑ d. Set the audit switch of File And Object Access to Success under Audit These Events.

❑ e. Set the priority of the printer to 99 (maximum) under the Scheduling tab on the printer's Properties dialog box.

Setting the auditing switches on the object is required to enable printer tracking. Therefore, answer a is correct. There isn't an auditing user right. Therefore, answer b is incorrect. Setting the master auditing switch to Audit These Events is required to track printer access. Therefore, answer c is correct. Setting the event type switch of File And Object Access to Success is required to track printer usage. Therefore, answer d is correct. Setting a printer's priority has nothing to do with tracking access. Therefore, answer e is incorrect.

Question 9

You need to gain access to a file named VENDORS.TXT in the
newly created \\Sales\Documents shared folder in the Sales
domain. You are a member of the Marketing group in the Sales
domain. What additional settings must be made to allow you access to the VENDORS.TXT file?

○ a. The Read permission on the Documents folder must be
set to your user account.

○ b. Your user account must be added to the Everyone group
in the Sales domain.

○ c. None, Full Control to all users is the default on all new
shares.

○ d. A new Sales group must be created and your account
added as a member.

Assigning specific permissions for the object to your user account is not
required because your account is a default member of the Everyone group
and a new share offers Full Control to this group by default. Therefore,
answer a is incorrect. Your user account automatically becomes a member
of the Everyone group when it is created. Therefore, answer b is incorrect.
**No action is required because your account is a member of the Sales
domain's Everyone group, which has Full Control to new shares by
default. Therefore, answer c is correct.** A new group is not required to gain
access to the new share. Therefore, answer d is incorrect.

Question 10

When you installed NT Workstation, you noticed that the backup
utility was installed automatically. When you try to use your tape
drive, nothing happens. What could be the cause of this?

○ a. Even though NT installs the NTBACKUP program, you
still must install the drivers for the tape drive.

○ b. You have to shut down your machine before you can run
NTBACKUP.

○ c. You must have the RAS service running.

○ d. You must have CSNW installed.

When NT is installed, NTBACKUP is installed automatically. However, you must still install the drivers for the tape backup. Therefore, answer a is correct. A workstation must be operating to provide access to its storage drives for a backup. Therefore, answer b is incorrect. NT's Remote Access Service is a communications program and has nothing to do with backups. Therefore, answer c is incorrect. The Client Service For NetWare is required for clients to communicate with a NetWare server; it has nothing to do with backups. Therefore, answer d also is incorrect.

Question 11

In what ways can the NTFS permission settings of a file be changed, altered, or modified? [Check all correct answers]

○ a. Through the CACLS command utility

○ b. By moving the file to a new partition

○ c. Through the Share Properties tab

○ d. By taking ownership

○ e. Through the Permissions button on the Security Properties tab

The CACLS command line utility is used to change the ACLs or permission settings on files and folders. Therefore, answer a is correct. Moving a file to a new partition causes the file to take on the settings of its new container, thus, its permissions are changed. Therefore, answer b is correct. The Share Properties tab can only change the permissions of a share, not the NTFS permissions of a file. Therefore, answer c is incorrect. Taking ownership gives a user the ability to change permissions, but the act of taking ownership does not alter the permissions on a file. Therefore, answer d is incorrect. The Permissions button on the Security Properties tab is the most common and easiest to use method of changing NTFS permissions. Therefore answer e is correct.

Question 12

You attempt to add new information into a document stored on a remote server. Using the Documents share, you are able to locate and open the document into your word processor. You have Full Control of the object. You are a member of the Sales group. The Sales group has Read access to the Documents share. You are unable to save your changes to the file, why?

○ a. You cannot edit documents over a network.

○ b. Your resultant permission for the file object is just Read.

○ c. The Sales group has the Save privilege revoked.

○ d. Only administrators can save files over the network.

It is possible to edit documents over a network—the only stipulation is you must have the proper access level to modify remote objects. Therefore, answer a is incorrect. **Accessing objects through shares results in the most restrictive shared permissions. Therefore, answer b is correct.** There isn't a Save privilege in the NT environment—the Sales group merely has Read access to the share. Therefore, answer c is incorrect. The ability to save documents (in other words, modify objects), is not limited to administrators. Therefore, answer d is incorrect.

Question 13

An important, new custom application is conflicting with an existing utility. The conflict seems to cause both programs to terminate prematurely. Which audit event type should be tracked to record some information about the conflict and which programs are affected?

○ a. File And Object Access

○ b. Security Policy Changes

○ c. Restart, Shutdown, And System

○ d. Process Tracking

○ e. Application Activity

File And Object Access is for tracking NTFS objects such as files and printers. Therefore, answer a is incorrect. Security Policy Changes tracks modifications to security and policies. Therefore, answer b is incorrect. Restart, Shutdown, And System tracks system restarts. Therefore, answer c is incorrect. **Process Tracking tracks threads and processes (that is, applications). Therefore, answer d is correct.** Application Activity is not a valid selection. Therefore, answer e is incorrect.

Question 14

> You attempt to access a file in the NTFS directory share \UserGuide. Sales has Change access to the share. Marketing has Read access to the share. Accounting has No Access to the share. You have Full Control of the object. You are a member of all three groups. What is your resultant access privileges?
>
> ○ a. No Access
>
> ○ b. Read
>
> ○ c. Change
>
> ○ d. Full Control

No Access results if any group of which you are a member has No Access. Therefore, answer a is correct. Read is the access for the Marketing group, but you are also a member of the Accounting group, which has No Access. Therefore, answer b is incorrect. Change is the access for the Sales group, but you are also a member of the Accounting group, which has No Access. Therefore, answer c is incorrect. You have Full Control of the object only when accessing it directly, but by using a share, you are restricted by your group settings that result in No Access. Therefore, answer d is incorrect.

Question 15

> Sheila is a member of the local group called Sales. She can back up files that she reads on a daily basis, but she cannot restore any files. What is the problem?
>
> ○ a. Sheila is not a member of Power Users.
>
> ○ b. Sheila is not a member of the Backup Operators, Users, and the Replicator group.
>
> ○ c. Sheila is not a member of the Backup Operators or the Administrator group.

Answer c is correct. You must be granted a right to restore data. Backup Operators and the Administrator groups both have the right to do this by default. Therefore, answer c is the only correct answer. Remember, if users can read a file, they can back up the file; but to restore the file, they must have the Restore Files And Directories right. The Power Users group does not have the right to restore files. Therefore, answer a is incorrect. The Users and Replicator groups do not have the right to restore files, thus, the stipulation of belonging to all three of these groups does not add the restore right to Sheila. Therefore, answer b is incorrect.

Need To Know More?

 Boyce, Jim, et al.: *Windows NT Workstation 4.0 Advanced Technical Reference.* Que, Indianapolis, IN, 1996. ISBN 0-7897-0863-9. Topics covered in this chapter are briefly discussed in various sections throughout this reference book. However, this reference should be used with caution because they seem to have overlapped and confused Workstation and Server details.

 Perkins, Charles, Matthew Strebe, and James Chellis: *MCSE: NT Workstation Study Guide.* Sybex Network Press, San Francisco, CA, 1997. ISBN 0-7821-1973-5. Chapter 6 contains detailed information about NT file and directory security, including shares, auditing, and backups. Also, Chapter 7 discusses object and ACL issues.

  Search the TechNet CD (or its online version through www.microsoft.com) and the *Windows NT Workstation Resource Kit* CD using the keywords "NTFS," "share," "backup," "audit," "ACL," and "permissions."

Windows NT System Security

8

Terms you'll need to understand:

√ Windows NT security model

√ Access control list (ACL)

√ Access token

√ Logon authentication

√ WINLOGON

√ Account policy

√ User rights policy

√ Auditing

√ Customizable environment options

√ Security Accounts Manager (SAM)

Techniques you'll need to master:

√ Understanding the Windows NT security model

√ Learning how user logons are authenticated

√ Creating customized settings for users

We've already introduced you to many of the security features built into NT Workstation. NTFS and share security, ACLs, and logon authentication were detailed in Chapters 6 and 7. Security and system policies were examined in Chapter 4. However, a few important aspects of NT security have not yet been addressed. Therefore, we include a "grab bag" of security issues in this chapter to adequately prepare you for the security questions on the Workstation exam.

The Windows NT Security Model

The Windows NT security model is designed to control access to data. As you know, security is often not a single barrier or restriction, but a collection of measures designed to prevent data loss of any kind. This includes theft, unauthorized disclosure, virus infection, and destruction of any kind—such as deletion, overwriting, and hardware failures. A security scheme is not impenetrable, but instead, a solid security deployment is one that makes gaining unauthorized access so difficult that it is easier to go elsewhere. NT provides numerous security features that make implementing an effective security scheme straightforward.

The security features of NT include access control lists (ACLs), access tokens, logon authentication, account policies, user rights policies, auditing, and customizable environment options. Many of these topics have already been mentioned or discussed in other chapters, but we'll at least review them here to give you a complete picture of NT security.

Logon Authentication

NT security starts with logon authentication. This is the process that goes on behind the scenes when Ctrl+Alt+Del is pressed at the NT splash screen and a user attempts to gain entry to the system. As discussed in Chapter 7, logging on to the system is controlled by the WINLOGON process and its communication with the security manager in the Executive Services of the Kernel.

There are four distinct parts to the logon process:

➤ **Mandatory logon** To gain access to the system, you must log on with a valid user account. Even if logon is automated by providing this information in the Registry (see the section titled "Customizing The Logon Process," later in this chapter), the logon process still occurs. The reason for this restriction is so that the access token for the user can be built.

> **User mode only** Without a valid logon with a current user account, no applications can be accessed or launched. This prevents the activation of Trojan Horse viruses that imitate the logon screen and steal passwords.

> **Physical logon** NT requires the Ctrl+Alt+Del keystroke to activate the WINLOGON dialog box. This keystroke combination activates a specific hardware interrupt that can only be generated from the keyboard, thus forcing users to be physically present at a computer to attempt logons.

> **User settings and preferences** A valid user account and password will grant a user entry to the system. From the account, NT will restore previously saved desktop and environmental settings, as well as generate an access token.

Access Tokens

When a valid user successfully logs in to Windows NT, an access token is generated by the security subsystem. This access token is used to launch the user's shell and establish the security context. The access token defines the user's access privileges and restrictions for his or her current logon session. Each time an object is accessed, the user's access token is compared to the object's ACL to verify the validity of the access requests.

An access token is built from three types of user data stored in the SAM database:

> **Security ID (SID)** The SID is a number assigned to each user, group, NT system, and many other objects that correlate to an entry in the SAM database. Each and every SID within a domain is unique. If a user or group is deleted, that specific SID is never reused. New groups or users with the same name and configuration will not regain the original SID or the previously granted permissions.

> **Group ID** A group ID is similar to a SID, except that it is not user specific—it's group specific. When a user joins a group, the group ID is added to that user's security list and included in the data used to create the access token. The group ID is linked to a group's security privileges and is compared to an object's ACL to grant or deny access.

> **Permissions** Permissions are specific access control settings granted to or restricted from a single user. If an object's ACL contains a specific user's SID, an additional element is added to a user's access token granting the specified access level to the object.

Each time a user logs in to Windows NT, he or she is assigned an access token generated from the current settings found in the SAM database. This access token is created by the Security Accounts Manager (SAM) and is returned to the WINLOGON process in the User mode. Once a valid access token is delivered to WINLOGON, that token is used to launch the user's primary process—the shell. Then, this process inherits the access token. WINLOGON removes itself from control and gives control to the user.

Each process launched by the user (or any user-controlled application or process) is governed by the access token inherited from the parent process. This inheritance scheme ensures that no process can be started with a higher security level than the parent. Thus, NT maintains control over user access levels through the initial access token assignment.

Objects And ACLs

We've already discussed objects and ACLs in Chapter 7. These are key features of the NT security system. If you are not already familiar and comfortable with the notion of objects and their associated ACLs, please review those sections in the previous chapter.

Customizing The Logon Process

The WINLOGON process has several customizable options to improve overall logon security and to force NT Workstation into compliance with your organization's security policy. All of these configuration settings must be made through the Registry in the WINLOGON key located at:

```
\HKEY_LOCAL_MACHINE\SOFTWARE\Microsoft\WindowsNT
\CurrentVersion\WinLogon
```

The available configuration changes for the Windows NT logon process are detailed in the next five sections.

Removing The Default User Name

By default, the user name of the last person to successfully log on to NT is displayed in the WINLOGON dialog box. Because a valid user name is half of the information needed by an intruder to gain access to your system, you can improve the security of your system by disabling the display of the last user's account name. You can set this feature by modifying the **DontDisplayLastUserName** string value in the Registry. Setting this entry to a value of 1 will display a blank user name field; setting this entry to a value of 0 will display the last user name.

Display A Security Warning Message

Some security policies require a message to be displayed about the ramifications of gaining unauthorized access to the computer system. NT can display a pop-up warning message just before displaying the WINLOGON dialog box. Each time a user presses Ctrl+Alt+Del, the warning will appear and the OK button must be clicked before logon can be attempted. Even if your security does not specify such a message, it is a good idea to help establish the culpability of intruders for criminal prosecution.

This feature is enabled through two entries to the Registry. The first is the title of the pop-up window for the message—it is called **LegalNotice Caption**. The second is the text to be displayed within the display window—it is called **LegalNoticeText**. These entries are already present in the Registry, but they are blank. To terminate the warning display, clear the contents of each value.

Designating The Shell

A shell is the foundation interface for a user environment. For Windows NT, the default shell is NT Explorer, but you can change the shell to some other custom or third-party application, depending on your needs or security policy. One common replacement for the default shell is the Program Manager (PROGMAN.EXE), a tool often more familiar to NT 3.51 and Windows 3.x users. However, by changing the default shell, the ability to access special NT 4 features such as My Computer, the Start menu, and the Taskbar will be severely limited.

To change the shell, modify the Registry entry named **Shell** to reflect the executable for the new shell. If the executable is not in the root Windows NT directory, you must provide a complete path.

Disabling The Shutdown Button

The WINLOGON prompt for Windows NT Workstation displays the Shutdown button, by default. This same button is disabled, by default, on Windows NT Server. You can choose which setting you prefer or require. The Registry entry that governs this button is **ShutdownWithoutLogon**. A value of 1 enables the button, and a value of 0 disables the button.

Logon Automation

Even though the logon process cannot be bypassed, it can be automated to eliminate the need to press Ctrl+Alt+Del, type in a user name and password, and then click Logon. If security is not an issue, this can simplify your computing experience, especially if you reboot often. To enable this feature, add three string values to the Registry: **DefaultUserName**, **DefaultPassword**, and **AutoAdminLogon**. The first two entries should be set to meet the standards set by your corporate security policy. **AutoAdminLogon** should be set to 1 to automate logon or 0 to disable.

Once enabled, the Shift key must be pressed during reboot or logoff to display the WINLOGON dialog box for an alternate user to gain access.

Exam Prep Questions

Question 1

A security scheme is put in place for which of the following reasons? [Check all correct answers]

❑ a. To prevent unauthorized disclosure

❑ b. To protect against virus infection

❑ c. To support privacy

❑ d. To deter unauthorized access

❑ e. To avert data loss

A security scheme should be put in place for any or all of these reasons. Therefore, answers a, b, c, d, and e are correct.

Question 2

Why is mandatory logon required by NT?

○ a. To force compliance with password policies

○ b. To initiate the generation of an access token

○ c. To enable user activity logging

○ d. To grant user access to shut down a machine

The only correct answer is the initiation of access token generation. Therefore, answer b is correct. Forcing password policy compliance, enabling user activity logging, and granting shutdown access are not reasons for mandatory logon. Therefore, answers a, c, and d are incorrect.

Question 3

> Which of the following components is responsible for the logon process?
>
> ○ a. SAM database
> ○ b. Executive Services
> ○ c. WINLOGON
> ○ d. User Manager
> ○ e. User mode

The SAM database is used by the security manager in the Executive Services when the WINLOGON process submits a user name and password for validation, but it is not in control of the logon process. Therefore, answer a is incorrect. The Executive Services are involved in the logon process, but they are not responsible for it. Therefore, answer b is incorrect. **The WINLOGON process is responsible for the logon process. Therefore, answer c is correct.** The User Manager is not associated with logon; it is used to manage user and group accounts. Therefore, answer d is incorrect. User mode is the section of the OS environment where WINLOGON operates, but it is not in control of the logon process. Therefore, answer e is incorrect.

Question 4

> Which of the following are components of NT security? [Check all correct answers]
>
> ❏ a. Sound schemes
> ❏ b. ACLs
> ❏ c. User rights
> ❏ d. Performance counters
> ❏ e. Auditing

A sound scheme is not a security device. Therefore, answer a is incorrect. ACLs, user rights, and auditing are all features of NT security. Therefore, answers b, c, and e are correct. Performance counters are not security devices. Therefore, answer d is incorrect.

Question 5

An access token is generated when a user successfully logs onto NT. What is the first action the action token performs?

❏ a. To load user preferences

❏ b. To launch the shell

❏ c. To initiate the User mode

❏ d. To allocate a virtual machine for applications

Loading user preferences occurs after a shell has been launched. Therefore, answer a is incorrect. **Launching the shell is the first action performed by the access token. Therefore, answer b is correct.** The User mode is initiated by the system during bootup and is only accessible after a successful logon. Therefore, answer c is incorrect. Virtual machines are created by the Executive Services, and processes within a virtual machine have the user's access token attached to them. Therefore, answer d is incorrect.

Question 6

What are the four parts or aspects of the logon process? [Check all correct answers]

❏ a. Physical logon

❏ b. User mode only

❏ c. ACLs

❏ d. Mandatory logon

❏ e. User preferences

Physical logon, user mode only, mandatory logon, and user preferences are the four aspects of the logon process. Therefore, answers a, b, d, and e are correct. ACLs are the permission settings on objects. Therefore, answer c is incorrect.

Question 7

An access token is generated by the security manager by pulling data, such as SID, group ID, and special permissions, from the SAM database.

○ a. True

○ b. False

The correct answer is a, true.

Question 8

Which setting of **AutoAdminLogon** is required to terminate the automatic logon process?

○ a. 1

○ b. 0

A value of 0 will disable the automatic logon feature of NT. Therefore, answer b is correct.

Question 9

How can the logon process be modified? [Check all correct answers]

❏ a. Prevent task list display

❏ b. Display warning message

❏ c. Remove pull-down list of user names

❏ d. Launching of an alternate shell

❏ e. Automating logon

There is no such control to prevent a task list display associated with the logon process. Therefore, answer a is incorrect. **Displaying a warning message is a customization option of the logon process. Therefore, answer b is correct.** There is no such control to remove a pull-down list of user names. Therefore, answer c is incorrect. **Launching an alternate shell and automating logon are two logon options. Therefore, answers d and e are correct.**

Question 10

By default, Windows NT Workstation does not enable the Shut-down button found on the WINLOGON dialog box.

○ a. True

○ b. False

Answer b, false, is correct. Windows NT Workstation does enable the Shut-down button, by default. NT Server disables this button, by default.

Need To Know More?

 Perkins, Charles, Matthew Strebe, and James Chellis: *MCSE: NT Workstation Study Guide.* Sybex Network Press, San Francisco, CA, 1997. ISBN 0-7821-1973-5. Chapter 7 discusses the Windows NT security features found in this chapter and those subjects referenced in the previous chapter.

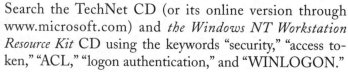 Search the TechNet CD (or its online version through www.microsoft.com) and *the Windows NT Workstation Resource Kit* CD using the keywords "security," "access token," "ACL," "logon authentication," and "WINLOGON."

9

Windows NT Networking

· ·

Terms you'll need to understand:

√ Protocol

√ Network Basic Input/Output System (NetBIOS)

√ NetBIOS Extended User Interface (NetBEUI)

√ Transmission Control Protocol/ Internet Protocol (TCP/IP)

√ NWLink Internetwork Packet eXchange/Sequenced Packet eXchange (IPX/SPX)

√ Data Link Control (DLC)

√ AppleTalk

√ Windows Sockets

Terms you'll need to master:

√ Installing and configuring network protocols

√ Familiarization with the Network applet in Control Panel

√ Implementing services that complement certain protocols

√ Understanding and configuring protocol bindings

√ Adjusting frame type settings

√ Remote Procedure Calls (RPC)

√ Network Dynamic Data Exchange

√ Frame type

√ Redirectors

√ Protocol binding

To enable communications on a computer network, you must tell NT how it's supposed to "talk" to other computers and peripheral devices. In the networking world, this is established through the use of protocols. Basically, a protocol is an agreed-upon set of standards that define how computers communicate. In this chapter, we explain what protocols are available with Windows NT and when to use which protocol, as well as the properties of each protocol. In keeping with the tone of this series, we cover only those details you need to know in order to pass the networking portion of the Workstation exam. Pointers are provided to additional resources for this topic.

Microsoft Network Component Architecture

The networking architecture implemented by Windows NT can be mapped to the International Standards Organization (ISO) model of networking in a near one-to-one relationship. But, you don't need to know the ISO model or how NT relates to it for the exam. There are, however, a few items within a handful of the components that you at least need to be aware of.

The Programming interface layer—which provides a standard for interaction between applications and the file system drivers and network services—supports important APIs. These include the following:

➤ **NetBIOS** All basic network communications within NT are performed using NetBIOS.

➤ **Windows Sockets** Provides a standard for application interaction with transport protocols such as TCP/IP over PPP.

➤ **Remote Procedure Calls** Handles network interprocess communications.

➤ **Network Dynamic Data Exchange** Supports DDE applications over a network; developed by Microsoft.

The File System Drivers layer supports all the storage types for NT, including the following:

➤ NTFS

➤ VFAT (includes FAT)

➤ CDFS

These topics are discussed in detail in Chapter 6, "Windows NT File Systems And Structures."

The Network Driver Interface layer complies with Network Driver Interface Standards 3.0 (NDIS 3.0). This allows multiple protocols to be bound to multiple adapters, and vice versa.

When Windows NT Workstation is installed, a few network system components are installed automatically. These are present to support both standalone operation and most of the low-level activities when connected to a network. Here are the default components:

➤ **NetBIOS interface** Supports NT's low-level system operation.

➤ **TCP/IP protocol** The default protocol.

➤ **Workstation service** Allows a machine to access network resources.

➤ **Server service** Allows other machines to access local resources and share resources.

➤ **Computer browser** Enables interaction with resource lists.

➤ **NIC driver** Enables NT to communicate with the network adapter.

➤ **RPC service** Manages network interprocess communications.

Built-In Windows NT Protocols

Windows NT Workstation comes with a number of protocols that can be enabled for interoperability and communication:

➤ NetBIOS Extended User Interface (NetBEUI)

➤ Transmission Control Protocol/Internet Protocol (TCP/IP)

➤ NWLink Internetwork Packet eXchange/Sequenced Packet eXchange (IPX/SPX)

➤ Data Link Control (DLC)

➤ AppleTalk

We define and explain all of these protocols and their uses in the following sections.

NetBEUI

NetBEUI is a simple network layer transport broadcast protocol developed to support NetBIOS networks. NetBEUI is not routable, so it really has no place on an enterprise network. NetBEUI is the fastest transport protocol available to NT. The benefits of NetBEUI include its speed as well as good error protection; also, it is easy to implement, with small memory overhead. The disadvantages of NetBEUI include the fact that it's not routable, there is very little support for cross-platform applications, and there are very few troubleshooting tools.

TCP/IP

TCP/IP is the most widely used protocol in networking today (due in part to the vast growth of the global Internet, which is a TCP/IP-based network). TCP/IP is the most flexible of the transport protocols and is able to span wide areas. In addition, it has excellent cross-platform support as well as routing capabilities. Also, TCP/IP has support for the Simple Network Management Protocol (SNMP), the Dynamic Host Configuration Protocol (DHCP), the Windows Internet Name Service (WINS), the Domain Name Service (DNS), as well as a host of other useful protocols, which are discussed in Chapter 10, "TCP/IP." On the other hand, TCP/IP is difficult to configure and demands a significant amount of overhead.

NWLink (IPX/SPX)

NWLink is Microsoft's "clean room" implementation of Novell's IPX/SPX protocol suite for NetWare networks. This protocol was included with NT to enable communication with NetWare servers. With NWLink, NT clients can access resources located on a NetWare server, and vice versa.

Put simply, Windows NT requires that NWLink be installed to enable communications with NetWare clients and servers. In addition, the File And Print Service For NetWare is also required in order for NetWare clients and servers to access NT files and printers. The Client Service For NetWare is designed for Windows NT Workstation computers that require a direct link to NetWare servers. The Gateway Service For NetWare lets Windows NT servers map a drive to a NetWare server, which provides access to NetWare server resources for Windows NT Workstations (via a gateway). Additional information about NWLink can be found in the section titled "NWLink Connectivity Issues" later in this chapter.

DLC

Windows NT uses the Data Link Control (DLC) protocol primarily for connectivity to SNA (Systems Network Architecture) gateways, and more importantly, for connecting to network-attached printers, such as the

Hewlett-Packard JetDirect. The use of DLC for network printing is detailed more in Chapter 14, "Windows NT Printing."

AppleTalk

It should come as no surprise that the AppleTalk protocol is used for communication with Macintosh computers. By enabling AppleTalk, you allow Mac clients to store and access files located on NT Server, print to NT printers, and vice versa. (Note that you must first install the NT Service For Macintosh before you can install AppleTalk; also, remember that Mac support is available only from an NTFS partition.) The only real benefit to NT users from the AppleTalk protocol is the ability to print to Macintosh color printers hosted on Macintosh computers. This is the only issue on the exam in relation to AppleTalk.

NetBEUI Connectivity Issues

NetBEUI is by far the easiest protocol to install and configure on an NT network. To install this protocol, perform the following steps:

1. Open the Control Panel (Start|Settings|Control Panel).

2. Double-click the Network icon.

3. In the Networks window, click the Protocols tab.

4. Click the Add button.

5. Select NetBEUI from the list of available protocols and click OK.

6. Enter the path to the installation CD or the location of the installation files.

7. If you have RAS installed, NT asks if you want to support it with this protocol. Click Cancel to leave it unsupported.

8. In the Network window, click the Close button.

9. Select Yes when NT asks to restart the computer.

NWLink Connectivity Issues

Put simply, NWLink is IPX for Windows NT: IPX is the protocol, and NWLink is the networking component that provides the protocol. NWLink is provided for connectivity to NetWare networks—both to allow NetWare clients to access NT servers and to allow NT clients to access NetWare servers. It is important to note, however, that NWLink by itself does not enable this type of communication; you must first install Gateway Service For NetWare (GSNW) on NT Server or Client Service For NetWare (CSNW) on NT Workstation. Basically, CSNW is a redirector, whereas GSNW is what makes file and print sharing on NetWare servers available to Microsoft clients.

IPX has a number of benefits: It supports routing between networks, it's faster than TCP/IP, and it's easy to install and maintain. Unfortunately, IPX doesn't have a sufficient central addressing scheme to prohibit multiple networks from making use of identical addresses, and it doesn't support the Simple Network Management Protocol (SNMP).

Installing NWLink

Installing the NWLink protocol is much like installing other protocols in Windows NT. There are, however, some special issues. To install NWLink, perform the following steps:

1. Open the Control Panel (Start|Settings|Control Panel).

2. Double-click the Network icon.

3. Click the Protocols tab in the Network dialog box.

4. Click the Add button.

5. Select NWLink IPX/SPX Compatible Transport from the list of available protocols.

6. Enter the path to the Windows NT Server installation CD in the path field of the setup dialog box. Then click Continue.

   If you have installed NT's Remote Access Service (RAS), NT then asks if you want to bind NWLink to RAS. Either click OK to enable binding or click Cancel.

7. Click the Close button and then click Yes when NT asks if you want to restart the computer.

 Although, in most cases, it's fine to leave the default frame type (auto) as is, some Ethernet adapters don't work well with this setting. For new installations, the Ethernet 802.2 setting is recommended.

To change the Ethernet frame type and IPX network number, perform the following steps:

1. Open the Control Panel (Start|Settings|Control Panel).

2. Double-click the Network icon.

3. Click the Protocols tab in the Network dialog box.

4. Double-click NWLink IPX/SPX Compatible Transport from the list of available protocols.

5. Click the Manual Frame Type Detection button.

6. Click the Add button.

7. Select your preferred frame type.

8. Type in the IPX network number for the adapter in the Network Number field.

9. Click the Add button.

10. Repeat the previous three steps for each frame type.

11. Click OK and then click the Close button.

12. Click Yes when asked to restart the computer.

There are more issues to consider when establishing communications between NT and NetWare networks. These details are covered in Chapter 11, "NetWare Connectivity."

TCP/IP Connectivity Issues

TCP/IP currently is the most-used networking protocol, as well as the standard protocol of the Internet. The beauty of the TCP/IP protocol suite lies in its ability to link many disparate kinds of computers and peripheral devices. Using this protocol stack, you enable most TCP/IP clients to access NT-based resources, and vice versa.

Because the following chapter is devoted to TCP/IP, the discussion of TCP/IP connectivity and configuration is not repeated here. Please refer to Chapter 10, "TCP/IP," for all of the details on TCP/IP.

InterProcess Communications

InterProcess Communications (IPC) provides a common communication path and language for clients to request resources and for servers to respond to requests. IPC is comprised of two types of elements: file systems and programming interfaces. The IPC file systems are named pipes and mail slots. These are connection-oriented and connection-less (respectively) communication channels. The IPC programming interfaces are those already mentioned in the network layer discussion in the section entitled "Microsoft Network Component Architecture" earlier in this chapter.

Very little information regarding IPC appears on the Workstation exam.

Redirectors

A redirector is a software service that intercepts requests for resources and directs those requests to the correct server hosting the required resource, whether local or over the network. There are four standard redirectors in NT:

➤ **Workstation service** Enables a client to request resources.

➤ **Server service** Enables a server to offer resources.

➤ **Multiple Universal Naming Convention Provider (MUP)** Links UNC requests, other redirectors, and applications together, thus isolating the redirection process from users and applications.

➤ **Multi-Provider Router** Handles non-UNC Win32 API naming convention resource requests (for example, C:\TEMP\ LEGAL.DOC).

If you can recognize these as redirectors, you already know more than you need to for the exam.

Network Configuration

Most (if not all) configuration of NT's network capabilities is done through the Network applet of the Control Panel. Some services provide additional utilities and applets, but they must first be installed through the Network applet. Each tab of this applet has important features and abilities.

Identification Tab

The Change button brings up the Identification Changes dialog box (see Figure 9.1). Here you can do the following:

➤ Change the name of the workstation.

➤ Switch membership between domain(s) and/or workgroup(s).

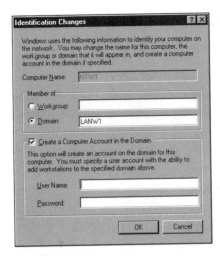

Figure 9.1   The Identification Changes dialog box.

➤ If a domain account does not already exist, you can input the name of the Administrator account and its password so that NT will create a computer account for this computer.

These changes do not alter the SID of the workstation; therefore, returning to a domain should not be a problem as long as the computer's account is not deleted.

Services Tab

On this tab, services can be added, removed, and configured. Each service has a different properties and configuration window. Unless service configuration is specifically highlighted in this book, you don't need to worry about it for the test. There is also an Update button to install new versions of services from Microsoft or from third parties.

Protocols Tab

On this tab, protocols are added, removed, and configured. Earlier in this chapter, details on installing and configuring the three central protocols of NT—TCP/IP, NWLink, and NetBEUI—were discussed in detail.

Adapters Tab

On this tab, network interface card drivers are installed. Because NT is not plug-n-play compatible and the user environment is isolated from the hardware, very little, if any, configuration changes can be made to a NIC through this tab.

Bindings Tab

Protocol binding is the process NT uses to link network components from various levels of the network architecture to enable communication between those components. This tab is where the bindings of installed network components are listed in order of upper-layer services and protocols to lower-layer network adapter drivers. By default, NT enables all possible bindings between services, protocols, and adapters.

Binding should be ordered to enhance the system's use of the network. For example, if your network has both TCP/IP and NetBEUI installed, and most network devices use TCP/IP, workstation bindings should be set to bind TCP/IP first and NetBEUI second. In other words, the most frequently used protocol should be bound first. This speeds network connections. Because servers use whatever protocol is sent to them by each workstation, the binding order needs to be changed on the workstations only. Network speed is affected by the binding order on the workstations, but not on the servers.

Exam Prep Questions

Question 1

> Which of the following are supported IPC elements? [Check all correct answers]
>
> ❏ a. NetBIOS
>
> ❏ b. Multi-Provider Router
>
> ❏ c. NetDDE
>
> ❏ d. Windows Sockets
>
> ❏ e. RPC

The programming interface elements of IPC are NetBIOS, NetDDE, Windows Sockets, and RPC. Therefore, answers a, c, d, and e are correct. Multi-Provider Router is a redirector and not an IPC element. Therefore, answer b is incorrect.

Question 2

> What protocols or services are installed by default in Windows NT Workstation? [Check all correct answers]
>
> ❏ a Server service
>
> ❏ b. DLC
>
> ❏ c. RPC
>
> ❏ d. NetBIOS
>
> ❏ e. RAS

The Server service, RPC, and NetBIOS are all installed by default. Therefore, answers a, b, and d are correct. DLC and RAS are not automatically installed. Therefore, answers b and e are incorrect.

Question 3

Your network uses multiple protocols. Where in NT is the binding order of the protocols changed to increase network speed?

○ a. On the domain controllers only

○ b. On the workstations only

○ c. On the servers only

○ d. On both the workstations and servers (including the domain controllers)

Because NT servers use the protocol sent to them by workstations, the binding order needs only to be changed on the workstations. Therefore, answer b is the correct choice. Network speed is affected by the binding order on the workstations, but not on the servers. Therefore, answers a, c, and d all are incorrect.

Question 4

Where is the workgroup membership for NT Workstation defined?

○ a. Workgroup applet

○ b. Network applet, Identification tab

○ c. Services applet, StartUp button

○ d. Server Manager, machine properties

There is no such utility as the Workgroup applet. Therefore, answer a is incorrect. The Identification tab of the Network applet is where workgroup membership is defined. Therefore, answer b is correct. The StartUp button applies to services, not workgroup membership. Therefore, answer c is incorrect. The Server Manager is not used to alter the workgroup membership. Therefore, answer d is incorrect.

Question 5

> Your NT workstation and the NT server has TCP/IP, NWLink, and
> NetBEUI protocols installed. Which protocol should you bind first
> to maximize throughput?
>
> ○ a. TCP/IP
> ○ b. NWLink
> ○ c. NetBEUI

NetBEUI uses the least overhead of the other protocols, and by binding it
first, it will be the protocol used by both the client and server to transfer
files. Therefore, answer c is correct. TCP/IP and NWLink are both larger
and more resource demanding than NWLink. Therefore, answers a and b
are incorrect.

Question 6

> You want to print a document to a color printer hosted on a
> Macintosh client in your workgroup. What protocol is required to
> support this activity?
>
> ○ a. DLC
> ○ b. NWLink
> ○ c. NetBEUI
> ○ d. AppleTalk

DLC is used for network attached printers. Therefore, answer a is incorrect. NWLink and NetBEUI cannot be used to communicate with a
Macintosh printer. Therefore, answers b and c are incorrect. The AppleTalk
protocol is required to support Macintosh printing. Therefore, answer d is
correct.

Question 7

> The Network Driver Interface, being NDIS 3.0 compliant, enables
> multiple protocols to be bound to multiple network adapters.
>
> ○ a. True
> ○ b. False

The NDIS 3.0 standard enables NT's Network Driver Interface to bind multiple protocols with multiple adapters. Therefore, answer a is correct.

Question 8

IPC is an NT mechanism used to support client/server applications.

○ a. True
○ b. False

IPC enables clients and servers to interact using a common language. Therefore, answer a is correct.

Question 9

What is the unified NT interface that isolates redirection and network processes from the user and application?

○ a. NetBIOS Extended User Interface (NetBEUI)
○ b. Multiple Universal Naming Convention Provider (MUP)
○ c. InterProcess Communications (IPC)
○ d. Internetwork Packet eXchange/Sequenced Packet eXchange (IPX/SPX)

NetBEUI is a protocol used by NT, but it is not the unified redirector hiding interface. Therefore, answer a is incorrect. **MUP is the unified redirector hiding interface. Therefore, answer b is correct.** IPC is not a redirector. Therefore, answer c is incorrect. IPX/SPX is the Novell protocol that Microsoft re-created as NWLink, and it is not a redirector. Therefore, answer d is incorrect.

Question 10

> Which network component is required for printer sharing on NT?
>
> ○ a. AppleTalk
>
> ○ b. Server
>
> ○ c. DLC
>
> ○ d. Workstation

AppleTalk is needed to access Macintosh hosted printers, but it is not required for printer sharing on NT. Therefore, answer a is incorrect. **The Server service is required to offer resources over the network. Therefore, answer b is correct.** DLC is used to interact with network connected printers, but it is not required to create a printer share. Therefore, answer c is incorrect. The Workstation service is only required to access a share, not to share a printer. Therefore, answer d is incorrect.

Need To Know More?

 Boyce, Jim, et al.: *Windows NT Workstation 4 Advanced Technical Reference.* Que, Indianapolis, IN, 1996. ISBN 0-7897-0863-9. This book contains a lot of NT network material in Chapters 15 through 19. However, we do not recommend this as a primary resource for the exam due to the lack of data density.

 Perkins, Charles, Matthew Strebe, and James Chellis: *MCSE: NT Workstation Study Guide.* Sybex Network Press, San Francisco, CA, 1997. ISBN 0-7821-1973-5. Chapter 8 has complete coverage of the networking systems of NT workstation.

 Search the TechNet CD (or its online version through www.microsoft.com) using the keywords "protocol management," "TCP/IP," "NWLink," "NetBEUI," and "internetworking."

  The *Windows NT Workstation Resource Kit* contains a lot of useful information about shares and share permissions. You can search the TechNet (either CD or online version) or the *Resource Kit* CD using keywords such as "protocols," "binding," and "networking services."

TCP/IP

Terms you'll need to understand:

- √ Transmission Control Protocol/ Internet Protocol (TCP/IP)
- √ Dynamic Host Configuration Protocol (DHCP)
- √ Windows Internet Naming Service (WINS)
- √ Domain Name Service (DNS)
- √ Serial Line Internet Protocol (SLIP)
- √ Point-To-Point Protocol (PPP)
- √ Point-To-Point Tunneling Protocol (PPTP)
- √ World Wide Web (WWW)

- √ File Transfer Protocol (FTP)
- √ Address Resolution Protocol (ARP)
- √ HOSTNAME
- √ IPCONFIG
- √ NBTSTAT
- √ NETSTAT
- √ PING
- √ ROUTE
- √ TRACERT
- √ Peer Web Services

Technique you'll need to master:

- √ Installing and configuring TCP/IP

TCP/IP is a large, complex, and multifaceted issue, especially in relation to networking with Windows NT. In this chapter, we give you an overview of TCP/IP in the world of NT, plus the specifics that apply to NT Workstation.

The TCP/IP Protocol Suite

Windows NT provides for a number of useful TCP/IP services. Included are the following:

➤ **Dynamic Host Configuration Protocol (DHCP)** This service enables the assignment of dynamic TCP/IP network addresses on a first- come-first-served basis, based on a specified pool of available addresses. When a network client configured for DHCP logs on to the network, the DHCP service assigns the next available TCP/IP address for that network session. This really simplifies address administration. The DHCP server is only available on a Windows NT Server machine; however, both NT Server and NT Workstation (as well as any other TCP/IP client) can request data from a DHCP server.

➤ **Windows Internet Naming Service (WINS)** This service enables the resolution of network names to IP addresses (similar to the Unix DNS). This way, you don't have to remember the IP address of the client with whom you are trying to communicate—you can enter the network name, and NT does the rest. Also, if a TCP/IP-based network does not have a WINS server, each time one computer tries to access another, it must send a b-node broadcast, which creates unnecessary network traffic and can slow a busy network to a crawl. WINS servers provide "computer name to IP address" resolution, reducing these broadcast messages and improving network performance. The WINS server is only available on a Windows NT Server machine; however, both NT Server and NT Workstation (as well as any other TCP/IP client) can use WINS server to resolve network names.

➤ **Serial Line Internet Protocol (SLIP)** SLIP originally was developed for the Unix environment and is still widely used among Internet providers. Although SLIP provides good performance with little system overhead requirements, it does not support error checking, flow control, or security features. SLIP is good for connecting to Unix hosts or Internet providers. This protocol is quickly being replaced by

PPP. SLIP is present on NT Workstation only for the purpose of connecting to a Unix server; it cannot be used for inbound RAS sessions.

➤ **Point-To-Point Protocol (PPP)** PPP addresses many of the insufficiencies of SLIP, such as providing the capability to encrypt logons as well as support for additional transport protocols, error checking, and recovery. In addition, PPP is optimized for low-bandwidth connections and, in general, is a more efficient protocol than SLIP. PPP is present on NT Workstation and is the preferred WAN protocol for RAS connections.

➤ **Point-To-Point Tunneling Protocol (PPTP)** Simply stated, PPTP is a protocol that creates secure connections between private networks over the Internet. Benefits of PPTP include lower administrative, transmission, and hardware costs than other solutions for this type of connectivity. PPTP on NT Workstation can be used to connect to any system supporting a compatible implementation of PPTP.

➤ **World Wide Web (WWW)** This service comes as a part of Peer Web Services (PSW). WWW makes it possible to publish Web pages, whether for an Internet-based Web site or for an internal intranet. It uses Hypertext Transfer Protocol (HTTP) to transfer Web documents and resources.

➤ **File Transfer Protocol (FTP)** This protocol is great for the fast transfer of files to and from a local hard drive to an FTP server located elsewhere on another TCP/IP-based network (such as the Internet). This service/protocol is part of Peer Web Services.

➤ **Gopher** This service, which predates HTTP (the Web protocol), serves text and links to other Gopher sites. Although Gopher sites are still out there, its use has been lessened because HTTP handles information transfer better than this outdated method. This service/protocol is part of Peer Web Services.

Installing And Configuring TCP/IP

You need to have a few items on hand when you install TCP/IP. The following list describes these items:

➤ **Your workstation's (Class C) IP address** This is the unique address that identifies a particular computer on a TCP/IP network. This number consists of four numbers, separated by periods (for example,

125.115.125.48). The first one to three numbers identify the network on which the computer is located, and the remaining numbers identify the computer on that network. If you do not have a permanent IP address assigned to you, you can configure your NT Workstation to poll a DHCP server to request an address.

➤ **Your network's subnet masks for each network adapter on the network** The subnet mask is a number mathematically applied to the IP address. This number determines which IP addresses are a part of the same subnetwork as the computer applying the subnet mask. This detail can also be requested from a DHCP server.

➤ **Your default gateway** The gateway is the computer that serves as a router, a format translator, or a security filter for a network. If the default gateway is not defined, the computer will be unable to communicate with machines outside its subnet. This detail can also be requested from a DHCP server.

➤ **The domain name server for the network** This is a computer that serves as an Internet host and performs translation of fully qualified domain names (FQDNs) into IP addresses.

➤ **Any DHCP and WINS information about your network** These nonmandatory name resolution services can expand the range of reachable services from your NT Workstation.

If you did not install TCP/IP when you first installed Windows NT Workstation, you must perform the following steps to install and configure this protocol suite:

1. Open the Control Panel (Start|Settings|Control Panel).

2. Double-click the Network icon.

3. In the Networks window, click the Protocols tab.

4. Click the Add button.

5. Select TCP/IP from the list of available protocols. NT may request the installation CD or the location of the installation files.

6. In the Network window, click the Close button.

7. Either enter the TCP/IP address of the computer or select Obtain An IP Address From A DHCP Server, whichever is appropriate for this installation. Then, specify the subnet mask and default gateway.

8. If your network has a DNS server or a constant Internet connection, click the DNS tab and enter the DNS address.

9. If your network has a WINS server, click the WINS tab and enter the WINS address.

10. Restart the computer.

Once your system reboots, TCP/IP will be fully installed. You can always return to the Protocols tab of the Network applet to modify the configuration of TCP/IP.

TCP/IP Tools

Once TCP/IP is installed and properly configured, you have access to a handful of TCP/IP utilities. These utilities are divided into two categories—diagnostic and connectivity.

Diagnostic commands:

➤ **ARP** Displays and modifies address translation tables used by the Address Resolution Protocol

➤ **HOSTNAME** Displays the name of the host

➤ **IPCONFIG** Displays all of the current local TCP/IP configuration values, including IP address, subnet mask, and WINS and DNS configuration

➤ **LPQ** Displays print queue status of an LPD printer

➤ **NBTSTAT** Displays protocol statistics and current TCP/IP connections using NetBIOS over TCP/IP

➤ **NETSTAT** Displays protocol statistics and current TCP/IP network connections

➤ **PING** Verifies existence of remote host

➤ **ROUTE** Modifies routing tables

➤ **TRACERT** Displays route taken by an Internet Control Message Protocol (ICMP) to a remote host

Connectivity commands:

➤ **FINGER** Displays information about a user (server must be running a FINGER service)

➤ **FTP** Used to transfer files to and from an FTP server

➤ **LPR** Sends files to an LPD printer

➤ **RCP** Used to copy files between a client and server running the RSHD service (remote shell)

➤ **REXEC** Executes commands on a remote system running the REXECD service

➤ **RSH** Executes commands on a remote system running the RSH service

➤ **Telnet** A terminal emulator for interacting with remote systems

➤ **TFTP** Transfers files using the Trivial File Transfer Protocol service (similar to FTP)

You can obtain the complete details of the syntax and usage of these commands by typing "/?" after their names at a command prompt or through the Help system of NT. You don't need to know anything about the actual use of these tools for the Workstation exam.

NT Names And Name Services

Computers interact with each other using long strings of complicated address numbers. Fortunately, Windows NT hides most of these unfriendly references behind easy-to-remember names. Name resolution is the activity of transforming a user-friendly name for a computer or network share into a computer-friendly network address. This process enables networks to quickly locate and request resources while shielding users from complicated and difficult-to-remember—much less type in—hardware-level addresses. Within Windows NT, there is a base resolution service (NetBIOS), three protocol-specific services (NetBEUI, NWLink, and TCP/IP), and additional services for TCP/IP (DHCP, DNS, and WINS).

> *Note: NetBEUI and NWLink name resolution is included in this chapter for convenience. They comprise too small a section to have placed them elsewhere. They are only included here to balance the discussion; there is no mention of either of these name resolution systems on the Workstation exams we have seen.*

NetBIOS Names In Windows NT

NetBIOS is automatically installed during NT installation. It is the underlying communication mechanism for many basic NT functions, such as browsing and interprocess communications between network servers. NetBIOS is an extremely fast protocol that requires very little communications overhead, which is why it's used by NT for basic operations. NetBIOS is an API used by all NT applications. It provides a uniform set of commands to access common low-level services.

All NT resources are identified by a unique NetBIOS name consisting of 15 characters or less. The NetBIOS namespace is not hierarchical, but flat. Therefore, every machine on the same network must have a unique NetBIOS name, even if the machines are in different domains. Each time a computer connects to the network, it broadcasts its presence by "shouting" its NetBIOS name. The Master Browser "hears" this broadcast and attempts to register the new machine. If another machine is already using the name that was broadcast by the newcomer, the registration is denied. That computer cannot go online until its NetBIOS name is changed or the other computer currently using the name goes offline.

A NetBIOS name is not the same as a host name. A host name is a substitute for a four-segment decimal notation IP address of an Internet host. These names are required for communication with the aliased machine (for example, www.microsoft.com equals 207.68.156.53). A NetBIOS name is a mandatory, unique name used by Windows NT for most network functions. Each time an Explorer interface such as an open file dialog box is activated, you are interacting with NetBIOS names.

As we discuss in Chapter 12 in the section on browsers, NetBIOS names are used to identify and list the resources currently available on a network. A computer announces itself and its resources upon booting up and once every minute thereafter. As it remains up and running, the interval increases to every 12 minutes. If a computer is gracefully shut down, it announces the removal of its resources as it leaves. If a computer goes offline otherwise, its resources can remain listed in the browser service for up to 51 minutes until the Master Browser removes the entries and the backup browsers are updated. Computers rebroadcast their existence and all their resources every 12 minutes, so the level of traffic can be quite high, even for a small network.

NetBEUI And Name Resolution

All name resolution over NetBEUI is done through NetBIOS. There-fore, there is no further configuration or installation required. Both users and computers use the NetBIOS name to call and access network system objects.

With NetBEUI, most of the network overhead is consumed by the NetBIOS announcement broadcasts. This is one of many reasons why NetBEUI should not be used on anything but the smallest of networks.

IPX And Name Resolution

IPX/SPX or NWLink uses NetBIOS Over IPX (NBIPX) to resolve NetBIOS names into IPX addresses. Because IPX addresses contain the MAC address of the host, no further resolution is required. NWLink caches NetBIOS names to perform the IPX address mappings. NWLink does not use an address mapping file or name service. Unlike Novell's implementation of IPX/SPX, NWLink from Microsoft does not issue Service Advertisement Protocol (SAP) broadcasts. Therefore, network overhead is greatly reduced.

IP And Name Resolution

Name resolution under TCP/IP is a complex but important issue. The reso-lution methods for IP include Dynamic Host Configuration Protocol (DHCP), Domain Name Service (DNS), and Windows Internet Name Service (WINS). These methods are discussed in the upcoming sections.

DHCP

DHCP is not exactly a name resolution system. Instead, it is an IP address–leasing system where a limited number of IP addresses can be shared among numerous computers, usually clients. DHCP dynamically assigns IP addresses to clients on a local subnet.

DHCP server is only available on Windows NT Server, but it is only cov-ered in detail on the TCP/IP exam. However, you need to be familiar with a few terms and the basic method of operation of DHCP.

When a client boots, it broadcasts a message requesting data from a DHCP server. The receiving DHCP server responds with an IP address assign-ment for a specified period of time (called a lease period). The client receives the data, integrates the data into its configuration, and completes the boot process.

A DHCP server can also distribute subnet masks and default gateway addresses. Each assignment from a DHCP server is for a predetermined length of time, called a lease period. When a lease expires, a DHCP server can reassign the address to another computer. An operating client can extend its lease simply by indicating that it is still using the address. When half of a lease period is reached, a client requests a lease extension, if needed. It continues to request an extension from the leasing DHCP server until 87.5 percent of its time period has expired. Then, it broadcasts the extension request to all DHCP servers. If no server responds by the time the lease expires, all TCP/IP communications of that client will cease.

A client's IP configuration and lease information can be displayed using **IPCONFIG** with the **/all** parameter. This utility can also end a lease by using the **/release** parameter or renew a lease by using the **/renew** parameter.

 Configuring a client to access a DHCP server is simple. To configure a client, all you have to do is open the TCP/IP Properties dialog box from the Protocols tab of the Network applet. Then, on the IP Address page, select the radio button labeled Obtain An IP Address From A DHCP Server.

If your DHCP server is located across a router, you'll need to use the DHCP Relay Agent to forward DHCP broadcasts. With the employment of the Windows NT DHCP Relay Agent, a single DHCP server can support multiple subnets connected by the NT Multi-Protocol Router (MPR). Without the DHCP Relay Agent, routers filter out the DHCP broadcasts instead of passing them through. The Relay Agent intercepts the DHCP broadcasts and then transmits the broadcasts directly to the DHCP server. The router still filters out the DHCP request, but the added agent intervenes and sends the important boot message to the supporting server.

The following steps describe how to install the DHCP Relay Agent:

1. Add the DHCP Relay Agent through the Services tab of the Network applet in the Control Panel.

2. Specify the IP address of the DHCP server in the IP Address tab of the TCP/IP Properties dialog box.

   The DHCP Relay Agent is enabled automatically and installed as a service.

3. Choose the DHCP Relay tab in TCP/IP Properties dialog box to change default values for the DHCP Relay Agent. The values are Seconds Threshold, Maximum Hops, and List Of DHCP Server Addresses.

DNS

DNS is used to resolve host names into IP addresses. Host names are user-friendly conveniences that represent the dotted decimal notation of IP addresses that are not required for the operation of communication, unlike NetBIOS names. A host name, such as www.microsoft.com, is much easier to remember than its IP address (207.68.156.51).

DNS server is only available on Windows NT Server, but it is only covered in detail on the TCP/IP exam. However, you need to be familiar with a few terms and the basic method of operation of DNS.

Early DNS used a lookup table stored on every machine in a file called "HOST." As networks expand, maintaining an updated and correct HOST file is increasingly difficult. To ease administration, centralized DNS was developed. A single server hosts the DNS data for the networks it supports, a hierarchy table of domains, and a list of other DNS servers to which it can refer requests.

DNS operates on user-friendly, fully qualified domain names (FQDN) to determine the location (IP address) of a system. For example, ftp2.dev.microsoft.com could represent the server named "FTP2" located in the ".dev" subdomain under the ".microsoft" domain within the ".com" top-level domain. This hierarchy structure enables DNS to quickly traverse its database to locate the correct IP address for the host machine.

DNS is essential on large networks, including the Internet. A client is configured to use a DNS server through the TCP/IP Properties dialog box. The DNS tab contains fields to define the host name of the client, the domain where the client resides, the IP addresses of DNS servers, and a search order of domains.

The configuration of a DNS server is a very complicated and convoluted endeavor. Microsoft has done an excellent job of simplifying this task, but it is still difficult. Unix-based DNS, such as that most commonly used on the Internet, can be likened to building an Apollo rocket. Microsoft Windows NT-based DNS can be likened to building a high-performance race car.

WINS

WINS is a name resolution service for NT-based TCP/IP networks. Similar to DNS, WINS maps NetBIOS names to IP addresses. But unlike DNS, WINS dynamically maintains the mapping database. The main WINS functions include:

➤ Mapping NetBIOS names to IP addresses

➤ Recognizing NetBIOS names on all subnets

➤ Enabling internetwork browsing

WINS server is only available on Windows NT Server, but it is only covered in detail on the TCP/IP exam. However, you need to be familiar with a few terms and the basic method of operation of WINS.

WINS reduced NetBIOS background tracking by eliminating the NetBIOS broadcasts. A WINS client communicates directly with a WINS server to send a resource notification, release its NetBIOS name, or locate a resource.

The original Microsoft solution to reduce NetBIOS broadcast traffic was the LMHOSTS file. This was a static file stored on each client that associated IP addresses with NetBIOS names. Just as with the DNS HOST file, it had to be manually maintained. Unfortunately, an LMHOSTS file is useless in a DHCP environment where relationships between IP addresses and NetBIOS names change.

WINS and DHCP work well together. Each time a DHCP client goes online, it can inform the WINS server of its presence. Thus, the dynamic relationship between IP addresses and NetBIOS names can be fully managed by these automatic services.

WINS clients are configured through the TCP/IP Properties dialog box of the Services tab of the Network application. The WINS Address tab enables you to configure two WINS servers. The second server is for fault tolerance.

WINS Vs. DNS

WINS and DNS, although similar, have significant differences that define when each should be used for name resolution. Table 10.1 displays a comparison chart to highlight the differences between WINS and DNS.

Within many private networks, both DNS and WINS are installed. This provides support for both NetBIOS and FQDN resolution. Both DNS and WINS can be configured to pass resolution requests to the opposing

Table 10.1   Differences between WINS and DNS.

WINS	DNS
Maps IP addresses to NetBIOS names	Maps IP addresses to fully qualified domain names (FQDNs)
Automatic client data registration	Manual configuration
Flat database namespace	Uses FQDN's hierarchical structure
Used on MS clients and networks	Used on TCP/IP-based hosts and networks
Only one entry per client	Each host can have multiple aliases
Enables domain functions such as logon and browsing	N/A

resolution service if the referenced name is not listed in the respective database.

Peer Web Services

Another important component of NT that you need to be aware of is the Peer Web Services (PWS). PWS is NT Workstation's equivalent of NT Server's Internet Information Server (IIS). The only significant difference between PWS and IIS is that PWS is limited to 10 simultaneous connections due to the licensing restrictions of NT Workstation.

NT Workstation ships with PWS version 2, but version 3 is the current standard for real-world implementation. For the Workstation exam, you only need to know the basics of this application in its version 2 form.

PWS is a file and application server that provides Web, FTP, and Gopher services. If you are not already familiar with the Internet and these three services, you should reference the following resources:

➤ *Internet For Dummies,* by John R. Levine, Carol Baroudi, and Margy Levine-Young, IDG Books Worldwide, 1996. ISBN: 0-76450-106-2.

➤ *The Internet Complete Reference,* by Harley Hahn, Osborne McGraw-Hill, 1996. ISBN: 0-07882-138-X.

These resources will bring you up to speed on the topics considered as prerequisites for the NT Workstation exam.

PWS can be used to support the Internet services of Web, FTP, and Gopher within a private TCP/IP-based network or over the Internet. The bulk of the PWS material on the Workstation exam focuses on the Web service, but you need to be at least minimally aware of the FTP and Gopher services.

Web

The Web, or World Wide Web, is a service based on the Hypertext Transfer Protocol (HTTP). HTTP is a client/server interprocess communications protocol that employs text and graphics as content. A Web server, such as PWS, sends out requested documents to a Web client, such as Microsoft Internet Explorer. PWS offers numerous configuration options, including the following:

➤ Anonymous access

➤ NT user account restricted access

➤ Activity logging

➤ IP or domain name restricted/granted access

➤ Virtual server configuration

One important configuration feature of PWS is that of custom directory roots and virtual servers. Multiple Web sites can be hosted from a single installation of PWS. Each Web site is stored in its own root directory. In addition, each hosted Web site can be identified with its own FQDN and IP address. To host multiple IP addresses on the same PWS server, additional IP addresses are assigned to the server's NIC through the TCP/IP properties.

If PWS is used on a network with Internet connectivity, no additional services are required. DNS is handled by InterNIC (Internet-based) servers, and WINS will not be needed at all. However, if PWS is used within a private isolated network, both DNS and WINS might need to be installed somewhere on the network to support local name resolution.

FTP

The File Transfer Protocol (FTP) is the service and protocol used on the Internet to transfer files from one machine to another. PWS offers this service to improve file distribution over the Internet and within large private networks. PWS's FTP service can host multiple sites, each stored in a separate directory; however, they must all be referenced by a common base domain name. Version 2 of PWS does not support FTP virtual servers, so you might need to look elsewhere if you want to provide FTP services to your users (or get the newest version of PWS).

Gopher

Gopher is a text-based, menu-like hierarchical organization of data. This service was extremely popular before the development of the Web. Because of this, bastions of Gopher sites can still be found on the Internet. No compelling reason exists for using Gopher within a private network. Like FTP, multiple Gopher sites can exist, but they are all referenced by a common base domain name.

Exam Prep Questions

Question 1

> What is the primary function of DHCP?
>
> ○ a. To maintain a dynamic relationship database between IP addresses and NetBIOS names
>
> ○ b. To route IP packets across routers to other subnets
>
> ○ c. To assign IP addresses to clients
>
> ○ d. To resolve FQDNs into IP addresses

The service that maintains a dynamic relationship database between IP addresses and NetBIOS names is WINS. Therefore, answer a is incorrect. The service that routes IP packets is RIP For IP, a subject not covered on the Workstation exam. Therefore, answer b is incorrect. **The service that assigns IP addresses to clients is DHCP. Therefore, answer c is correct.** The service that resolves FQDNs to IP addresses is DNS. Therefore, answer d is incorrect.

Question 2

> What is an advantage of SLIP over PPP?
>
> ○ a. SLIP supports security, whereas PPP does not support security.
>
> ○ b. SLIP supports error checking, whereas PPP does not support error checking.
>
> ○ c. SLIP supports flow control, whereas PPP does not support flow control.
>
> ○ d. SLIP requires less system overhead than PPP.

SLIP does not support error checking, flow control, or security—these are features of PPP. Therefore, answers a, b, and c are incorrect. **SLIP does, however, require less system overhead than PPP. Therefore, d is the correct choice.**

Question 3

> You want to install TCP/IP on an NT Workstation in a nonrouted
> network. You have already assigned an IP address manually to
> the machine. What other parameter must you specify to install
> TCP/IP on the server?
>
> ○ a. The subnet mask
>
> ○ b. The default gateway
>
> ○ c. The DHCP server IP address
>
> ○ d. The WINS server IP address

When installing TCP/IP on a nonrouted network, the IP address and
subnet mask parameters must be specified. Therefore, answer a is correct.
If a default gateway is not specified, the machine can only communicate
with other machines within its subnet; however, it is not a mandatory element. Therefore, answer b is incorrect. DHCP and WINS are not mandatory fields to define. Therefore, answers c and d are incorrect.

Question 4

> A DNS server links what types of information together? [Check all
> correct answers]
>
> ❑ a. NetBEUI names
>
> ❑ b. FQDNs
>
> ❑ c. Subnet masks
>
> ❑ d. IP addresses
>
> ❑ e. MAC addresses

DNS maintains a relationship between FQDNs and IP addresses in such
a way that both forward and reverse lookups are possible. Therefore, only
answers b and d are correct. NetBEUI names are stored by WINS. Therefore, answer a is incorrect. Subnet masks can be distributed by a DHCP
server, but a link table does not exist. Therefore, answer c is incorrect. MAC
addresses are linked through NWLink's and NetBEUI's cached name resolution. Therefore, answer e is incorrect.

Question 5

You need to set up two new virtual Web servers to be hosted on your small private network using only a single installation of PWS. Each Web site will require its own directory, a unique URL, and a unique IP address. What should you do to implement this configuration? [Check all correct answers]

❑ a. Install RIP For IP on the PWS server.

❑ b. Assign each of the IP addresses to be used to the NIC in the PWS server; then, associate each IP address with the appropriate Web directory.

❑ c. Set up the DHCP Relay Agent.

❑ d. Configure DNS so it contains the FDQN for each site and correlates that name to its IP address.

❑ e. Configure WINS by adding the NetBIOS names and IP addresses of the sites to the static list of sites.

RIP For IP should not be used in this situation, plus, you do not know if there is more than one NIC in the server. Therefore, answer a is incorrect. **Assigning the additional IP addresses to the server's NIC is an important step. Therefore, answer b is correct.** The DHCP Relay Agent does not apply to this situation. Therefore, answer c is incorrect. **Because this site is within a private network, you'll need both DNS and WINS to support name resolution. Therefore, answers d and e are correct. Thus, only answers b, d, and e are correct.** The trick to this question is realizing that even though NT Workstation does not host DNS or WINS servers, it can be the subject of a reference in a DNS or WINS server resolution database.

Question 6

What are the functions of WINS? [Check all correct answers]

❑ a. Enables internetwork browsing

❑ b. Maps FQDNs to IP addresses

❑ c. Maps NetBIOS names to IP addresses

❑ d. Maps NetBIOS names to MAC addresses

❑ e. Assigns clients IP addresses

Enabling internetwork browsing and mapping NetBIOS names to IP addresses are two of the three functions of WINS; the third function is recognizing NetBIOS names on all subnets. Therefore, only answers a and c are correct. Mapping FQDNs to IP addresses is a function of DNS. Therefore, answer b is incorrect. Mapping NetBIOS names to MAC addresses happens in both NWLink and NetBEUI. Therefore, answer d is incorrect. Assigning clients IP addresses is a function of a DHCP server. Therefore, answer e is incorrect.

Question 7

What is an LMHOSTS file?

○ a. A static list of NetBIOS names mapped to IP addresses

○ b. A dynamic list of NetBIOS names mapped to IP addresses

○ c. A static list of FQDNs mapped to IP addresses

○ d. A dynamic list of FQDNs mapped to IP addresses

LMHOSTS is the predecessor to WINS and is a static list of NetBIOS names mapped to IP addresses. Therefore, answer a is correct. A dynamic list of NetBIOS names mapped to IP addresses is WINS. Therefore, answer b is incorrect. The HOST file is a static list of FQDNs mapped to IP addresses. Therefore, answer c is incorrect. There is no dynamic list of FQDNs mapped to IP addresses. Therefore, answer d is incorrect.

Question 8

You need users to access the office NT network across the Internet. How can you establish Internet-based access without compromising security?

○ a. Implement the SLIP protocol

○ b. Implement the FTP protocol

○ c. Implement the Point-To-Point Protocol

○ d. Implement the Point-To-Point Tunneling Protocol

The Point-To-Point Tunneling Protocol (PPTP) uses the Internet as a connection medium while still maintaining network security. Therefore, answer d is correct. SLIP cannot be used to connect to an NT system. Therefore, answer a is incorrect. The FTP protocol cannot be used to establish a network connection between NT systems; it is only used to transfer files between TCP/IP systems supporting the FTP protocol. Therefore, answer b is incorrect. PPP will only encrypt the initial password, and all other data is not encrypted. Therefore, answer c is incorrect.

Question 9

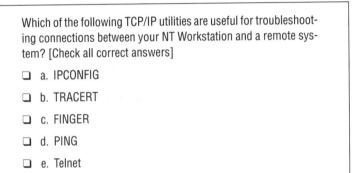

Which of the following TCP/IP utilities are useful for troubleshooting connections between your NT Workstation and a remote system? [Check all correct answers]

❑ a. IPCONFIG

❑ b. TRACERT

❑ c. FINGER

❑ d. PING

❑ e. Telnet

The IPCONFIG utility is only useful for identifying local TCP/IP configurations. Therefore, answer a is incorrect. **The TRACERT utility displays the route taken by packets to the remote system. Therefore, answer b is correct.** The FINGER utility is used to obtain user information; it does not offer connection diagnostics. Therefore, answer c is incorrect. **The PING utility indicates whether or not a remote system is currently online. Therefore, answer d is correct.** The Telnet utility is used to establish a terminal emulation session with a remote system; it does not offer connection diagnostics. Therefore, answer e is incorrect.

Question 10

How are the HOST and LMHOSTS files different?

○ a. A HOST file maps host names to IP addresses; an LMHOSTS file maps IP addresses to NetBIOS names.

○ b. An LMHOSTS file maps host names to IP addresses, whereas a HOST file maps IP addresses to NetBIOS names.

○ c. A HOST file maps host names to IP addresses, whereas an LMHOSTS file maps host names to NetBIOS names.

○ d. An LMHOSTS file maps host names to IP addresses, whereas a HOST file maps host names to NetBIOS names.

A HOST file maps host names to IP addresses, whereas an LMHOSTS file maps IP addresses to NetBIOS names. Therefore, only answer a is correct.

Need To Know More?

Boyce, Jim, et al.: *Windows NT Workstation 4.0 Advanced Technical Reference*. Que, Indianapolis, IN, 1996. ISBN 0-7897-0863-9. Chapters 21 through 26 contain detailed information about TCP/IP and its related issues.

Perkins, Charles, Matthew Strebe, and James Chellis: *MCSE: NT Workstation Study Guide*. Sybex Network Press, San Francisco, CA, 1997. ISBN 0-7821-1973-5. Chapter 19 discusses most of the TCP/IP issues raised in this chapter.

Search the TechNet CD (or its online version through www.microsoft.com) and the *Windows NT Workstation Resource Kit* CD using the keywords "TCP/IP," "name resolution," "Peer Web Services," "DNS," "WINS," "LMHOSTS," "HOST," and "DHCP."

11

NetWare Connectivity

. . . .

Terms you'll need to understand:

√ NetWare

√ NWLink Internetwork Packet eXchange/Sequenced Packet eXchange (IPX/SPX)

√ Client Service For NetWare (CSNW)

√ Gateway Service For NetWare (GSNW)

√ File And Print Services For NetWare (FPNW)

√ Frame type

Techniques you'll need to master:

√ Installing, configuring, and enabling NWLink (IPX/SPX)

√ Installing, configuring, and enabling CSNW

√ Installing, configuring, and enabling GSNW

√ Implementing FPNW

√ Adjusting frame type settings

199

By making NetWare connectivity part and parcel of Windows NT, Microsoft has made it possible to integrate its products directly and easily with existing networks all over the world. Considering the built-in NetWare access capabilities as well as the add-ins available at low cost from Microsoft for Windows NT to enhance these capabilities, it's clear that NetWare interoperability is an important concern in Redmond.

Even if you don't have any NetWare servers on your Windows NT network, you must still understand what Microsoft offers by way of NetWare compatibility and access in order to pass the Workstation exam (as well as the NT Server 4 and NT Server 4 in the Enterprise tests). Although much of this material will be old hat to those who work in hybrid NetWare–Windows NT environments, those who don't have the benefit of direct exposure should study this chapter carefully. It will help with the three to six NetWare-related test questions that can be expected on the exam.

You might find the detail in this chapter a bit overwhelming. We've included as much detail as possible to give you a solid understanding of everything going on when interoperating with NetWare. The few questions on the exam related to this topic can be fairly esoteric; therefore, it is important to know what each component is as well as what it isn't. There is just as much weight placed on your knowledge of GSNW, an NT Server service, as there is on CSNW, a service of both NT Server and Workstation. These items and much more are detailed in this chapter.

Protocols And Compatibility Issues

To avoid paying royalties to Novell, Microsoft built its own implementation of the Internetwork Packet eXchange/Sequenced Packet eXchange (IPX/SPX) protocol suite, called "NWLink" (to avoid infringing on Novell trade names). Surprisingly, some comparisons between Novell's IPX/SPX client implementations and Microsoft's NWLink have shown the latter implementation to be slightly faster than the former. In other words, these guys are serious about their NetWare compatibility, and they have done a pretty good job.

Although NetWare supports multiple protocols—primarily IPX/SPX and TCP/IP—it's most common to find IPX/SPX used to communicate between NetWare's clients and its servers. In fact, Novell does not support any protocols other than IPX/SPX for versions of NetWare older than 3.x (which usually means version 2.2).

If you see an exam question that mentions NetWare 2.2, it's safe to assume that IPX/SPX is the protocol used to communicate between the NetWare server and its clients.

When Novell implemented IPX/SPX, it also elected to use a special frame format for the protocol on Ethernet and other network types. Even though the emerging standard at the time (which has since become the official standard) was to use 802.2 frame formats for networked communications, Novell elected to use what's often called a "raw 802.3" frame format for its implementation of IPX/SPX on Ethernet.

To make a long and complex story as short as possible, the upshot of Novell's initial decision, and its subsequent divergence from industry standard frame types, introduced the possibility of a frame type mismatch when using IPX/SPX (or NWLink). You'll see one or possibly two questions on the test referring to problems communicating on a network or requiring an understanding of NWLink's ability to detect automatically 802.2 IPX frame types on a Windows NT machine.

Here's what you need to know to deal with such questions:

➤ Although NWLink is provided primarily for NetWare access and interoperability, Windows NT-based networks can only use NWLink, where no NetWare is present. Don't be surprised if this shows up on a test question.

➤ Until NetWare 3.12 shipped, NetWare's default frame type was raw 802.3, which Microsoft calls simply "802.3 frame type."

➤ For NetWare 3.12 and all 4.x versions (including IntranetWare), the default frame type uses 802.2 headers atop the native frame type for the network technology in use. Microsoft calls this the "802.2 frame type," without regard to technology.

➤ The total battery of frame types you're most likely to encounter is:

    ➤ 802.2 frame type (industry standard; default for NetWare 3.12 and higher-numbered versions)

    ➤ 802.3 frame type (so-called "raw 802.3 header" format, developed by Novell; default for older, pre-3.12 versions of NetWare)

➤ 802.3 with SNAP header (sometimes called "Ethernet_SNAP frame type" in Microsoft terminology)

➤ 802.5 frame type (the native format for Token Ring networks)

➤ 802.5 frame type with SNAP header (sometimes called "Token_Ring_SNAP" in Microsoft terminology)

Note: SNAP stands for SubNetwork Access Protocol, and it provides a mechanism that permits nonstandard, higher-level protocols to appear within a standard IEEE logical link control frame like the frame types previously mentioned. It's often used to transport AppleTalk or SNA in IP network environments. It's not necessary to understand the subtleties of this technology for this MCSE test, however.

➤ If any workstation (or server) is configured for an incorrect IPX frame type (that doesn't match the rest of the population), an improperly configured machine will not be able to interact with the network. This can occur even though the network may otherwise work properly, and all other machines are able to communicate successfully.

➤ Although Windows NT 4 can detect 802.2 frame types automatically, it cannot detect any other type of IPX frame automatically. This means that on networks where versions of NetWare older than 3.12 occur, Manual Frame Type Detection *must* be chosen when configuring NWLink. It also means that the IPX network numbers to which Windows NT are attached and all IPX frame types in use must be identified explicitly as part of NWLink configuration.

➤ For client/server applications, such as SQL Server database access, or NetBIOS-based applications, native NetWare clients using IPX/SPX can communicate directly with Windows NT running such an application without requiring anything other than NWLink and the server side of the application to be installed on that machine. In essence, the client side of the client/server application supplies everything the client and server need to communicate, as long as they have a protocol in common. Because the assumption is that native NetWare clients use IPX/SPX, a Windows NT machine must install NWLink to communicate with such clients across the network.

Gateway Service For NetWare

Microsoft often refers to Gateway Service For NetWare by its acronym—GSNW. But there's more to this component than meets the eye, and this can lead to some confusion. The complete name of the software component as it appears in the Add dialog box on Windows NT Server, generated from Control Panel|Network applet|Services is Gateway (And Client) Services For NetWare.

You may be surprised to learn that GSNW includes Client Service For NetWare (CSNW; discussed later in this chapter) in its capabilities and functionality. In English, this means that any Windows NT Server with GSNW installed also can function as a client to a NetWare server. This explains why you must remove existing NetWare client software—especially Novell's NetWare Client For Windows NT—from any Windows NT Server before installing GSNW on that machine.

 Keep in mind that the Gateway Service For NetWare is not a service available in Windows NT Workstation; rather, it is an NT Server service. However, you must have an understanding of this service for the Workstation exam. Therefore, the following discussion is from the Server standpoint, not Workstation.

Understanding GSNW

The Workstation exam questions that touch on GSNW only require that you understand what it does on NT Server. The issues involved with installing GSNW are not covered in the Workstation exam; rather, these are left to the Server and Server in the Enterprise exams.

Generically speaking, the term "gateway" refers to a software component permitting computers that do not share a common set of protocols and services to communicate with one another. In other words, the gateway translates from one protocol and service world to another, and vice versa.

GSNW is no exception: What GSNW does is make it possible for ordinary Microsoft Network clients (PCs running Windows 3.x, Windows 95, or even Windows NT Workstation or Server) to access resources on a NetWare server by translating requests from those clients stated in MS Network terms into NetWare terms, and then translating the accompanying responses from the NetWare server from NetWare terms back into MS Network terms. The gateway is in the middle of these communications.

Here's the "trick" that makes this work: The Windows NT computer where GSNW runs exports a logical volume from the NetWare server through the gateway that MS Network clients can access as if it were any other NT-based network share. The gateway also can create a similar function for NetWare-based printers and make NetWare-based print services available to MS Network clients. The chief selling point for GSNW is that it provides access to NetWare resources for MS Network clients without requiring any additional software (or software changes) to be made to those clients themselves.

If you can understand and appreciate the material in the two preceding paragraphs, you'll know enough about GSNW to be able to answer any test questions in which it may appear.

Installing, Configuring, And Enabling GSNW

As already mentioned, installing GSNW on NT Server is not covered on the Workstation exam, but the details are listed here to help you gain a more rounded understanding of this interoperability service from Microsoft.

Gateway Service For NetWare is an optional network service included as part of Windows NT Server: This means it's included with the distribution media for the Server product, but not installed by default whenever you install the core operating system. To install GSNW (see Figure 11.1), you must open the Network applet in Control Panel, select the Services tab,

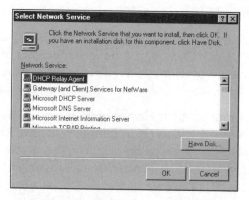

Figure 11.1 You can install GSNW (and CSNW) on Windows NT Server through the Select Network Service dialog box in the Network applet in Control Panel.

and then click the Add button in the resulting display. This produces the Select Network Service screen, where GSNW appears as the second choice in the list. To begin the process of installing GSNW, highlight its entry and then click the OK button at the bottom of the window. This brings up a prompt for the NT Server CD.

 Occasionally, a test question may reference NWLink separately from GSNW. It's important to note that if you elect to install GSNW on an NT Server that does not already have NWLink running, NWLink will be installed automatically as a part of the GSNW installation process. Thus, although NWLink is required for GSNW to run, it's not necessary to install it in advance, nor is it a problem if NWLink has already been installed.

Here's a high-level overview of the GSNW installation process, emphasizing those elements and information that must be supplied during installation that are most likely to appear in GSNW-related test questions:

1. Before installing and configuring GSNW, you must create the following accounts on the NetWare server where the gateway will connect:

    a. A user account on the NetWare server with rights to the NetWare file system directories that gateway users from the NT side will need.

    b. A group account named NTGATEWAY on the NetWare server with rights to all file and print resources that gateway users will need.

    Note: All users who go through a single GSNW gateway have the same access and the same rights to the NetWare resources; the only way to create different collections of accesses and rights is to set up multiple gateways—only one instance of GSNW per individual Windows NT Server is permitted.

2. To install GSNW, you must log on to Windows NT Server as an administrator. In the Network applet in Control Panel, select the Services tab, click the Add button, and then select Gateway (and Client) Services For NetWare (as shown in Figure 11.1). Supply the NT installation CD or point to a copy of the \i386 directory where the necessary source code files reside. The software will more or less install itself.

3. To configure GSNW, double-click the GSNW icon in Control Panel. The Gateway Service For NetWare dialog box appears.

   a. Click the Gateway button to elicit the Configure Gateway dialog box.

   b. Check the Enable Gateway box to enable the Gateway Service.

   c. In the Gateway Account field, enter the NetWare user name you created in Step 1a. Enter the password into the Password field and then confirm that password in the Confirm Password field.

   d. Click the Add button to create a NetWare share for use by Microsoft networking clients. The New Share dialog box appears.

   e. In the Share Name flield, enter a name through which the NetWare directory will be shared.

   f. In the Network Path field, enter a UNC name for the NetWare directory that's being shared. For the SYS:Public directory on a server named NETONE, the syntax is \\NETONE\SYS\ PUBLIC.

   g. In the Comment field, you can add an optional descriptive phrase that will appear in the Browse window for MS Clients on the network.

   h. In the Use Drive field, select a drive letter on the Windows NT Server to be assigned to the NetWare directory. This drive letter remains taken as long as GSNW runs on the Windows NT Server (by default, Z is the letter assigned to the first such share name).

   i. The User Limit box permits administrators to limit the number of users who can access the NetWare share simultaneously. Because the gateway bogs down under increasing load, it's a good idea to limit the number of users to 10 or so (unless the server is extremely fast or only lightly loaded).

   j. Click OK to save all changes. You'll return to the Configure Gateway dialog box. Click OK again to exit the Gateway Service For NetWare dialog box. All changes will take effect upon the next system logon.

4. The only way to create NetWare shares is through the interface described in Steps 3d through 3j (not through Explorer or My Computer, as is the case for normal Windows NT shares). Likewise, you must use the GSNW applet in Control Panel to set permissions for NetWare shares. Here's how:

   a. From an administrative logon, launch the GSNW applet from Control Panel.

   b. When the Gateway Service For NetWare dialog box appears, choose the Gateway button.

   c. In the Configure Gateway dialog box, highlight the NetWare share name and choose the Permissions button. Use this interface to set permissions for the NetWare share.

5. Using NetWare Print Resources through the Gateway requires none of the shenanigans needed to establish and set permissions for the NetWare shares. Instead, configure NetWare print queues through the Printers icon in Control Panel (as with any other Windows NT Server-attached printer). Here's what's involved:

   a. From an administrative logon, launch the Printers applet. Select the Add Printer icon. This displays the Add Printer Wizard window.

   b. Select the Network Printer radio button and then click the Next button. This brings up the Connect To Printer dialog box.

   c. In this dialog box, you'll see two icons: one labeled "NetWare Or Compatible Network" and the other labeled "Microsoft Windows Network." You can expand and navigate the NetWare Or Compatible Network directory tree the same way you would the Microsoft Windows Network tree: Open Control Panel, double-click Network, select a server, and then double-click and select the printer you want to manage.

   Otherwise, the procedure is exactly the same as installing an ordinary Windows NT network printer. (This is covered in Chapter 14.)

Remember that it is necessary to map a drive on the Windows NT computer for the NetWare share, and that NetWare shares and their permissions only can be managed through the GSNW applet, not through ordinary file management tools. NetWare printers, on the other hand, can be handled like any other network printer (that is, through the Printers applet), once GSNW has been installed in Windows NT.

Client Service For NetWare

GSNW makes NetWare resources available to ordinary MS Network clients, but CSNW works only with Windows NT machines to make them act as native clients to NetWare servers elsewhere on the network. This system component is called CSNW only on Windows NT Workstation 4, which ships without GSNW; however, CSNW is part and parcel of GSNW on Windows NT Server 4 machines. In either case, its job is to let Windows NT machines link up to and browse NetWare resources alongside Microsoft Windows Network resources.

CSNW is installed through the Services tab of the Network applet. Once it's installed and your system is rebooted, you can configure the service. A new applet called CSNW appears in the Control Panel, which is where all the configuration of this service takes place. This includes selecting and defining a preferred server (for NetWare 3.1x servers) or default tree and context (for NetWare 3.x servers), setting print options (add form feeds, notify print completion, and print banner), and whether or not to run logon scripts. If no settings are made, NT attempts to log in to the closest NetWare server it can find.

The first time you attempt to access a NetWare resource, you'll need to provide an account and password valid on that NetWare network/server. NT should remember this information for all future accesses and perform automatic validation (like the RAS AutoDial feature) the next time NetWare resources are requested.

Due to this auto-reconnect feature, you might need to rearrange your redirector bindings to force NT to search local or NT networks first before NetWare networks. This is done through the Network applet on the Services tab. After CSNW is installed, an additional button is present at the bottom of this tab. The Network Access Order button displays the known networks; through this dialog box, you can reorder networks so that Microsoft networks are searched before NetWare networks.

Resources hosted from a NetWare server are seen to NT clients the same as any other NT-hosted resource. CSNW and GSNW hide the translation between the differing networks from the user by listing NetWare resources in standard browser lists. Printing from NT to a NetWare-hosted printer is no different than printing to any other type of network printer. Simply create a new printer using the Add Printer wizard and link to the network-shared device. NT handles all the issues related to NetWare print servers, drivers, and queues, making the use of non-NT network resources seamless.

File And Print Services For NetWare

FPNW, as it's usually called, is not included with Windows NT 4; it must be purchased separately (at the time of writing, it costs $100 in the U.S. market). What GSNW is to MS Network clients, FPNW is to native NetWare clients: It makes resources from a Windows NT server available to NetWare clients, without requiring any additional software or configuration changes to those clients. In other words, FPNW makes a Windows NT server look like a NetWare 3.11 server to any native NetWare clients on a network.

NetWare-Aware Applications

Some NetWare-aware applications can be used on NT. If they require only those DLLs for NetWare, they are provided by the NetWare client for Windows, CSNW, or GSNW. Some NetWare-aware utilities will only function if the NetWare link has already been established. The only way to really know is to test the applications yourself.

Several of the NetWare administration tools will not function from NT, but there are command prompt equivalents that can be used in their stead. (See Table 11.1.)

However, there are many utilities that can be launched from NT, without significant problems. These include the following:

CHKVOL, COLORPAL, DSPACE, FLAG, FLAGDIR, FCONSOLE, FILER, GRANT, HELP, LISTDIR, MAP, NCOPY, NDIR, PCONSOLE, PSC, PSTAT, RCONSOLE, REMOVE, REVOKE,

Table 11.1 The unsupported NetWare commands and their NT equivalents.

Unsupported NetWare Command	NT Equivalent
ATTACH	NET USE
CAPTURE	NET USE
LOGIN	NET LOGON
LOGOUT	NET LOGOFF
SLIST	NET VIEW

RIGHTS, SECURITY, SEND, SESSION (search mapping not supported), SETPASS, SETTTS, SLIST, SYSCON, TLIST, USERLIST, VOLINFO (slow execution if interval=5), and WHOAMI.

NetWare Troubleshooting

Troubleshooting NetWare interoperability problems is a bit beyond the scope of the Workstation exam. Basic familiarity with troubleshooting techniques and a handful of NetWare-resource-specific fixes will suffice to carry you through the minimal NetWare material on the test.

The first step is to determine where the difficulty is occurring. Is it with the hardware, the network connection, the NT network, or the NetWare network? If the location can be isolated, you can apply the appropriate measures to eliminate the issue.

If the problem lies with NetWare, here are a few things to try:

1. Make sure the NetWare server is booted and functioning.

2. Verify that the workstation can connect to other Microsoft-hosted resources.

3. Double-check that NWLink and CSNW are installed properly on the NT Workstation or that GSNW is on the NT Server.

4. Check the preferred server and tree/context settings.

5. Reset frame types and network numbers for both the NetWare systems and the NT systems.

There is a lot more to troubleshooting interoperability between NT and NetWare, but it is not covered on the Workstation exam.

 Unless you work in a mixed NetWare/NT environment, you'll want to review the basics about GSNW, CSNW, FPNW, and NWLink before you take any NT 4 test. If these sound like gibberish, check the glossary first; then, reread this chapter (and at least one of the references in the "Need To Know More?" section at the end of the chapter) before you even *think* about taking the exam! For those who feel like they're better prepared, here are some questions for you to study.

Exam Prep Questions

Question 1

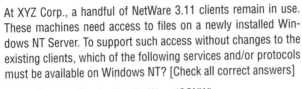

At XYZ Corp., a handful of NetWare 3.11 clients remain in use. These machines need access to files on a newly installed Windows NT Server. To support such access without changes to the existing clients, which of the following services and/or protocols must be available on Windows NT? [Check all correct answers]

❑ a. Gateway Service For NetWare (GSNW)

❑ b. Client Service For NetWare (CSNW)

❑ c. File And Print Services For NetWare (FPNW)

❑ d. The NWLink protocol

GSNW provides mediated access to NetWare services for Microsoft Network clients. Therefore, it's not required, meaning answer a is incorrect. Likewise, CSNW makes it possible for NT workstations and servers to obtain direct access to a NetWare server. Therefore, answer b is also incorrect. **File And Print Services For NetWare makes an NT server look like a NetWare server to NetWare network clients, so it's what provides file access. Therefore, answer c is correct.** Native NetWare 3.x clients need IPX/SPX to access real NetWare servers, or Windows NT computers running FPNW. Therefore, NWLink is Microsoft's implementation of IPX/SPX, meaning answer d is also correct. Thus, answers c and d are the only correct answers.

Question 2

> You have CSNW installed on your NT Workstation. You also have
> a logical printer defined for a NetWare-hosted HP LaserJet. You
> have numerous small documents to print, but you share the
> printer with many other users. How can you force each print job
> to be labeled so that your documents are easily identified after
> printing?
>
> ○ a. Define a separator page within the properties for the
>   logical printer.
> ○ b. The NetWare print server must be configured to print
>   separator pages.
> ○ c. The Print Banner option should be selected in CSNW.
> ○ d. Enable the sort option on the print device.

The logical printer on your NT Workstation does not have the ability to
alter the control of a NetWare-hosted printer. Therefore, answer a is incorrect. The NetWare print server may offer a print separator page option, but
you do not need to enable this feature for everyone. Therefore, answer b is
incorrect. **Enabling the Print Banner option in CSNW is the best way to
force NetWare to print a separator page before each of your print jobs.
Therefore, answer c is correct.** Most printers do not have a sort option, and
this option would not be useful or practical in this situation. Therefore,
answer d is incorrect.

Question 3

> With CSNW installed on an NT Workstation, which of the follow-
> ing NetWare command-line utilities can be launched from your
> workstation?
>
> ○ a. SLIST
> ○ b. LOGOUT
> ○ c. SYSCON
> ○ d. CAPTURE
> ○ e. ATTACH

The only utility from this list that can be launched from NT is SYSCON. Therefore, answer c is correct. All of the other utilities are not supported by NT, but their functions can be performed using NT's net command equivalents. Therefore, answers a, b, d, and e are incorrect.

Question 4

One of the PCs on a network is unable to establish a working connection, but all other computers are working correctly. The only protocol in use on the network is NWLink. Of the following possibilities, which is the most likely to be the cause of this problem?

○ a. Faulty network interface devices

○ b. A protocol mismatch

○ c. A PC memory conflict

○ d. An incorrect IPX frame type

The key to answering this question correctly is careful reading. Anyone who knows anything about networks knows that loose connections are the most common cause of problems, but that appears nowhere in this list of choices. Because the problem statement includes an indication that only *one* PC is having problems and gives "faulty network interface *devices*" as a possibility, this knocks out what typically might be the next most obvious cause, namely a faulty Network Interface Card, thereby eliminating answer a from further consideration. Answer b patently is false because the only protocol in use is NWLink (or IPX/SPX, if you prefer). Answer c is possible, but unlikely, because most memory conflicts will cause a machine to crash rather than simply rendering network access inoperative. The clue to answering the question correctly lies in the statement "the only protocol in use on the network is NWLink." **Because IPX does not require a fixed frame type, but works with multiple frame types, a frame type mismatch easily can render a machine unable to communicate successfully with the network, even though the hardware is working correctly. Therefore, answer d is correct.**

Question 5

On a network that contains multiple versions of NetWare, some clients are configured for NetWare 2.2, while others are configured for NetWare 4.11. Among other protocols, NWLink is in use on this network. The NetWare 2.2 clients use an 802.3 raw frame type, whereas the NetWare 4.11 clients use the 802.2 frame type. What kinds of information must be supplied in the NWLink IPX/SPX Properties dialog box to allow the same Windows NT Workstation to recognize both flavors of NetWare clients on this network?

○ a. Select Auto Frame Type Detection and add the clients' IPX network numbers and frame types to the frame type configuration list.

○ b. Select Manual Frame Type Detection and add the network numbers and frame types for both 2.2 and 4.11 clients to the frame type configuration list.

○ c. Select only Auto Frame Type Detection; the rest is automatic.

○ d. Select Manual Frame Type Detection and add the 2.2 clients' network numbers and frame types to the frame type configuration list.

The secret to answering this question is to understand how automatic frame type detection works in NT. As long as the only frame type in use is 802.2, automatic detection works fine. But because older NetWare clients—especially NetWare 2.2 clients—use only 802.3 frames, Manual Frame Type Detection must be selected during the configuration process. This eliminates answers a and c. Answer d is incorrect because Manual Frame Type Detection requires entry of all frame types and network numbers in use. Only answer b covers all these requirements and is therefore the only correct choice.

Question 6

> Widgets Corp. seeks to make its NT Workstation and Windows 95
> clients able to access a NetWare server without installing NetWare
> client software on their machines. How can this objective be met
> most effectively?
>
> ○ a. Install Gateway Service For NetWare on a Windows NT
>   server on the same network.
>
> ○ b. Install NWLink on the NT Workstation and Windows 95
>   computers.
>
> ○ c. Install Gateway Service For NetWare on the NetWare
>   server.
>
> ○ d. Install File And Print Services For NetWare on a Windows
>   NT server on the same network.

The whole point of a gateway is to permit clients to access services that
their current configurations would otherwise make inaccessible. For that
reason, answer a is the only correct answer, because it opens a gateway for
the NT Workstation and Windows 95 clients to access NetWare resources
with no change to their current configurations. Answer b is incorrect,
because by adding NWLink to the clients, it not only violates the requirement that no NetWare client software be added to those machines, it does
not do the complete job (additional software is necessary for these
machines to communicate with a NetWare server). Answer c mentions the
right software product, but puts it on a NetWare server rather than on a
Windows NT server, where it was designed to be run. Finally, File And
Print Services For NetWare lets native NetWare clients access Windows
NT, not native Microsoft Networking clients access NetWare (thus completely missing the point of the question).

Question 7

> On a NetWare network, your NT Workstation is configured to Auto Detect, which detects the IPX frame types in use. What kinds of frame types will your NT Workstation be able to identify successfully? [Check all correct answers]
>
> ❏ a. 802.2 frame type
> ❏ b. 802.3 frame type
> ❏ c. 802.3 frame type with SNAP header
> ❏ d. 802.5 frame type
> ❏ e. 802.5 frame type with SNAP header

The secret to this question is understanding that Auto Detect is aimed at newer versions of NetWare (3.12 and higher), which support only 802.2 headers by default, in keeping with common practice for most networks. **Auto Detect will not be able to detect anything but 802.2, which means the only correct answer to this question is a.**

Question 8

> Once you've successfully installed CSNW, what additional configuration steps are necessary to actually use the gateway? [Check all correct answers]
>
> ❏ a. Define a tree and context.
> ❏ b. Set the preferred server.
> ❏ c. Select printer options.
> ❏ d. Enable or disable logon scripts.
> ❏ e. No additional steps are necessary.

After CSNW is installed, no additional steps are necessary in order to connect to a NetWare server. An account and password are required, but these are not defined through CSNW. NT will attempt to connect to the nearest NetWare server without any additional settings. Therefore, only answer e is correct. Defining a tree and context and setting a preferred server are not required, and they are mutually exclusive. **Therefore, answers a and b are incorrect.** Setting printer and logon script options are also not required in order to use CSNW. Therefore, answers c and d are incorrect.

Question 9

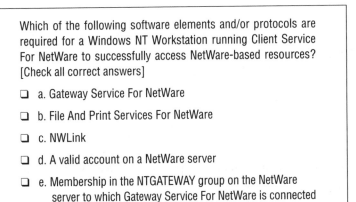

Which of the following software elements and/or protocols are required for a Windows NT Workstation running Client Service For NetWare to successfully access NetWare-based resources? [Check all correct answers]

❑ a. Gateway Service For NetWare

❑ b. File And Print Services For NetWare

❑ c. NWLink

❑ d. A valid account on a NetWare server

❑ e. Membership in the NTGATEWAY group on the NetWare server to which Gateway Service For NetWare is connected

With CSNW in use, the NT Server service of GSNW is not required in order to connect to NetWare resources. Therefore, answer a is incorrect. Answer e is also incorrect because no membership in the GSNW NTGATEWAY group is needed. File And Print Services For NetWare is an add-on to enable NetWare clients to access NT resources this is also not required for an NT Workstation to access NetWare resources. Therefore, answer b is incorrect. **As it happens, both of the remaining answers are necessary to make successful use of CSNW. Answer c supplies the necessary protocol to communicate from client to server and answer d provides the necessary permission to access the NetWare server once communication commences. Therefore, answers c and d are correct.**

Need To Know More?

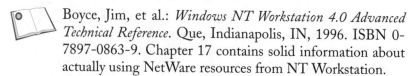

Boyce, Jim, et al.: *Windows NT Workstation 4.0 Advanced Technical Reference*. Que, Indianapolis, IN, 1996. ISBN 0-7897-0863-9. Chapter 17 contains solid information about actually using NetWare resources from NT Workstation.

Gaskin, James E.: *The Complete Guide to NetWare 4.11/ IntranetWare, 2nd Edition*. Sybex Network Press, Alameda, CA, 1997. ISBN 0-7821-1931-X. For a comprehensive look at NetWare networking, there's no better reference than this one. Use it to deal with NetWare specifics and the NetWare side of any NetWare-to-NT connection.

Heywood, Drew: *Inside Windows NT Server*. New Riders, Indianapolis, IN, 1995. ISBN 1-56205-472-4. Chapter 16, "Windows NT Server and NetWare," explains the salient software, communications issues, and connectivity concerns likely to appear on the test.

Minasi, Mark, Christa Anderson, and Elizabeth Creegan: *Mastering Windows NT Server 4, 4th Edition*. Sybex Network Press, Alameda, CA, 1997. ISBN 0-7821-2067-9. Minasi's been an NT guru ever since the product appeared; his experience and practical orientation show in Chapter 13, "Novell NetWare in an NT Server Environment." This book is worthwhile because of the tips and tricks it provides, and it's a good overview as well.

Perkins, Charles, Matthew Strebe, and James Chellis: *MCSE: NT Workstation Study Guide*. Sybex Network Press, San Francisco, CA, 1997. ISBN 0-7821-1973-5. Chapter 10 has a detailed account of NT Workstation interoperability with NetWare resources.

Siyan, Karanjit S: *Windows NT Server 4 Professional Reference*. New Riders, Indianapolis, IN, 1996. ISBN 1-56205-731-6. Chapter 12, "Integrating NetWare with Windows NT Server," brings Siyan's usual depth of coverage and details to this topic; this is the best available preparation material for NetWare questions for this test and the Server Enterprise test.

Strebe, Matthew, Charles Perkins, and James Chellis: *MSCE: NT Server 4 Study Guide.* Sybex Network Press, San Francisco, CA, 1996. ISBN 0-7821-1972-7. Chapter 13, "Interoperating with NetWare," covers this ground well (only Siyan offers more depth and details).

 Search the TechNet CD (or its online version through www.microsoft.com) using the keywords "NetWare," "NWLink," "Gateway Services," and related product names. The *Windows NT Concepts and Planning Manual*, which is also on TechNet, also includes useful information on making NT-to-NetWare connections, and vice versa.

 The *Windows NT Workstation Resource Kit* contains a lot of useful information about NetWare and related topics. You can search the TechNet (either CD or online version) or the CD accompanying the *Resource Kit*, using the keywords "NetWare," "NWLink," and "Gateway Services." Useful NetWare-related materials occur throughout the *Networking Guide* volume.

Workgroups, Domains, And Browsing

12

Terms you'll need to understand:

√ Workgroups

√ Domain

√ Primary Domain Controller (PDC)

√ Backup Domain Controller (BDC)

√ Trusts

√ Browsers

√ Logon scripts

√ Replication

Techniques you'll need to master:

√ Understanding the workgroup concept

√ Learning and implementing domain controllers

√ Implementing trusts between domains

√ Exploring the Windows NT Browser Service

Within the Windows NT networking world are two types of networks—workgroups and domains. In addition to network type, NT uses a resource list called the "browse list" to inform users and computers of available resources. In this chapter, we introduce you to these concepts and focus on the material found on the NT Workstation exam.

Workgroups

A workgroup is a network of computers in which no single machine has control over the operation, activity, or access to the entire network. Within a workgroup, each machine is a peer—meaning that each machine has equal administrative control. A workgroup computer is only able to regulate access to the resources it hosts—it is not able to restrict access to resources hosted by other peers.

Here are a few important points to remember about workgroups:

➤ No central control

➤ Share-level security

➤ All user accounts must be created on each member

A workgroup is a useful networking type, but only if you have 10 computers or fewer to tie together. Windows NT Workstation can participate in a workgroup simply by defining the workgroup name in the appropriate place. That place is the Identification tab of the Network applet. Clicking the Change button on that tab causes the Identification Changes dialog box to appear (see Figure 12.1). By selecting the Workgroup radio button and defining the name of the workgroup, you can transform NT Workstation from a client in a domain to a peer in a workgroup.

The process is easily reversed by redefining the domain using the same dialog box. However, for either change, you'll need to reboot the computer for the changes take effect. Also, a workstation cannot be a member of both a workgroup and a domain simultaneously, but it can switch back and forth as needed.

A Simple Look At Domains And Controllers

Put simply, a domain is a collection of networked workstations and servers that are managed as a group. In Windows NT, each domain must have a

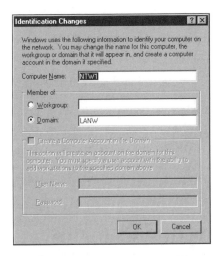

Figure 12.1   The Identification Changes dialog box.

domain controller to administer user rights for that domain. The first NT Server installed in a domain is the Primary Domain Controller (PDC). The PDC houses the security policy and database for the domain; therefore, the server is responsible for authenticating that domain's users at logon.

The next NT server to be installed should take on the role of Backup Domain Controller (BDC). The BDC maintains a copy of the security policy and domain database (it synchronizes with the PDC at specified intervals to maintain up-to-date copies of these security features). If the PDC goes down for any reason, the BDC continues to authenticate users. A BDC can be promoted to a PDC, but this is not an automatic process. Although it is not required that you have a BDC on an NT network, we highly recommended.

You can promote a BDC to a PDC manually if you need to take the PDC down for maintenance purposes. It is important, however, to promote the BDC *before* the PDC goes down; otherwise, some account information that might not have yet been replicated between the controllers may be lost. BDC promotion is performed with the Server Manager tool found only on NT Server.

Note: When a PDC is not present in a domain, no changes to the security database can be made. A BDC can only authenticate—it cannot modify or create entries in the security database.

Obviously, Microsoft's description of a domain is highly tainted by its configuration and construction of a domain. Here are a few more tidbits to remember about domains:

➤ They provide central control and administration.

➤ They only have user-level security.

➤ User and group accounts are created once and used across the network.

According to Microsoft, a domain should be used when you have more than 10 users/computers.

Workstations And Domains

Workstations can become members of a domain in two ways. The first way is to create a computer account in the domain for the workstation. This is done through the NT Workstation utility Server Manager. Once an account is created, the workstation joins the domain simply by being named the same name as the account that was created. Once it joins, the domain controller records that machine's SID so that no other machine can impersonate it. The second way for a workstation to join a domain is to supply an administrative account and password during the installation. This account will be used by the setup program to log onto the PDC and create a computer account when it is needed.

Trusts

PDCs and BDCs control access to resources on a particular domain, but what if a user needs access to a resource on another domain? Then you must establish a trust relationship between domains.

By establishing trust relationships, you allow secure access between domains. However, users in one domain are not required to be defined in another domain. Trusted domains make Windows NT a more scaleable network scheme, especially in enterprise-wide networks. If it weren't for the use of trusted domains, large NT-based networks would not be workable due to the huge amount of administration involved. With the trusted-domain concept, for example, the Sales department can have its own little part of the network, separate from the rest of the network. If it's necessary for the Sales domain to share information and resources with the Marketing department domain, NT can easily provide the cross-access needed via domain trusts.

Trusts can only be created through the NT Workstation utility User Manager For Domains. However, once a trust is established, the entire domain participates in that trust.

It is important to note that trusts are "one way" by default. This means that although the Production domain (the trusting domain) grants a trust to the Engineering domain (the trusted domain) to access the Design share, Production does not have any additional rights to the Engineering domain unless this is defined in the Trust Relationships dialog box in the User Manager For Domains. Two-way trusts are simply two one-way trusts between domains.

Workstation Logon

To log onto a workstation, you must press Ctrl+Alt+Del to access the WinLogon dialog box. By providing a valid name and password, you are given access. However, the type of access depends on the type of user account used to log in. NT Workstation can support logons of two types—workstation and domain. A workstation account is a user account that only exists on the local computer. This is the type of user account used in a workgroup, but it can still be created if the workstation is a member of a domain. When a workstation account is used, the user is limited to local resources and may not be able to access anything on the network. A domain account is a user account administrated by the domain controller, thus it grants the user access to all network resources (or at least the ones to which he or she has authorized access).

In instances where both a workgroup and a domain account share the same name, the account type to access is selected by choosing the local computer name or the domain name in the bottom box of the WinLogon logon screen labeled "From:". If the account name and the password are the same for both types of accounts, then local and network access will be granted regardless of which account is used to gain initial access.

Browsers

The NT Browser Service maintains a list of all network resources within a domain and provides lists of these domains, servers, and resource objects to any Explorer-type interface that requests them (for example, browse lists).

Each computer within a domain participates in the Browser Service. Each time a computer is brought up within the domain, it announces itself and the resources it has to share (if any). This is the most common level of participation for computers within a domain. The most important role within the Browser Service is that of the Master Browser. The Master Browser maintains the main list of all available resources within a domain (including links to external domains).

> *Note: On some TCP/IP networks, another role—the Domain Master Browser (DMB)—is used to enable resource lists to be communicated across subnets within the same domain. By default, the DMB is the PDC. Also, a Master Browser is present within each subnet.*

Two other important roles are the Backup Browser and the Potential Browser. The Backup Browser maintains a duplicate list of the resources and acts in a similar way within the Browser Service as does the BDC with domain control. The Backup Browser can serve lists of resources to clients. A Potential Browser can be any machine capable of becoming a Backup or Master Browser. As needed, the Browser Service changes the role of a machine from Potential Browser to Backup Browser. Within any domain, the Browser service attempts to maintain the maximum of three Backup Browsers, but any number of Potential Browsers can exist.

Only the following computer setups can serve as Potential Browsers:

➤ NT Server 3.5 or higher

➤ NT Advanced Server 3.1

➤ NT Workstation 3.1 or higher

➤ Windows 95

➤ Windows For Workgroups 3.11

Any of these computer setups can also be set to be non-browsers so that they will not participate in supporting the browser lists, except to announce themselves upon bootup.

In the next few sections, we continue our discussion of the Browser Service. This includes how networks are chosen (elected), in addition to how the browse list is maintained and how it can be managed through the Windows NT Registry.

Browser Election

When a Master Browser goes offline, or when another machine that has the capability to claim the role of Master Browser comes online, an election occurs. The results of the election determine which machine becomes the active Master Browser. An election packet is transmitted by the new computer or by a Backup Browser once the Master Browser is no longer detected. This packet travels to each Potential Browser within the domain. The winner of the election is determined by the following hierarchy of criteria (presented in order of priority):

➤ **Operating system** NT Server, NT Workstation, Windows 95, Windows For Workgroups

➤ **Operating system version** NT versions 4, 3.51, and 3.5; and Windows 95, 3.11, and 3.1

➤ **Current browser role** Master Browser, Backup Browser, Potential Browser

➤ **Alphabetical** Further election is resolved through the alphabetical order of the computer names

List Maintenance

When a computer comes online, it announces itself. Initially, it announces itself once a minute, with the interval decreasing to once every 12 minutes. This repeated announcement is used by the Master Browser to determine if a resource is still available. The Master Browser maintains the list of resources for any machine for three missed announcements to accommodate performance dips and communication bottlenecks. Therefore, after a machine has been up and running for a reasonable time and then goes offline, its resources can remain in the Master Browser's list for up to 36 minutes.

Backup Browsers poll the Master Browser every 15 minutes to request an updated version of the browse list. Therefore, a failed resource can remain in the Backup Browser's list for up to 51 minutes. If a Backup Browser requests an update from the Master Browser and receives no response, it initiates an election.

Browser And The Registry

The status of any Potential Browser can be altered through two Registry parameters. The parameters are located in HKEY_LOCAL_MACHINE\

SYSTEM\CurrentControlSet\Services\Browser\Parameters. The first value, **MaintainServerList**, determines whether a machine can be a Potential Browser. It can have a value of **No, Yes,** or **Auto. No** sets the machine to be a non-browser. **Yes** forces the machine to be a Master Browser or Backup Browser. And, **Auto** allows the Browser service to determine the role as needed. The second value, **IsDomainMaster**, sets the machine to be the Master Browser. It can have the value of **True** or **False**.

Exam Prep Questions

Question 1

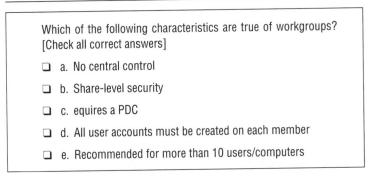

Which of the following characteristics are true of workgroups? [Check all correct answers]

❑ a. No central control

❑ b. Share-level security

❑ c. equires a PDC

❑ d. All user accounts must be created on each member

❑ e. Recommended for more than 10 users/computers

Workgroups have no central control, use share-level security, and user accounts must be created on each member. Therefore, answers a, b, and d are correct. Workgroups do not require a PDC and are recommended for 10 or fewer users/computers. Therefore, answers c and e are incorrect.

Question 2

A Workstation can be a member of a domain and a workgroup member at the same time.

○ a. True

○ b. False

Answer b, false, is correct. A workstation can be a member of either a workgroup or a domain at any given time, but not both simultaneously.

Question 3

What must be or what can be supplied by the user in order to log into an NT Workstation? [Check all correct answers]

❑ a. User account name

❑ b. Domain name

❑ c. IP address

❑ d. Password

❑ e. Workstation name

To log into the domain, the user must supply the user account name, password, and domain name (the later can be selected from a pull-down list). Therefore, answers a, b, and d are correct. To log into the local workstation, the user must supply the user account name, password, and the workstation name (the later can be selected from a pull-down list). Therefore, answer e is also correct. The IP address is not a valid entry for gaining access to an NT machine. Therefore, answer c is incorrect. The "trick" to this question is that, if you don't read the question carefully, you could automatically select the steps for a only workstation or domain login rather than for both. Always read questions very carefully.

Question 4

Which of the following computer systems can act as a Potential Browser? [Check all correct answers]

❑ a. NT Server 4

❑ b. Windows 3.1

❑ c. NT Server 3.1

❑ d. Windows For Workgroups 3.11

❑ e. NT Workstation 3.5

❑ f. OS/2 Warp

NT Server 4, Windows 3.1, Windows For Workgroups 3.11, and NT Workstation 3.5 are all valid system types that can be Potential Browsers. Therefore, answers a, b, d, and e are correct. NT Server 3.1 and OS/2 Warp are invalid system types for Potential Browsers. Therefore, answers c and f are incorrect.

Question 5

> When the PDC on a domain fails, what can you do with your NT
> Workstation? [Check all correct answers]
>
> ❑ a. Log on locally to the Workstation
>
> ❑ b. Maintain a current active session on the network
>
> ❑ c. Change your password
>
> ❑ d. Log on to the network

Without a PDC, you can still log on locally, maintain current network
access, and log on to the network (through BDC authentication). Therefore, answers a, b, and d are correct. You cannot change your password
because a BDC cannot modify the SAM database. Therefore, answer c is
incorrect.

Question 6

> An NT Workstation can participate as a Master Browser.
>
> ○ a. True
>
> ○ b. False

True, answer a is correct. An NT Workstation can be a Master Browser;
however, it is unlikely because any NT Server within a domain will have a
better chance of winning the browser election due to its OS type.

Question 7

> If a client hosting a network printer goes offline, how long could
> the browser list entry for that printer remain before it is removed
> from a Master Browser's resource list?
>
> ○ a. 12 minutes
>
> ○ b. 15 minutes
>
> ○ c. 36 minutes
>
> ○ d. 51 minutes

Twelve minutes is the interval of how often a machine announces itself to the Master Browser; it takes three intervals before the Master Browser removes a missing resource from its list. Therefore, answer a is incorrect. Fifteen minutes is the interval of how often a Backup Browser polls the Master Browser for a list update. Therefore, answer b is incorrect. Thirty-six minutes is the maximum length of time a missing resource can remain in a Master Browser's list. Therefore, answer c is incorrect. **Fifty-one minutes is the maximum length of time a missing resource can remain in a Backup Browser list, because it polls for an updated list every 15 minutes and a Master Browser can have a bad resource listed for 36 minutes. Therefore, answer d is correct.**

Question 8

What is the process by which a computer becomes a Master Browser?

○ a. Domain synchronization

○ b. Browser election

○ c. Replication

Domain synchronization is the process by which the SAM of a PDC is duplicated to all BDCs in the domain. Therefore, answer a is incorrect. **A browser election is the process by which a computer can become a Master Browser. Therefore, answer b is correct.** Replication is the process by which logon files are distributed across a network to speed authentication. Therefore, answer c is incorrect.

Question 9

Which of the following characteristics are true of domains? [Check all correct answers]

❑ a. Central control and administration

❑ b. User-level security

❑ c. Requires a PDC

❑ d. All user accounts must be created on each member

❑ e. Recommended for 10 or fewer users/computers

Domains have central control and administration, user-level security, and require a PDC. Therefore, answers a, b, and c are correct. Domains do not require accounts to be created on each member and are recommended for more than 10 users/computers. Therefore, answers d and e are incorrect.

Question 10

> If no domain controller of any type is present, the NT Workstation can still be logged onto locally.
>
> O a. True
> O b. False

Answer a, true, is correct. If no PDC nor BDCs are present, the NT Workstation can be logged onto locally if a user account has been created to do so. Workstation can maintain local accounts separate and distinct from domain accounts used to access the network.

Need To Know More?

Perkins, Charles, Matthew Strebe, and James Chellis: *MCSE: NT Workstation Study Guide.* Sybex Network Press, San Francisco, CA, 1997. ISBN 0-7821-1973-5. Chapter 11 discusses workgroups, domains, and browsing.

Search the TechNet CD (or its online version through www.microsoft.com) and the *Windows NT Workstation Resource Kit* CD using the keywords "workgroup," "domain," and "browser."

Remote Access Service (RAS)

13

Terms you'll need to understand:

√ Remote Access Service (RAS)

√ RAS clients

√ Telephony Application Programming Interface (TAPI)

√ RAS Phonebook

√ Encryption

√ AutoDial

√ Logging

√ Null modem

√ Name resolution

Techniques you'll need to master:

√ Installing and configuring RAS

√ Configuring the RAS Phonebook

√ Implementing RAS security measures

Remote Access Service (RAS) is a secure and reliable method of extending a network across communication links to remote computers. Modems and other communication devices act just like a network interface card (NIC) over a RAS connection. A remote RAS client can access and operate everything a standard network-attached client can. In this chapter, we provide the details you need to know to pass the Workstation exam.

NT RAS

RAS in Windows NT 4 is a significant improvement over the communications capabilities of version 3.51. Many of its advances were borrowed from Windows 95, including the ease of installation, process of configuration, and the look and feel of the service itself. NT Server RAS is able to support 256 simultaneous connections, act as a firewall, gateway, or router; and maintain tight security; NT Workstation RAS is limited to one inbound connection.

The communication links through which RAS can connect include the following:

➤ Public Switched Telephone Network (PSTN)

➤ Integrated Service Digital Network (ISDN)

➤ X.25 packet switching network

Standard LAN protocols are used over the RAS connection. Thus, TCP/IP, IPX/SPX, or NetBEUI can be used for network communication over the link established by RAS. Because the actual network protocol is used, the remote RAS client acts just as if it were connected to the network locally. The only difference is that the speed of data transfer is slower over the RAS connection than it would be if the computer accessing the server were physically attached to the network. On the Workstation exam, there are questions that test your understanding of this. Always remember that a client is a client is a client, whether locally connected or using RAS.

RAS Clients

A RAS client is any machine that is able to dial in or connect to a RAS server and establish an authorized connection. Although optimized for the integration of Microsoft-based operating systems, other system types can gain access with the proper software, protocols, and configuration.

The links established between a client and a server using RAS are called Wide Area Network (WAN) links. Because RAS is most often used to connect a computer (or an entire LAN) to a centrally located network over a long distance, it is considered to create a WAN link. The communication protocols used to establish a RAS connection are called WAN protocols. Windows NT supports two WAN protocols:

➤ **SLIP** The Serial Line Internet Protocol connection supports TCP/IP, but it does not support IPX/SPX and NetBEUI. Every client using SLIP must have a statically assigned IP address. SLIP does not support encrypted passwords, either. This protocol is provided only as a means for an NT Server to act as a client when dialing in to a Unix server; it cannot be used to accept inbound connections on NT.

➤ **PPP** The Point-To-Point Protocol supports several protocols, including AppleTalk, TCP/IP, IPX/SPX, and NetBEUI. It was designed as an improvement to SLIP. PPP supports DHCP and encrypted passwords. PPP is the most common and widely supported WAN protocol.

Windows NT Workstation can act as a RAS client whenever it dials out over a modem (or other communication link device) to establish a connection with an NT Server or some other type of computer system. The most common situation in which NT is a RAS client is when it connects to the Internet.

RAS Servers

Windows NT Workstation can support only one incoming RAS connection. (NT Server can support up to 256.)

 Important points to remember about NT as an RAS server include the following:

➤ NT only supports PPP clients—SLIP is not supported for dial-up.

➤ A NetBIOS gateway is established between the RAS server and PPP-attached RAS client to sustain standard NT network operations.

➤ RAS supports both IP and IPX routing.

➤ RAS supports NetBIOS and Windows Sockets applications.

➤ NT supports Point-To-Point Tunneling Protocol (PPTP) connections, which makes it possible for Windows NT computers to communicate securely over the Internet. In addition, it also supports Multilink PPP (MP), where numerous connections can be aggregated to create a larger amount of bandwidth.

Point-To-Point Tunneling Protocol (PPTP)

PPTP enables "tunneling" of IPX, NetBEUI, or TCP/IP inside PPP packets in such a way as to establish a secure link between a client and server over the Internet. PPTP connections are useful for establishing Virtual Private Networks (VPNs) in small companies that cannot afford expensive leased lines for network communications over long distances. PPTP enables users anywhere in the world to connect to the home office's network. PPTP uses a powerful encryption security scheme that is more secure than standard communications over the network itself. Thus, all traffic over the Internet using PPTP is safe.

Like all other network protocols, PPTP must be installed through the Protocols tab of the Network applet.

Multilink PPP (MP)

Windows NT has the capability to combine the bandwidth of multiple physical links, which increases the total bandwidth that could be used for a RAS connection. This aggregating of multiple communication links can be used as an inexpensive way to increase the overall bandwidth with the least amount of cost. MP must be supported by both the client and server systems. MP cannot be used with the callback security feature (discussed in detail later in this chapter in the section entitled "RAS Callback").

The checkbox to enable MP on a RAS server is located on the Network Configuration dialog box (see Figure 13.1, later in the chapter). MP is enabled through Dial-Up Networking's Phonebook configuration windows where multiple modems and phone numbers can be defined.

For the test, you can assume MP can aggregate different types of links, such as a regular telephone link and ISDN, into a single pipeline. However, in reality, MP only works when all of the links are of the same type.

Telephony API (TAPI) Properties And Phonebooks

In Windows NT, the Telephony Application Programming Interface (TAPI) provides a standard method of controlling communications over voice, data, and fax. Although the hardware is not provided with NT, TAPI can be used to control many PBX systems and communication devices for automated activity.

When you install a modem or the RAS components of NT, TAPI automatically is installed. It is required to control any communications device. Each time a dial-out connection is attempted, TAPI controls the modem and moderates the connection. Once the connection is established, TAPI continues to oversee the operation of the communication link.

The Dialing Properties dialog box (reached through the Modems applet in Control Panel) controls how TAPI uses your modem to place calls. You can control long-distance dialing, calling card use, prefix numbers, and tone/pulse dialing. You can also define multiple configurations based on physical location. If you travel with an NT Workstation notebook, you can define a dialing property profile for each of the cities you visit regularly.

TAPI is also the controlling entity for the Phonebook entries used to establish RAS connections. All of the functions and features of the modem and the communication types established over a modem are configured through a TAPI-controlled interface.

Installing RAS

RAS is installed through the Services tab of the Network applet. Installing RAS correctly does take some preparation and know-how. When performing the installation, you must remember the following:

1. Physically install or attach the modem first. During installation, if a modem has not been installed, you will be forced to install one.

2. Install RAS through the Services tab of the Network applet.

3. Select the communications port.

4. Add an installed modem as a RAS device.

5. Configure the port for one of the following:

    ➤ Dial Out Only

    ➤ Receive Calls Only

    ➤ Dial Out And Receive Calls

6. Select the LAN network protocols (see Figure 13.1).

    ➤ If Dial Out Only was selected, only the outbound protocols can be chosen.

    ➤ If Receive Calls Only was selected, only the inbound protocols can be configured.

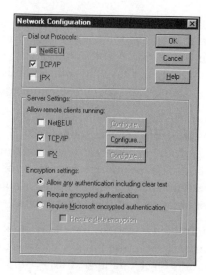

Figure 13.1 The Network Configuration dialog box for RAS.

> ➤ If Dial Out And Receive Calls was selected, both outbound and inbound protocols can be configured.

7. Select protocol-specific configuration for each inbound protocol (see Figures 13.2 and 13.3).

Once RAS is installed, you need to check your port and modem configuration through the Port and Modem applets of the Control Panel. If RAS is configured to receive calls, the port and modem cannot be used by any

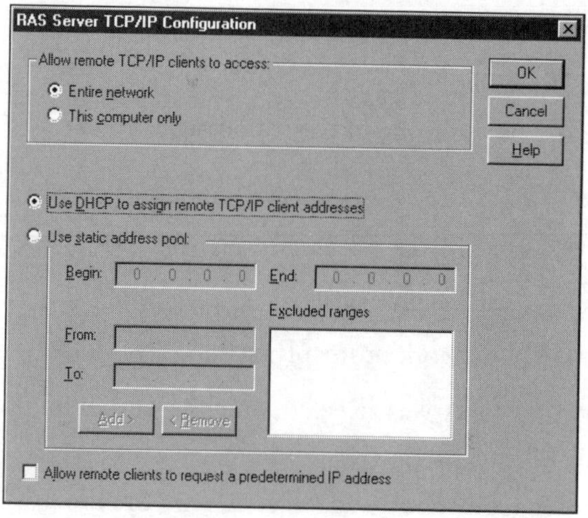

Figure 13.2 The RAS Server TCP/IP Configuration dialog box.

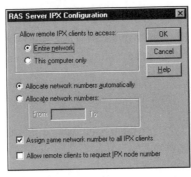

Figure 13.3   The RAS Server IPX Configuration dialog box.

other application. RAS locks the port to maintain control to monitor for inbound calls.

RAS Routing, Gateway, Firewall

You can select whether to let RAS clients using network protocols access just the RAS server or the entire network. When you limit RAS clients to the RAS server, you are using RAS as a firewall; no access of any kind off the RAS server is permitted. If you allow RAS clients to access the entire network, you are using RAS as a router. If NetBEUI is the only protocol in use, RAS acts as a gateway to enable the nonroutable protocol of NetBEUI to access the network.

RAS Phonebook

The dial-out capabilities of RAS are controlled and accessed through the RAS Phonebook. This utility, Dial-Up Networking (DUN), is found in the Programs|Accessories folder of the Start menu. The first time DUN is launched, the RAS Wizard appears to help you create your first Phonebook entry. Every time after that, the Phonebook dialog box appears. Through this interface, you can create and modify dial-up parameters for every RAS connection.

Phonebook entries consist of the following:

➤ Name, phone number, and modem to use

➤ Server type and protocol settings

➤ Connection scripts

➤ Security settings

➤ X.25 settings (if applicable)

RAS Security

RAS has numerous levels and types of security that protect your network from unauthorized remote access. The following sections highlight these security features.

RAS Encryption

Windows NT can be configured to increase or decrease connection security through the following:

➤ The Security tab of a Phonebook entry for outbound RAS links

➤ The Network Configuration dialog box for inbound RAS links (as shown in Figure 13.1)

Here are the three settings available for RAS data encryption:

➤ **Allow Any Authentication Including Clear Text** This is the most permissive setting. It should be used when the user is not concerned about passwords. This option allows a connection using any authentication provided by the server; therefore, it is useful when connecting to a non-Microsoft server.

➤ **Require Encrypted Authentication** This option is beneficial when the transmission of clear text password is not desired and when you are connecting to a non-Microsoft server.

➤ **Microsoft Encrypted Authentication** For this setting, the Microsoft Challenge Authentication Handshake Protocol (MS-CHAP) must be used; therefore, it is useful when calling a Microsoft server. If the Require Encrypted Authentication box is checked, all the data sent over the wire is encrypted. Data encryption is provided by Windows NT using the Rivest-Shamir-Adleman (RSA) Data Security Incorporated RC4 algorithm. If the data sent fails to encrypt, the connection automatically is terminated.

RAS Callback

Callback is a security feature in which a RAS connection is established only after the server has disconnected the inbound call and then has called the user back. Setting callback is performed via the User|Properties option in User Manager For Domains or the User|Properties command of the Remote Access Manager, by selecting from the following:

➤ **No Call Back** This is the default setting. It means that when a user is establishing a RAS connection, he or she will not be called back.

➤ **Set By Caller** Callback can be set by the user. This is a good way to save on long-distance charges, because the server calls the client back at the number set by the caller.

➤ **Preset To** You can configure the callback for a preset number. This heightens security because the user must call from a predetermined phone number.

The RAS Logon Process

With Windows NT, you can log on to a domain via RAS at the Logon prompt by selecting the Connect Via Dial-In option and providing the proper domain. This allows you to establish a RAS connection to the remote network without requiring you to log on locally first.

 When you are using TCP/IP via a slow RAS connection, an LMHOSTS file might speed up network access and name resolution. Place an LMHOSTS file on the RAS client. Ensure that LMHOSTS entries have the **#PRE** tag so that the IP addresses will be cached.

Additional RAS Features

There is much more to RAS than is listed in this chapter. You'll need to review the reference materials listed at the end of this chapter for more RAS information. However, we have included a short list of important features or options to RAS, and these are the most important to know for the exam.

AutoDial

AutoDial is the ability of NT to remember the location of resources accessed over a RAS connection. This is done by maintaining a map that correlates a network address to a Phonebook entry. When that resource is referenced, RAS reestablishes the WAN connection to regain access to that resource without additional user interaction. AutoDial is enabled by default. AutoDial does not yet function over IPX/SPX, but it works with TCP/IP and NetBEUI.

DUN Monitor

Once you've established a RAS connection so that your NT Workstation is a client on another network, you can obtain realtime status information about the connection using the DUN Monitor. It appears, by default, in the taskbar, but it can be set to appear as an icon in the tray (the area next to the time on the taskbar). Device statistics, connection statistics, and errors are some of the data sets presented by the utility. This is often the first place you should start when troubleshooting a RAS connection because data about connection speed, duration of link, users connected, protocols in use, and the RAS device are clearly listed.

Logging

Troubleshooting RAS difficulties is much simpler when the logging capabilities are employed. There are two logging features of NT that record RAS-related activities. The first is the MODEMLOG.TXT file, which records the activities of the modem. This is enabled through a modem's properties in the Modems applet in the Advanced Connections Settings area. This file is placed in the NT root directory.

The second log file is DEVICE.LOG. This file only can be enabled through the Registry. The "Logging" value located in \HKEY_LOCAL_ MACHINE\SYSTEM\CurrentControlSet\Services\RasMan\Parameters should be set to 1. The DEVICE.LOG file will be stored in the \%winntroot %\system32\ras directory.

The Event Viewer captures RAS information that may be useful for troubleshooting and deciphering RAS. By default, all server errors, user connect attempts, disconnects, and so on, are logged in the System Log.

Null Modem

A null modem is a serial cable that enables two computers to connect without the need for a modem. These special cables are common peer-to-peer attachment devices, but they can be used by NT RAS to establish a standard NT network connection. A null modem can be installed through the Modems applet by selecting it from the standard modems. A cable is not actually required for the setup, and this offers you a way out when installing RAS if you don't already have the modem at hand. Once installed, a null-modem cable can be used just like a modem, which is itself used by RAS just as if it were a NIC—that is, a workstation attached via a null-modem cable can fully participate in a domain, but at a slower data transfer rate.

Multiple Protocols

A RAS link uses both a WAN protocol and a LAN protocol to enable the network communications. Most often, the WAN protocol is PPP. The LAN protocol can be any of the protocols installed on your RAS server, which may or may not be the same set of protocols on the NT Workstation client. However, even if you use multiple protocols elsewhere, only a single LAN protocol is used over the RAS connection. The first common protocol identified between the client and server is used. Therefore, the proper bonding order of protocols to the RAS dial-up adapter on the client should be configured so that the most important protocol has the highest priority.

Name Resolution

In situations where static lookups occur, the configuration with optimal resolution speed and WAN link traffic is to store the HOST (DNS) and the LMHOSTS (WINS) files on the local hard drives of the RAS clients. This configuration makes it somewhat difficult to maintain the newest version of the files on multiple remote clients.

Exam Prep Questions

Question 1

Your NT Workstation is unable to maintain a connection to your office RAS server. Where should you start looking to investigate this problem?

O a. The System Log through the Event Viewer

O b. The DUN Monitor

O c. The DEVICE.LOG file

O d. The Remote Access Admin application located in Start|Programs|Administrative Tools

The best place to start investigating RAS connection problems is the DUN Monitor, because details about connection speed, protocols, and link duration might instantly pinpoint the problem. Therefore, answer b is correct. The System Log will contain little if any information about RAS connections. Therefore, answer a is incorrect. The DEVICE.LOG file is the second step in RAS troubleshooting, because it focuses on the activity of the RAS device, which might not be the problem. Therefore, answer c is incorrect. The Remote Access Admin application is not a tool to use for troubleshooting—it's for monitoring traffic, granting permissions, and controlling the RAS server. Therefore, answer d is incorrect.

Question 2

Which of the following statements about PPP and SLIP are true? [Check all correct answers]

❑ a. PPP supports encrypted passwords; SLIP does not.

❑ b. SLIP supports NetBEUI, IPX/SPX, and TCP/IP; PPP only supports TCP/IP.

❑ c. PPP supports DHCP; SLIP does not.

❑ d. SLIP is used to access Unix servers.

❑ e. PPP is the most commonly used WAN protocol.

PPP supports encrypted passwords; SLIP does not. Therefore, answer a is correct. PPP supports NetBEUI, IPX/SPX, and TCP/IP, but SLIP only supports TCP/IP. Therefore, answer b is incorrect. PPP supports DHCP; SLIP does not. Therefore, answer c is incorrect. SLIP is used to access Unix servers. Therefore, answer d is correct. PPP is the most commonly used WAN protocol. Therefore, answer e is also correct. Thus, answers a, c, d, and e are correct.

Question 3

Which of the following NT networking activities are supported by a PPP RAS connection? [Check all correct answers]

❏ a. Printer share access

❏ b. Named pipes

❏ c. WinSOCK API applications over TCP/IP

❏ d. InterProcess Communications (IPC)

❏ e. User logon authentication

Because a RAS-connected client is no different than a direct-connected client (other than in its speed of data transfer), all standard network activities still occur over the WAN link. Therefore, all answers are correct.

Question 4

While connected to the office LAN, you create a shortcut on your desktop that points to a documents folder located on the LAN's file server. After working with a few files from this folder, you close your RAS session. Later, you attempt to reopen the files you edited earlier. What happens?

○ a. Access is denied because no link to the LAN exists.

○ b The file is pulled from the network cache.

○ c A file with a similar name on your local hard drive is accessed instead.

○ d. RAS AutoDial attempts to reconnect to the office LAN.

Only answer d is correct. RAS maintains a map list of the resources accessed over WAN links. When one of these resources is referenced, it will attempt to use AutoDial to regain a connection to the server hosting the resource. Answer a would be the result if AutoDial was not enabled, but you always should assume the default configuration for computers in Microsoft exam questions unless indicated otherwise. Therefore, answer a is incorrect. Answers b and c are fictitious activities that do not occur. Therefore, they are incorrect.

Question 5

> Where can you find information related to RAS problems to aid in troubleshooting? [Check all correct answers]
>
> ❑ a. Event Viewer
>
> ❑ b. DEVICE.LOG
>
> ❑ c. Dr. Watson
>
> ❑ d. MODEMLOG.TXT
>
> ❑ e. NT Diagnostics

Event Viewer, DEVICE.LOG, and MODEMLOG.TXT can be useful troubleshooting tools for RAS problems. Therefore, answers a, b, and d are correct. Dr. Watson does not track RAS events; it focuses on applications. Therefore, answer c is incorrect. NT Diagnostics will not provide useful information related to RAS. Therefore, answer e is incorrect.

Question 6

> Your NT Workstation has an ISDN modem with two B channels and an analog modem with a dedicated data POTS line. You need to establish a RAS connection to an NT Server that hosts multiple ISDN and POTS lines. Assuming Multilink is supported on the RAS Server, how should you configure your Phonebook entry to maximize throughput?
>
> ○ a. Create three Phonebook entries—one for the POTS modem line and one for each ISDN B channel.
>
> ○ b. Create two Phonebook entries—one for the POTS modem and one for the ISDN modem.
>
> ○ c. Create a single Phonebook entry so that it uses the POTS modem and both channels of the ISDN modem.
>
> ○ d. Create a single Phonebook entry for the ISDN modem.

Creating a single Phonebook entry that uses all of the RAS devices in a Multilink aggregation is how DUN should be configured for maximum throughput. Therefore, answer c is correct. Creating multiple Phonebook entries will not allow the separate lines to be aggregated, only a single Phonebook entry can be active at any time. Therefore, answers a and b are incorrect. By using only the ISDN modem, you do not get the maximum bandwidth possible if the POTS connection was aggregated in through MP. Therefore, answer d is incorrect.

Question 7

> You have a field technician who travels extensively around the country. Her schedule changes often, and she rarely visits the same place twice. It is important that she is able to connect to the office LAN periodically, but your organization's security policy requires callback security on all RAS connections. How can you configure her account so that she is able to gain access, while also supporting your organization's security?
>
> O a. Set the callback security to No Call Back only for her account.
>
> O b. Enable callback security with Set By Caller selected.
>
> O c. Set the callback security to Preset To with her home phone number.
>
> O d. Set the callback security to Roaming and give her the page number to configure the callback number remotely.
>
> O e. Turn on the callback Caller ID capture.

Setting the No Call Back option will violate the organization's security policy. Therefore, answer a is incorrect. **Setting the Set By Caller option will allow her to input the callback number each time she needs to connect. Therefore, answer b is correct.** Setting the Preset To number will not allow her to gain access to the network because she is never in the same place. Therefore, answer c is incorrect. There is not a Roaming callback setting. Therefore, answer d is incorrect. NT does not have a Caller ID capture setting, but this can be obtained through third-party software; however, it is not required for this situation. Therefore, answer e is incorrect.

Question 8

Which protocols can be used over a RAS connection?

○ a. TCP/IP, NetBEUI, but not NWLink

○ b. TCP/IP, NWLink, but not NetBEUI

○ c. Only TCP/IP

○ d. TCP/IP, NetBEUI, and NWLink

TCP/IP, NetBEUI, but not NWLink is the restriction for the AutoDial feature, but this is not a limitation of RAS as a whole. Therefore, answer a is incorrect. TCP/IP, NWLink, but not NetBEUI are the protocols that can be routed over RAS, but this is not a limitation as to which protocols can be used. Therefore, answer b is also incorrect. Only TCP/IP can be used over SLIP, but RAS is not limited to SLIP. Therefore, answer c is incorrect. **TCP/IP, NetBEUI, and NWLink can all be used over RAS. Therefore, answer d is correct.**

Question 9

What are the possible uses of a null-modem cable? [Check all correct answers]

❑ a. Attach a workstation to a domain

❑ b. Enable subnet routing

❑ c. Test a RAS server locally

❑ d. Establish a VPN over the Internet

❑ e. Temporarily connect two LANs

Attaching a workstation to a domain is a use for a null-modem cable. There- fore, **answer a is correct.** Subnet routing can be implemented only when two NICs are installed on the same machine. Therefore, answer b is incor- rect. **A RAS server can be tested using a null-modem cable to simulate a remote client. Therefore, answer c is correct.** A VPN over the Internet can be established only with PPTP and a connection to the Internet, requiring a modem. Therefore, answer d is incorrect. **Two closely adjacent LANs can be connected over a null-modem cable. Therefore, answer e is correct. Thus, answers a, c, and e are correct.**

Question 10

Your LAN uses both NetBEUI and NWLink protocols. Your RAS server supports NetBEUI and TCP/IP, bound in that order. A RAS client also uses both NetBEUI and TCP/IP, bound in that order to the dial-up adapter. Which of the following activities cannot occur over a RAS connection made between the client and the server?

○ a. Accessing a directory list of NetBIOS share names

○ b. Accessing resources on the LAN

○ c. Accessing resources on the RAS server

○ d. Accessing WinSOCK applications

The bind order of the protocols on the client determine what single LAN protocol is used over the RAS connection, resulting in a NetBEUI connection. WinSOCK applications based on the Windows TCP/IP API cannot be used, because TCP/IP is not a protocol being communicated over the link. Therefore, **answer d is correct.** The other activities can occur using the NetBEUI protocol. Therefore, answers a, b, and c are incorrect.

Question 11

If static name resolution is used, what is the proper location of the HOST and LMHOSTS files to optimize the lookup time?

○ a. Both HOST and LMHOSTS should be stored on the RAS clients.

○ b. HOST should be stored on the RAS server, and LMHOSTS should be stored on the RAS clients.

○ c. Both HOST and LMHOSTS should be stored on the RAS server.

○ d. HOST should be stored on the RAS clients, and LMHOSTS should be stored on the RAS server.

The fastest lookup time will occur when the HOST and LMHOSTS files are stored on the local hard drive of each RAS client, because no WAN traffic must occur to resolve a resource location. Therefore, **answer a is correct.** All others answers are incorrect because they discuss storing these files somewhere other than on the client, which increases the lookup time.

Need To Know More?

 Boyce, Jim, et al.: *Windows NT Workstation 4.0 Advanced Technical Reference*. Que, Indianapolis, IN, 1996. ISBN 0-7897-0863-9. Chapter 20 contains detailed information about Dial-Up Networking.

 Perkins, Charles, Matthew Strebe, and James Chellis: *MCSE: NT Workstation Study Guide*. Sybex Network Press, San Francisco, CA, 1997. ISBN 0-7821-1973-5. Chapter 12 focuses on the Remote Access Service. It includes numerous exercises to walk you through the installation process.

 Search the TechNet CD (or its online version through www.microsoft.com) using the keywords "RAS," "Remote Access," "PPP," and "modems."

 The *Windows NT Workstation Resource Kit* contains some discussion of RAS in scattered articles. Performing a search on the TechNet (either CD or online version) or the CD accompanying the *Resource Kit* using "RAS" or "Remote Access" will locate these quickly.

Windows NT Printing

14

. . . .

Terms you'll need to understand:

√ Connecting to a printer

√ Creating a printer

√ Network interface printer

√ Print client

√ Print device

√ Print job

√ Print resolution

√ Print server

√ Print spooler

√ Print driver

√ Printer/logical printer

√ Queue/print queue

√ Rendering

Techniques you'll need to master:

√ Installing and configuring a printer

√ Managing printing clients

√ Managing the print spooler

√ Setting up print priorities

√ Establishing logical printers and printing pools

It's the job of the network administrator to make sure that users have access to needed resources—and the printer is one of the most often-used resources. One of the biggest complaints about other network operating systems has been their inability to handle printers effectively and efficiently. Microsoft has developed an intuitive and simple way to manage this much-used resource. This chapter focuses on the Microsoft approach to printing and defines a few Microsoft-specific printing terms—both with an eye toward preparing you for the printing section of the Workstation exam.

The Windows NT Print Lexicon

The following list contains Microsoft-specific printing terminology that must be mastered. It is very important for successful exam taking that you know and fully understand all of these terms and concepts. Exam questions about printing can be tricky, especially when they deal with this specialized terminology.

➤ **Client application** A network program that originates print jobs (this can be located on a print server or client computer on the network).

➤ **Connecting to a printer** The process of attaching to a network share that resides on the computer on which the logical printer was created (performed through the Add Printer Wizard, accessed from the Start menu's Printers option).

➤ **Creating a printer** The process of naming a printer, as well as defining settings for, installing drivers for, and linking a printing device to the network. In Windows NT, this process is performed through the Add Printer Wizard.

➤ **Network interface printer** Built-in network interface cards for print devices that are directly attached to the network—for example, the Hewlett-Packard JetDirect.

> *Note: The DLC protocol must be installed to communicate with directly attached print devices.*

➤ **Print client** A computer on a network (called a "client computer") that transmits the print jobs to be produced by the physical printing device.

➤ **Print device** Commonly referred to as the "printer." In other words, it is the physical hardware device that produces printed material. This is very confusing to most people. Just remember that the print device is the piece of hardware that actually spits out paper with your material printed on it. But you should also realize that a printer can also be a fax modem, a slide maker, or even a CAD plotter.

➤ **Print job** The code that defines the print processing commands as well as the actual file to be printed. Windows NT defines print jobs by data type, depending on what adjustments must be made to the file for it to print accurately (that is, one data type can be printable as-is, whereas another might need a form feed to conclude the data stream for the print job to be executed properly).

➤ **Print resolution** The measurement of pixel density that is responsible for the smoothness of any image or text being printed. This is measured in dots per inch (DPI)—the higher the DPI, the better the quality of the printed material.

➤ **Print server** The server computer that links physical print devices to the network and manages sharing those devices with computers on the network.

➤ **Print Server services** Software components located on the print server that accept print jobs and send them to the print spooler for execution. These components, such as Services For Macintosh, enable a variety of client computers to communicate with the print server to process print jobs.

➤ **Print spooler** The collection of dynamic link libraries (DLLs) that acquires, processes, catalogues, and disburses print jobs. A print job will be saved to disk in a spool file. Print despooling is the process of reading what is contained in the spool file and transmitting it to the physical printing device.

➤ **Printer driver** Programs that enable communications between applications and a specific print device. Most hardware peripherals, such as printers, require the use of a driver to process commands.

➤ **Printer/logical printer** The logical printer (Microsoft calls this "the printer") is the software interface that communicates between the operating system and the physical printing device. The logical printer handles the printing process from the time the print command is issued. Its settings determine the physical printing device that renders the file to be printed as well as how the file to be printed is sent to the printing device (for example, via a remote print share or local port).

➤ **Queue/print queue** In printing terms, a queue is a series of files waiting to be produced by the printing device.

➤ **Rendering** The process by which Windows NT prints is as follows: A client application sends file information to the Graphics Device Interface (GDI), which receives the data, communicates that data to the physical printing device driver, and produces the print job in the language of the physical printing device. The printing device then interprets this information and creates a file (bitmap) for each page to be printed.

Printing With Windows NT Workstation

Windows NT print settings are managed through the Printers folder, which is accessible from the Control Panel or the Start menu (under Settings).

> *Note: The Printers folder replaces the old Windows NT 3.51 Print Manager.*

This approach is extremely straightforward compared to earlier versions of NT and other network operating systems.

Windows NT takes a modular approach to printing, as shown in Figure 14.1. Each component has a specific use and interfaces with the other components in the print architecture.

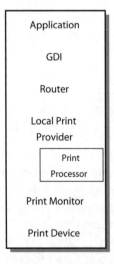

Figure 14.1 The Windows NT print architecture components work together to render print jobs for the user.

The following list defines each component of the NT printing architecture:

➤ **Graphics Device Interface (GDI)** The component that provides network applications with a system for presenting graphical information. The GDI works as a translator between the application's print requests and the device driver interface (DDI) to make sure a job is rendered accurately.

➤ **Print device** The physical hardware device that produces printed output.

➤ **Print driver** The software component that enables communication between the operating system and the physical printing device.

➤ **Print monitor** The component that passes the print job (which has been translated to the print device's language) to the physical printing device.

➤ **Print processor** The component that makes any necessary modifications to the print job before passing the job to the print monitor. NT actually has two print processors—one for the Windows platform and one for the Macintosh.

➤ **Print router** The component that directs the print job to the appropriate printing device.

➤ **Print spooler** The component that accepts print jobs from the router, calls the processor to make any needed changes to the print job, and transfers the jobs one at a time to the print monitor. It is also called the "print provider."

Printing From Windows NT Clients

This is where NT's approach to printing really shines. Client computers need access to print devices, so they must add the printer via the Add Printer Wizard. Previously, all client computers required that the print driver be installed on each client machine that needed access to a printing device. No more! All that is needed for printing from an NT client is that the driver be installed on the print server. That's it! This simplifies the printing process, because if an updated print driver is released, it just needs to be installed on the server, not on every client machine.

Printer Installation

Configuring or installing printers under NT is extremely simple, even if the drivers for the printer are not on the shipping distribution CD-ROM. There are two types of printer setup—local and network.

A local printer is simply the situation where a print device is physically attached to your workstation. In such a case, your machine will act as the print server. Once you've physically connected the printer, use the Add Printer Wizard from the Printers folder to install the proper drivers. Select the My Computer option at the first prompt. You'll be asked for the port, the printer make and model (if not listed you can click the Have Disk option to load drivers from a floppy), and a name for the printer. If you want to offer access to the printer across the network to other clients, you should select the Shared option and define a share name. By default, the Everyone group will have Print access, Print Operators and Administrators will have Full Control, and you'll be the Owner and also have Full Control. You should now see a printer icon in the Printers folder (hit Refresh if it does not appear) with a hand under the printer if it has been shared.

A network printer is simply a software redirector that guides print jobs from your workstation to the actual location of the print server and ultimately the printer itself. Attaching to a network printer is simple. Once again, use the Add Printer Wizard from the Printers folder, but select Network Printer Servers at the first prompt. A list of all printer shares on the network will be displayed. Make a selection and opt to print a test page. If the test document prints, you've connected successfully. If you notice, you do not install a printer driver when connecting to a network printer if you are working from a Windows NT client. Instead, the driver is downloaded from the print server each time a print job needs to be created.

Printer Configuration

Once a printer has been installed, you can alter its configuration and setup to better suit your needs. Through the Properties dialog box of the printer, you have numerous features and options. These include General, Ports, Scheduling, Sharing, Security, and Device Settings. You'll need to be familiar with each of these tabs.

General

On the General tab, you can do the following:

> ➤ Comment about the printer

> ➤ Describe the printer's location

> ➤ Change, update, or reinstall the driver for the printer

> ➤ Define a separator page that prints between print jobs

> ➤ Set the print processor, such as allowing Unix or Macintosh print jobs, and data type, such as **EMF, RAW, RAW (FF Appended), RAW (FF Auto), TEXT,** and **PSCRIPT,** for the printer

> ➤ Print a test page

Ports

On the Ports tab, you can do the following:

> ➤ Set the attached port, including add, delete, and configure ports

> ➤ Enable bidirectional support so that print jobs and the printer status can be communicated simultaneously

> ➤ Enable printer pooling

Scheduling

On the Scheduling tab, you do the following:

> ➤ Set time restrictions where all print jobs sent outside of the valid time period are spooled and printed during the next interval

> ➤ Prioritize print jobs.

> ➤ Spool documents directly to the printer

> ➤ Print spooling documents immediately or after the entire job has been spooled

> ➤ Hold mismatched documents

> ➤ Print spooled documents first

> ➤ Keep documents after they have printed

Sharing

On the Sharing tab, you can do the following:

➤ Share or not share

➤ Share name

➤ Select additional 95 or versions of NT drivers to install

Security

On the Security tab, you can do the following:

➤ Set permissions for users and/or groups to Full Control, Manage, Print, or No Access (the settings operate the same way as File and Directory permissions)

➤ Set print-related auditing for users and/or groups (the settings operate the same way as file and directory auditing)

➤ Take ownership

Device Settings

On the Device Settings tab, you can set most of the printer-specific settings. These are the settings that you would otherwise interact with through the device's on-board LCD screen and buttons or the manufacturer-supplied configuration software utility. However, the interface is easier to use and displays all possible options, plus it offers some additional help and information.

Print Job Management

Managing print jobs is a fairly simple task with Windows NT. As a print operator, printer owner, or print job owner, you can manipulate a job that is listed in the queue. To do this, open the printer queue window through the main Printers folder. The printer queue window is shown in Figure 14.2. By opening the Properties dialog box for a print job, you can manipulate how it is printed by the printer, its priority, and who to notify when it is completed. Changing a print job's priority alters how quickly it will be sent to the printer. Working with the queue as a whole, you have the privilege of using the following commands from the Document menu to control the queue:

➤ **Pause** Halts a print job.

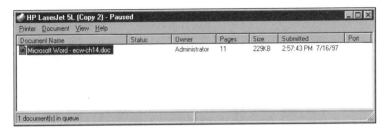

Figure 14.2   The print queue window of a logical printer.

➤ **Resume** Continues printing where paused.

➤ **Restart** Starts current print job over. Any document can be restarted if it has not been deleted from the spooler.

However, you only have the ability to manage your own documents unless you are a printer owner or a member of either the Print Operators or Administrators groups.

Printer Shares

One of the most useful capabilities of a network is that of sharing a single printer with multiple users. The process of enabling other network users to access a printer is just as simple as giving users network access to a directory or a drive—you create a printer share. This is done through the Sharing command located in the File menu of the main Printers folder or the Printer menu of the individual Printers folder (under Settings). All you need to do is assign a share name and everyone on the network can print to that printer (provided they have the printer drivers available).

To tighten security on a printer, you must access the Permissions button located on the Security tab of a printer's Properties dialog box. The Printer Permissions dialog box acts the same as the File Permissions NT version. The only real change is the types of access possible with printers:

➤ **No Access** Grants no access other than viewing the NetBIOS name

➤ **Print** Enables users to print and manage their own documents, but they can only see others' documents

➤ **Manage Documents** Allows users to print documents and manage all print jobs

➤ **Full Control** Allows users to print, manage print jobs, change permissions, and install drivers

The default settings for a newly created printer share are:

➤ **Full Control** Administrators, Server Operators, and Print Operators

➤ **Manage Documents** Creator owner

➤ **Print** Everyone

To restrict access to a printer, you must remove the Everyone group and then add group(s) and user(s) as needed.

Multiple Printers: Physical And Logical

Many of the exam questions that deal with printers involve multiple groups requiring printer access, with one of the groups printing large, nonurgent documents. More often than not, these situations are resolved by defining multiple logical printers for a single physical printer and altering the priority or access times.

Keep in mind that:

➤ A single physical printer can be served by multiple logical printers.

➤ A single logical printer can serve multiple physical printers (pooling).

➤ Multiple logical printers can serve multiple physical printers.

Print Auditing

A printer is just another NT object. Therefore, you can use NT's audit system to monitor access, use, and errors. (For more details about NT's audit system, refer to Chapter 4.) You need to enable File And Object Access-level auditing (Success and/or Failure) to track Printer events. To set the events to Audit By User/Group, go to the Audit button on the Security tab of the Properties dialog box of a printer. This dialog box operates the same way as the File version.

The events you can audit are:

➤ Print

➤ Full Control

➤ Delete

➤ Change Permissions

➤ Take Ownership

Events captured through print auditing are listed in the System or Security log, depending on the nature of the event.

Ownership

The creator of a logical printer is the owner of that printer. Only an administrator or a user with Full Control access can take ownership of a printer (just like every other object within NT). In addition to the ability to change permissions on an owned printer, the owner can also modify form-to-tray assignments, install font cartridges, and adjust the halftone settings.

Spooling

When a user sends out a print job, it goes to the print spooler, which is responsible for tracking the print job through the printing process, routing jobs to the correct ports, and assigning priorities to print jobs.

Print Priorities

By default, the spooler prints jobs in the order in which they are received. It is possible, however, to ensure that print jobs from certain users are printed before any other job. To adjust priority levels for individual users or groups, you must create a different logical printer to a particular printing device (this is discussed in detail in the "Logical Printers And Printing Pools" section, later in the chapter). To assign higher priority to print jobs from certain users, the following steps must be performed on a logical printer:

1. Go to the Printers folder (Start|Settings|Printers).

2. Select Server Properties from the File menu for the logical printer to be adjusted.

3. Select the Scheduling tab.

4. Adjust the slide bar to assign a higher priority (this can be set anywhere from 1 to 99, with 1 being the lowest—as well as the default setting).

Separate Spool Files

If the printers on your network are hit with many print jobs at one time, the print spooler can get fairly large. It is important to make sure that the spooler file is big enough to handle all the jobs that are sent to it, the size of this file varies with the capabilities of the printer and its print server. It might become necessary, therefore, to create individual spool files for each printer on the network. This is performed through the Registry by creating files under the following Registry key:

```
HKEY_LOCAL_MACHINE\SYSTEM\CurrentControlSet\Control\Printers
```

 It is possible for print jobs to get stuck in the spooler. To remedy this, stop and restart the spooler service by performing the following steps:

1. Go to the Control Panel (Start|Settings|Control Panel).

2. Double-click the Services icon.

3. Highlight the entry labeled "Spooler" in the list of services.

4. Click the Stop button and confirm that you want to stop the service.

5. Click the Start button.

6. Click Close on the Services dialog box.

Changing The Spool Location

The default directory for the print spooler is *SystemRoot*\System32\Spool. Here are the steps for changing the location of the spooler directory:

1. Go to the Printers folder (Start|Settings|Printers).

2. Select Server Properties from the File menu.

3. Select the Advanced tab.

4. Enter the path to the new spool directory in the Spool Folder text box.

You may want to change this setting because the drive for the default path has limited space for storing print jobs. (Note: You must restart the print server before these changes take effect.)

Logical Printers And Printing Pools

A logical printer is the software interface that enables communication between Windows NT and the physical printing device. You can create multiple logical printers that send print jobs to a single print device (and, conversely, a single logical printer that sends jobs to multiple print devices).

It is necessary to create different logical printers (with different share names) to assign priorities to various groups and users printing to a single print device. All of this is defined through the Add Printer Wizard in the Printers folder. You simply provide different settings (such as access rights, access times, and priorities) for different shares that attach to the same physical print device.

When a printer services multiple printing devices, it creates what is called a "printer pool." Put simply, a single logical printer spools out jobs to the next available printing device in the printer pool. It is necessary for all of the print devices in a printer pool to be of the same type. With this setup, the printer assigns files to be printed to whichever print device is free in the printer pool.

DLC

The DLC protocol is typically used to interoperate with IBM mainframes, but it is also used to provide connectivity to network-attached print devices. Most commonly, and for the exam, the DLC protocol is used for Hewlett-Packard network-attached printers and/or JetDirect interfaces (for example, a printer NIC).

The DLC protocol is installed using the Protocols tab of the Network Control Panel applet. There are no configuration options; however, the binding order of DLC is important. The order in which adapters are bound (that is, prioritized) to DLC is the reference number used by DLC applications—the first adapter is value 0, the second is value 1, and so on. Windows NT DLC can support up to 16 physical adapters.

To use DLC for printing, you must install both the DLC protocol and the Hewlett-Packard Network Port monitor on the server that is designated as the print server. You can designate any server to be the print server because the print device is attached to the network directly and not through a parallel cable to a computer. The DLC protocol must be installed first, and then the HP Network Port monitor (HPMON.DLL) should be installed through the Add Printer Wizard Add Port command. Once installation is complete, the logical printer on the print server can be shared across the network and used as any other printer.

The Hewlett-Packard Network Port monitor can be configured so that the managed ports are either "job-based" or "continuous connection," which is set at port creation. A job-based setting disconnects from a printer when the print job is complete. Thus, other print servers can connect and print.

A continuous connection setting does not release the printer; therefore, other servers cannot connect.

TCP/IP And Unix Printers

If your network has Unix workstations, you can use the Microsoft TCP/IP Printing service. TCP/IP only needs to be installed on the printer server hosting the physical printer. The path of the TCP/IP Print Services is the Line Printer Daemon (LPD) and Line Printer Remote (LPR). LPD servers and LPR clients are often Unix systems, but these utilities are available for most platforms, including NT.

TCP/IP Print Services is installed through the Services tab of the Network applet in the Control Panel. After installation, you can change its startup settings in the Services applet from Manual (the default) to Automatic. If the printer is hosted on a Windows NT machine, use the New Printer Wizard to create a new port of type "LPR Port" and direct it to the proper location of the printer, whether an NT print share or a Unix-hosted queue.

Logical printers are created to send documents to the TCP/IP printer through the Add Printer Wizard. This is done by using the IP address print server and the name of the printer, as defined by the print server.

Printer Troubleshooting

When working with printers, there seems to be an infinite number of issues to resolve before normal operation is restored. Many printer problems are either simple or obvious, so check these before moving on to the more complicated solutions:

➤ Always check the physical aspects of the printer—cable, power, paper, toner, and so on.

➤ Check the print queue for stalled jobs on the logical printer on both the client and server.

➤ Make sure the printer driver has not become corrupted by reinstalling it.

➤ Attempt to print from a different application or a different client.

➤ Print using Administrator access.

➤ Stop and restart the spooler using the Services applet.

➤ Check the status and CPU usage of SPOOLSS.EXE using the Task Manager.

➤ Check the free space on the drive hosting the spooler file and change its destination.

Exam Prep Questions

Question 1

> Several users are trying to print to a print server. You receive many complaints from the users that they have sent several jobs to the print server, but the jobs have not printed and cannot be deleted. How do you resolve this problem?
>
> ○ a. Verify that the Pause printing option is not checked on the print server.
>
> ○ b. Delete the stalled printer from the print server, create a new printer, and tell the users to resend their jobs to the new printer.
>
> ○ c. Delete all files from the spool folder on the print server and tell the users to resend them.
>
> ○ d. Stop the spooler service and then restart it.

There isn't a Pause printing option. Therefore, answer a is incorrect. There's no need to re-create the printer from scratch. Therefore, answer b is also incorrect. You should never have to involve users in the problem-solving process (other than to gather information from them). Therefore, answer c is also incorrect. **Choice d is the correct answer. This scenario is a quintessential example of a stalled print spooler. To fix the problem, select Services in the Control Panel, stop the spooler service, and then restart it.**

Question 2

You have an HP LaserJet attached to your NT Workstation that is acting as the print server for 20 other Windows NT computers on your network. Hewlett-Packard has just released an updated printer driver. What must be done to distribute the updated driver to all the computers that print to this print server?

○ a. Install the updated driver on all client computers; there is no need to update the server.

○ b. Install the updated driver on the print server and do nothing more.

○ c. Install the updated driver on the print server and on all client computers.

○ d. Create a separate logical printer with the updated driver on the print server and tell all the users to print to the new printer.

○ e. Install the updated driver on the print server and instruct all client computers to download the updated driver from the server.

The best way to update a printer driver is to update the driver on the print server. Therefore, b is the only correct answer. There is no need to update the driver manually on each client computer running NT. Therefore, answer a is incorrect. When a client computer sends a print job to the print server, the updated driver is automatically copied to the client. Therefore, answers c, d, and e are also incorrect.

Question 3

You run a network for a small consulting firm. You have only a single printer on the network. The company executives have asked that you configure printing so that all documents from the executives print before other documents. How is this performed?

- ○ a Create a separate logical printer, assign rights to the executive group, and set the printer priority to 1.

- ○ b. Create a separate logical printer, assign rights to the executive group, and set the printer priority to 99.

- ○ c. Create a separate logical printer for the executive group and configure the printer to start printing immediately.

- ○ d. Create a separate logical printer for the executive group and configure the printer to print directly to the physical print device.

It is possible to set priorities between groups of documents by creating different logical printers for the same physical print device and setting different priority levels on the printers. To set printer priority, select the Scheduling tab in Printer Properties dialog box. The lowest priority is 1. Therefore, answer a is incorrect. **The highest priority is 99. Therefore, b is the correct answer.** There is no Start Printing Immediately option. Therefore, answer c is incorrect. Any NT printer automatically prints to the print device. Therefore, answer d is incorrect.

Question 4

You just installed a new printer on your print server. You send a print job to the printer, but it comes out as pages of nonsense. What is the most likely cause of the problem?

- ○ a. The DLC protocol is not installed.

- ○ b. The print spooler is corrupt.

- ○ c. An incorrect printer driver has been installed.

- ○ d. There is not enough hard disk space for spooling.

A print job won't print at all if the wrong protocol is used. Therefore, answer a is incorrect. Likewise, nothing will print without the spooler. Therefore, answer b is incorrect. **If an incorrect printer driver has been installed, documents might print illegibly. Therefore, choice c is correct.** As in answer b, a print job won't print without proper spooling. Therefore, answer d is incorrect.

Question 5

You want to create a printer pool with five print devices. Which condition must be present for you to create this printer pool?

○ a. All print devices must use the same protocol.

○ b. All physical print devices must be connected to the same logical printer.

○ c. All print devices must use the same printer port.

○ d. All print devices must be located in the same room.

It is not necessary for all print devices to use the same protocol. Therefore, answer a is incorrect. **To create a printer pool, all print devices must be connected to the same print server. Therefore, answer b is the correct choice.** All print devices also should be identical. Answers c and d are both incorrect because you don't have to use the same port for multiple printer devices, and printers don't have to be in the same room.

Question 6

You have a printer pool that consists of Printer 1 and Printer 2. Printer 1 is printing a job and Printer 2 is idle. A paper jam occurs on Printer 1's print device. What will happen to the rest of the job that was being printed?

○ a. The print job will be completed on Printer 2.

○ b. The print job will be canceled.

○ c. The print job will be completed on Printer 2 because Printer 2 has a higher priority level.

○ d. The print job is held for completion by Printer 1 until the device is fixed.

The print job will not be sent to Printer 2. Therefore, answer a is incorrect. The print job will not be canceled if the device fails. Therefore, answer b is also incorrect. Priority levels have nothing to do with failed devices. Therefore, answer c is wrong as well. **If a physical print device in a printer pool fails in the middle of a print job, the print job is retained at that physical print device until the device is fixed. Therefore, choice d is correct.** Any other print jobs sent to the printer pool will continue to print to other physical print devices in the printer pool.

Question 7

You want to configure a Windows NT computer to be the print server for an HP network interface print device. However, you are unable to locate the option to install a port for the printer. Why is this?

○ a. PostScript printing is enabled on the print device and must be disabled.

○ b. You didn't install the print driver on the print server.

○ c. The print processor is corrupt and must be fixed.

○ d. The DLC protocol is not installed on the print server.

PostScript printing has nothing to do with print device installation. Therefore, answer a is incorrect. You can't install a print driver if NT can't recognize the print device. Therefore, answer b is incorrect. The print processor is not involved in the installation of printers. Therefore, answer c is also incorrect. **For Windows NT to provide support for HP network interface print devices, you must install the DLC (Data Link Control) protocol. Therefore, answer d is correct.**

Question 8

During the printing of a 43-page document, your printer jams on the second page. You pause the printer through the Printers folder. After you remove the jam and reset the physical printer, what command should you enter?

- O a. Open the Printers folder for the printer and select Resume from the Document menu.

- O b. Open the Printers folder for the printer and select Restart from the Document menu.

- O c. Open the Printers folder for the printer and select Resume from the Printer menu.

- O d. Open the Printers folder for the printer and select Restart from the Printer menu.

Resume will start printing from the last place in the print job and will not resend the destroyed page or the data lost from the printer buffer. Therefore, answer a is incorrect. **Restart will restart the print process from the beginning. Therefore, answer b is correct.** Resume is located in the Document menu, not the Printer menu, and it is the wrong command. Therefore, answer c is incorrect. Restart is located in the Document menu (therein lies the "trick"), not the Printer menu. Therefore, answer d is incorrect.

Question 9

What is the advantage of connecting to a printer as opposed to creating a new printer with Windows NT?

- O a. More options over the scheduling of accessibility

- O b. Local spooling of print jobs

- O c. The print driver does not have to be manually installed

- O d. Local print queues

There are no additional scheduling options in either case. Therefore, answer a is incorrect. There is no local spooling of print jobs for network connection over printers; a logical printer is simply a redirector to the real print server where all spooling takes place. Therefore, answer b is incorrect. **Print drivers do not need to be installed locally on each NT Workstation** that connects to a network share printer. **Therefore, answer c is correct.** The logical printer used to connect to the print share will display a print queue, but it is the entire print queue for the printer as seen by the print server that is displayed. There is not an individual print queue for each local machine; however, only those print jobs owned by the workstation user can be manipulated by that user. **Therefore, answer d is incorrect.**

Question 10

You want to share the printer attached to your NT Workstation with the rest of the network. There are Windows 95, Windows NT 4, and Windows NT 3.51 systems on the network that need access to your printer. What is the simplest way to allow them access?

○ a. Install printer drivers on each machine.

○ b. Install the needed drivers on your printer server.

○ c. Run serial cables to each machine and use a multiport switchbox.

○ d. Upgrade all machines to NT 4 and then access the print share.

Installing a print driver on each machine is a waste of time, especially with these three OS types. **Therefore, answers a, c, and d are incorrect. Because Windows 95 and NT machines don't need the drivers, answer b is the correct choice;** the driver only needs to be installed on the print server.

Need To Know More?

 Boyce, Jim, et al.: *Windows NT Workstation 4.0 Advanced Technical Reference.* Que, Indianapolis, IN, 1996. ISBN 0-7897-0863-9. This book contains scattered references to print topics, but lacks a dedicated chapter.

 Heywood, Drew: *Inside Windows NT Server.* New Riders, Indianapolis, IN, 1995. ISBN 1-56205-472-4. Chapter 6, "Managing Print Services," details the issues relating to printing and printer permissions and management.

 Perkins, Charles, Matthew Strebe, and James Chellis: *MCSE: NT Workstation Study Guide.* Sybex Network Press, San Francisco, CA, 1997. ISBN 0-7821-1973-5. Chapter 13 has a detailed account of the print system of NT Workstation.

 Siyan, Karanjit S.: *Windows NT Server 4 Professional Reference.* New Riders, Indianapolis, IN, 1996. ISBN 1-56205-731-6. A nice discussion of using Windows NT print services is located in Chapter 17, "Windows NT Printing."

 Strebe, Matthew, Charles Perkins, and James Chellis: *MSCE: NT Server 4 Study Guide.* Sybex Network Press, San Francisco, CA, 1996. ISBN 0-7821-1972-7. Chapter 14 contains detailed information about creating and maintaining your printing environment.

 Search the TechNet CD (or its online version through www.microsoft.com) using the keywords "printing," "logical printers," "print management," and "print devices."

 The *Windows NT Workstation Resource Kit* contains a lot of useful information about printers and printer management. You can search the TechNet (CD or online version) or the *Resource Kit* CD, using keywords such as "shares," "resource management," and "user management."

Tuning And Monitoring Windows NT Workstation

15

Terms you'll need to understand:

√ Performance Monitor

√ Optimization

√ Objects

√ Counters

√ Baselining

√ Update Interval

√ Task Manager

√ Paging file

√ Priorities

Techniques you'll need to master:

√ Using Performance Monitor

√ Understanding what network characteristics to monitor

√ Viewing network data with Chart view, Alert view, Report view, and Log view

√ Logging network statistics

√ Establishing a baseline

√ Setting administrative alerts

Performance tuning and monitoring on Windows NT Workstation involves numerous applications and configuration screens. In this chapter, we look at many of the tools and methods used to monitor and increase performance, with a focus on the material covered on the Workstation exam. Specifically, we look at the Task Manager, Performance Monitor, and the NT paging file. In addition, we look at managing process priorities and optimizing system settings.

Task Manager

The Task Manager is a new utility to the Windows NT environment. This tool enables you to view and control the processes currently active on your machine. Three types of information are available through the Task Manager (each displayed on its own display tab).

The three types of information available through the Task Manager are:

➤ **Applications** This tab shows a list the applications currently in use and their status, whether running or nonresponsive. (See Figure 15.1.)

➤ **Processes** This tab displays a list of all processes in memory with details on the CPU and memory usage. (See Figure 15.2.)

➤ **Performance** This tab shows a graphical and numerical display of system performance metrics—including CPU and memory usage graphs; totals for handles, threads, and processes; physical memory statistics; committed memory changes (memory allocated to the system or an application); and Kernel memory statistics. (See Figure 15.3.)

The Task Manager can be reached using two different methods:

➤ Press Ctrl+Alt+Del and then click the Task Manager button.

➤ Right-click over a blank area of the taskbar and then select the Task Manager from the pop-up menu.

The Task Manager is an invaluable tool used for fast investigation of system activity and instant corrective actions, such as the following:

➤ Identifying nonresponsive applications and terminating them to release their hostage resources (Applications tab).

➤ Identifying runaway processes and terminating them to return the system to normal operational levels (Processes tab).

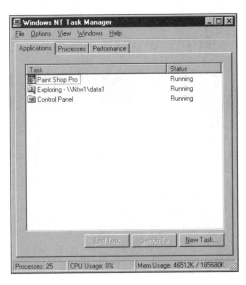

Figure 15.1   The Task Manager's Applications tab.

➤ Ascertaining the memory use levels to determine the need for additional RAM (Performance tab).

The Task Manager also enables you to launch new processes, switch to a new foreground application, view separate graphs for each CPU, display the Kernel access time, and alter the priority of processes (see the "Managing Process Priorities" section later in this chapter).

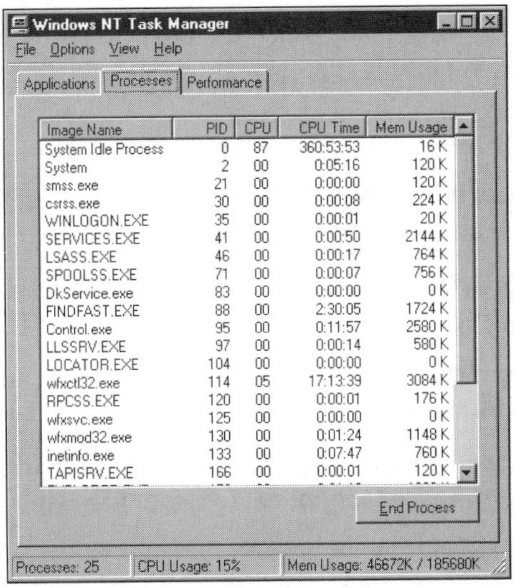

Figure 15.2   The Task Manager's Processes tab.

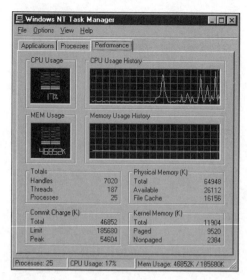

Figure 15.3 The Task Manager's Performance tab.

Performance Monitor

The NT Performance Monitor (also called the PerfMon) is a solid utility that you can use to inspect the performance and activity of processes, resources, physical components, networks, and remote machines. The use and operation of Performance Monitor is rather simple. However, knowing what metrics and counters to watch and what to do about them is not always so easy. We'll take a look at the controls and commands of PerfMon and then look into how to use it to evaluate NT's performance.

Performance Monitor has four views: Chart, Alert, Log, and Report.

The four views of the Performance Monitor are:

➤ **Chart view** Allows users to view realtime data in line graph or histogram form. (See Figure 15.4.)

➤ **Alert view** Allows users to set and view alerts and alert statistics.

➤ **Log view** Allows users to create and save a log of system performance.

➤ **Report view** Allows users to create custom reports of Performance Monitor data. All four views revolve around

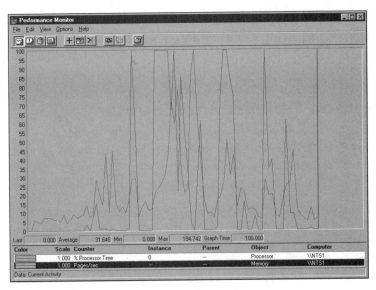

Figure 15.4   The Performance Monitor in Chart view, monitoring processor time and memory page swaps.

counters. A counter is a measurable aspect of an object used to evaluate the performance of that object. No matter which view you use, the Add To command in the Edit menu is how you add counters. When you initiate this command, a dialog box appears that allows you to select counters based on the counter's computer, object, and instance.

The following is a list of what information is required to monitor an object:

➤ **Computer** Most computers on the network provide counters that PerfMon can read and display; however, as the OS gets farther away from NT, the number of useful counters decreases.

➤ **Objects** Any component on the specified computer that can be measured, such as the processor, the memory, the physical disk, and so forth, is listed as an object.

➤ **Instances** This identifies which instance of an object should be monitored. Instance 0 is the first or only occurrence of an object, instance 1 is the second occurrence, and so on. If it is not possible for an object to have multiple instances (for example, the Workstation service), then this area is blank.

➤ **Counters** This identifies the available counters for a specific instance of an object on the chosen computer.

A cursory interaction with PerfMon might leave you baffled as to which counters are important. Because this book is geared toward passing the Workstation exam, the next section only looks at counters that matter for the test.

Common Objects And Counters

In the real world of networking, you might have to be familiar with more counters than the ones listed in this section. Fortunately, if you don't quite understand a counter, you can highlight it in the Add To dialog box and click the Explain button to get a brief but helpful definition of that counter.

Most questions that refer to PerfMon seem to focus on the following counters, so if you have a good grasp of these, the questions that deal with the PerfMon should be a breeze:

➤ **Processor: %Processor Time** When you suspect a processor upgrade is necessary, measure this counter. If the processor counter measures 80 percent or more for an extended period of time, this could be a good indication that the processor is in need of an upgrade.

➤ **System: Processor Queue Length** This can also be measured to determine if a processor upgrade is necessary. If the number of threads waiting to be processed is greater than two, the processor might be a bottleneck for the system.

➤ **Processor: Interrupts/sec.** When you suspect a hardware device is malfunctioning in the system, measure this counter. If the Processor: Interrupts/sec. increases and the processor time does not, a hardware device might be sending bogus interrupts to the processor. Locate the hardware device and replace it.

➤ **Memory: Cache Faults, Page Faults, and Pages/sec.** When you suspect that there is not enough memory in the system, these counters should be measured. They indicate how frequently your system needs to swap pages to the hard disk swap file. If this counter is high, chances are the need for memory is high as well.

➤ **PhysicalDisk/LogicalDisk: %Disk Time** When you suspect the hard disk is a system bottleneck, measure this counter—it shows you how much processor time is being spent servicing disk requests. Measure this counter against Processor: %Processor Time to see if the disk requests are using up a notable amount of processor time.

➤ **PhysicalDisk/LogicalDisk: Disk Bytes/Transfer** When you are trying to find out how fast your hard disks are transferring data, measure this counter.

➤ **PhysicalDisk/LogicalDisk: Current Disk Queue Length** When you are thinking about upgrading your hard disk, measure this counter. This counter shows you how much data is waiting to be transferred to the disk. If the disk queue is long, processes are being delayed by disk speed.

Note: The PhysicalDisk object counters apply to the entire physical storage device and are best used for suspected hardware troubleshooting. The LogicalDisk object counters focus on a specific volume and are best used for Read/Write performance investigations.

Monitoring Disk Performance

By default, the PhysicalDisk and LogicalDisk counters are not activated. The process of gathering disk counters has a significant effect on the performance of storage devices. To turn on the disk counters, you need to execute **diskperf -y** and then reboot your system. Once you complete your monitoring, turn off the disk counters with **diskperf -n** and then reboot. You must be logged on as Administrator to execute either of these commands. Until **diskperf** is executed, all PhysicalDisk and LogicalDisk counters will display a reading of **0**.

Monitoring Network Performance

Unlike Windows NT Server, Workstation has only a limited capability for analyzing network performance. A network service tool called Network Monitor Agent (NMA) gathers counter readings from network-related objects. These readings can be viewed through the Performance Monitor from the Network Segment object. Without NMA installed, these counters will report null readings. The NMA statistics can also be gathered remotely by a Windows NT Server machine running the built-in or the SMS version of Network Monitor.

Using The PerfMon Views

In the following sections, we explore the various views you can use in Performance Monitor to examine network data. These views include Chart, Alert, Log, and Report.

Using Charts

Once you've selected and added counters to your Chart view, you can make some adjustments through the Options|Chart command. This command brings up a dialog box where you can alter the maximum value of the vertical axis, change between graph and histogram, add grid lines, and change update intervals.

Configuring Alerts

You can use the Windows NT Performance Monitor to configure system alerts. For example, an administrator could be informed when a storage device approaches 85 percent capacity. To work with alerts, you must switch to the Alert view from the View menu. You add counters through the Edit|Add To Alert command (the same way they are added in Chart view). The Add To Alert dialog box is the same as the one for a chart, with the addition of an alert trigger level and program/script to run when an alert occurs.

The remaining alert configuration options are accessed through the Options|Alert command. From there, you can instruct PerfMon to switch to Alert view when an alert is triggered, write the alert in the Application log, and send a notification message to a user or machine.

Working With Logs

The Log view creates a stored record of the performance of one or more objects to be analyzed or compared at another time. You must use the Edit|Add To Log command to add objects for the log to record. Note that the Log view does not offer a selection at the counter level. It records all possible counters for the selected objects.

Once you've selected the objects to log, you need to define the update interval and file name of the log file. This is done through the Options|Log command. You will be prompted for a file name and how often to capture the counters for the objects.

Creating Reports

A report of your gathered metrics can be created through the Report view. Counters to include in a report are added the same way that counters are added in the other views, through the Edit|Add To Report command. After you select the counters to list in the report, you need to set the update interval using the Options|Report command.

Miscellaneous Commands And Controls

All PerfMon view selections have numerous commands in common, including the following:

➤ **File|Save [View] Settings As** Saves a view's settings to be used at another time.

➤ **File|Save Workspace** Saves all view settings in a single file.

➤ **File|Export** Saves the current view's captured data in a tab- or comma-delimited file.

➤ **Add|Edit** Edits the counter's parameters or settings.

➤ **Add|Delete** Removes the counter.

➤ **Options|Data From** Displays data from the active network or from a log file.

> *Note: No matter which view is being used, Performance Monitor must remain up and running (that is, as an active process) to display realtime charts, record logs, send alerts, or create reports.*

Now that we have discussed the Performance Monitor's views, let's move on to the process of baselining.

Baselining

Baselining, or establishing a baseline, is the process of recording the parameters of a fully functional system. This is done through the Log view. Once you've recorded a log of an operating system with "normal" parameters, you can use the log in the future to evaluate the performance of the system. Some objects you should include in your baseline are:

➤ Processor

➤ PhysicalDisk

➤ Memory

➤ System

➤ Any installed protocols

However, just grabbing a short interval of data won't provide a useful baseline for comparison. Instead, you should record a log file for each counter over a 24-hour interval with a counter reading 5, 10, or 15 minutes. Repeat this process for a few days or even a week. This provides you with a look into the network's performance during an entire day, covering both peak and off-peak hours. Furthermore, it is a good idea to repeat the process of collecting a baseline once a month. This not only establishes a timeline of "normal" performance, but it provides a regular interval to investigate the activity of your network. The regular inspection can help reveal new bottlenecks or failures that you would otherwise not be aware of until production came to a standstill.

NT Paging File

You should remember that NT uses disk space to expand the available memory for the system. The Virtual Memory Manager (VMM) swaps pages from physical RAM to the paging, or swap, file stored on a hard drive. Generally, the VMM handles everything about the paging file automatically, but you can control its maximum size and destination drive.

Changes to the paging file are made through the Performance tab of the System applet in the Control Panel. An area in the middle of this display tab, labeled "Virtual Memory," indicates the total size of the pagefile (see Figure 15.5). Click the Change button to alter this setting.

Through the Virtual Memory dialog box, you can change the size of the paging file on any storage device. The paging file can reside on a single drive or in areas on multiple drives. However, the overall speed of NT is determined by how fast the VMM can swap sections of memory from physical RAM to the swap file. Therefore, the speed of the storage device is important.

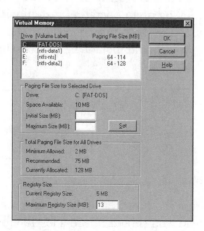

Figure 15.5 The Virtual Memory dialog box.

The two parameters you must define for each drive that will support a paging file are "initial size" and "maximum size." The initial size is the space VMM initially allocates and uses for the swap file. The maximum size is the most space the VMM will use on the drive for the paging file. The VMM is able to expand or shrink the paging file as needed between these two settings. However, neither of these settings guarantees that the disk will have enough free space for a pagefile of the specified size.

Here are some hints on how to speed up the paging file:

➤ If your system is comprised of multiple physical disks, the paging file may be spread across these disks.

➤ If you move the paging file off the drive that contains the Windows NT system files, it keeps the paging files from competing with the operating system files.

➤ As a general rule, your paging file should be the size of your physical RAM plus 12 MB. Therefore, if your machine has 32 MB of RAM, you should set the pagefile to 44 MB.

➤ While NT is operating, PAGEFILE.SYS (the name of the paging file) cannot be deleted. If for some reason the paging file is deleted, NT will re-create it during boot-up.

If your system is "thrashing"—when the disk drive is in constant activity swapping pages between the drive and physical RAM—you need to take one of the following steps to solve the problem:

➤ Add more physical RAM to your system

➤ Place your paging file on a faster storage device

➤ Spread the paging file across multiple disks

Each of these solutions is an inexpensive way to improve performance; the next step is to upgrade your motherboard and CPU.

Managing Process Priorities

NT's multiprocessing environment requires that some processes have a higher execution priority than others. The kernel handles the setting of priorities for each process and has the capability to increase or decrease the priority of a process to improve or alter how it executes. There are 32 priority levels (0 through 31). The higher-numbered priorities are executed before the lower numbered priorities.

Although the system has the capability to use all 32 levels directly, you have only a limited ability to set priorities. By default, all user- and administrator-launched applications are assigned a base priority of **8** (**/normal**). However, users can launch applications with **4** (**/low**) or **13** (**/high**) priority and an administrator can launch with **24** (**/realtime**) priority. To launch an application with an alternate priority level, use the following syntax at a command prompt:

```
start [/low|/normal|/high|/realtime] application
```

NT offers two other priority controls to alter the levels of running processes. The first is a slide bar to control the performance boost for foreground applications. A foreground application is the process that is the active window on your screen, usually indicated by a colored title bar. This slide control is located on the Performance tab in the System applet in the Control Panel (see Figure 15.5, shown earlier in this chapter). By default, foreground applications have a priority of **10** (maximum). You can move the slider to set foregrounds with an additional priority level of **1** (middle tick) or **0** (none).

The second control is accessed via the Task Manager. By selecting any of the listed processes on the Process tab or any application on the Applications tab, you can change the priority to low, normal, high, or paused through the View|Update Speed command in the menu bar. On the Processes tab, you can change the priority of a selected process to low, normal, high, or realtime with the Set Priority command located in the right-click pop-up menu.

Exam Prep Questions

Question 1

Which of the following is the best way to establish a baseline for system performance counters?

○ a. Capture performance counters from the System object for 30 minutes during nonworking hours.

○ b. Capture performance counters from the System object for 30 minutes during the peak hour, capture performance counters from the System object for 30 minutes during a nonworking hour, and then average these two measurements.

○ c. Capture performance counters from the System object for 30 minutes each day at a preselected time for a week.

○ d. Capture performance counters from the System object at regular intervals throughout the day for three days.

Answer a will not provide an adequate baseline because the captured data covers only a brief off-peak interval. Therefore, answer a is incorrect. Answer b will not provide an adequate baseline because the captured data represents only a brief off-peak and peak interval. Furthermore, the averaging of the times makes the data even more useless. Therefore, answer b is incorrect. Answer c will not provide an adequate baseline because recording a brief period every day does not reflect the overall picture of the network activity. Therefore, answer c is incorrect. **Answer d will provide an adequate baseline because the data collected will represent all levels of use over a multiple-day period. Therefore, answer d is correct.**

Question 2

You want to monitor PhysicalDisk performance counters of a local drive. With a standard installation of Windows NT Workstation, what additional operation must be performed to enable the
monitoring of the PhysicalDisk counters?

- ○ a. Install Network Monitor Agent.
- ○ b. Run the **diskperf** utility with the **-y** option.
- ○ c. Install Network Monitor Agent and run the **diskperf** utility
  with the **-n** option.
- ○ d. No additional operations are required. The PhysicalDisk
  counters are accessible by default.

The Network Monitor Agent is not required to monitor PhysicalDisk performance counters. It is only needed to access Network Segment object
counters. Therefore, answer a is incorrect. The "diskperf -y" command is
needed to enable the PhysicalDisk counters. Therefore, answer b is correct. The Network Monitor is not required, but the **diskperf** command is;
however the -n option turns off the PhysicalDisk counters. Therefore, answer c is incorrect. The **diskperf** command is required because PhysicalDisk
counters are not enabled by default. They must be turned on before PerfMon
can access them. Therefore, answer d is incorrect.

Question 3

As a domain user on a Windows NT Workstation, what priority
levels can you set for the process you launch? [Check all correct
answers]

- ❏ a. Realtime (**24**)
- ❏ b. High (**13**)
- ❏ c. Normal (**8**)
- ❏ d. Low (**4**)
- ❏ e. System (**32**)

Only administrators have the privilege of setting process priority to Realtime.
Therefore, answer a is incorrect. As a non-administrator, any user can set a
priority process of High, Normal, or Low. Therefore, answers b, c, and d

are correct. Only the system itself can launch processes with the highest level of priority—System—therefore, answer e is incorrect.

Question 4

Which of the following utilities can be used to display the current level of CPU utilization? [Check all correct answers]

❑ a. Performance Monitor

❑ b. Network Monitor

❑ c. Task Manager

❑ d. Windows NT Diagnostics

❑ e. Server Manager

The Performance Monitor can display the Processor CPU Utilization counter. Therefore, answer a is correct. Network Monitor and Server Manager are NT Server tools not found on NT Workstation. Therefore, answers b and e are incorrect. The Task Manager displays CPU utilization. Therefore, answer c is correct. Windows NT Diagnostics cannot display CPU utilization. Therefore, answer d is incorrect. Thus, only answers a and c are correct.

Question 5

Which view available through Performance Monitor should you use to create a baseline?

○ a. Chart

○ b. Log

○ c. Report

○ d. Graph

Chart view displays the realtime values of counters but cannot record the data as it is gathered. Therefore, answer a is incorrect. Log view records object counters and should be used to create a baseline. Therefore, answer b is correct. Report view creates a snapshot of the performance levels of counters from realtime gathering or a recorded log. Therefore, answer c is incorrect. Graph is not a view but rather a display selection in the Chart view. Therefore, answer d is incorrect.

Question 6

Users on your peer-to-peer network are experiencing up to twice the normal time to access files from your NT Workstation, but all other activities are relatively unaffected. Your system has three physical hard disks with two partitions on each. Which of the following is the best type of object counter to monitor in order to investigate this problem?

O a. System object counters

O b. LogicalDisk object counters

O c. Server object counters

O d. PhysicalDisk object counters

O e. Memory object counters

System, Server, and Memory object counters will provide little help toward a storage device performance problem. Therefore, answers a, c, and e are incorrect. **LogicalDisk object counters are the best selection because they will provide data on space usage and levels of Read/Write activities on volumes. Therefore, answer b is correct.** PhysicalDisk object counters are useful for hardware troubleshooting and affect an entire drive. The question focuses on the time to access files within a partition and not necessarily the entire drive, making the LogicalDisk counters more effective. Therefore, answer d is incorrect.

Question 7

After an application has been launched, which of the following are possible settings for the priority level on the Applications tab of the Task Manager? [Check all correct answers]

❏ a. Low

❏ b. Realtime

❏ c. System

❏ d. Normal

❏ e. Kernel

❏ f. High

Low, High, and Normal are three of the four selections available on the Applications tab—the fourth is Pause. Therefore, answers a, d, and f are correct. Realtime is only available on the Process right-click pop-up menu. Therefore, answer b is incorrect. There are no System or Kernel priority settings. Therefore, answers c and e are incorrect. Thus, only answers a, d, and f are correct.

Question 8

> Which are possible functions of the Task Manager? [Check all correct answers]
>
> ❏ a. Switch the foreground application
>
> ❏ b. View committed memory changes
>
> ❏ c. Launch new processes
>
> ❏ d. Set the increase in priority for foreground applications
>
> ❏ e. View multiple CPUs in separate graphs

The Task Manager is able to switch the foreground application, view committed memory changes, launch new processes, and view multiple CPUs in separate graphs. Therefore, answers a, b, c, and e are correct. The Task Manger cannot set the increase in priority for foreground applications. This is done through the System applet. Therefore, answer d is incorrect.

Question 9

> You just doubled the size of your server's physical RAM to 128 MB. The pagefile is currently hosted on the same drive as the NT system files, not on the drive containing only your user data files. What change should be made to your pagefile?
>
> ○ a. No change to the pagefile size is recommended, but it should be placed on the data drive.
>
> ○ b. The pagefile should be increased to 140 MB and placed on the data drive.
>
> ○ c. The pagefile should be increased by 12 MB.
>
> ○ d. The pagefile should be increased to 140 MB.

The pagefile size is recommended to be the size of physical RAM plus 12 MB. Therefore, answer a is incorrect. **The pagefile should be 140 MB and placed on a different drive than the one hosting the system files if possible. Therefore, answer b is correct.** The pagefile should be the size of physical RAM plus 12 MB. Therefore, answer c is incorrect. The pagefile should be 140 MB and placed on a different drive than the one hosting the system files if possible. Therefore, answer d is incorrect. **You have to read this question carefully to be able to determine that you need to add 12 MB to the 128 MB of installed RAM and that it should reside on a different drive. Always read the questions (and answers) carefully!**

Question 10

What can be done to improve performance on an NT Workstation computer if excessive paging is occurring? [Check all correct answers]

❑ a. Add more physical RAM.

❑ b. Reduce the size of the paging file.

❑ c. Spread the paging file across several drives.

❑ d. Move the paging file to a drive other than the one hosting the NT system files.

Adding more RAM, using multiple drives, and avoiding the boot partition are all methods of improving performance due to excessive paging. Therefore, answers a, c, and d are correct. Reducing the size of the paging file will degrade performance further and possibly prevent the system from functioning properly. Therefore, answer b is incorrect.

Need To Know More?

Boyce, Jim, et al.: *Windows NT Workstation 4.0 Advanced Technical Reference.* Que, Indianapolis, IN, 1996. ISBN 0-7897-0863-9. Chapter 8 discusses the Performance Monitor and has a brief section on the Task Manager.

Perkins, Charles, Matthew Strebe, and James Chellis: *MCSE: NT Workstation Study Guide.* Sybex Network Press, San Francisco, CA, 1997. ISBN 0-7821-1973-5. Chapter 14 has detailed information about Performance Monitor and using its features to optimize your system.

Search the TechNet CD (or its online version through www.microsoft.com) and the *Windows NT Workstation Resource Kit* CD using the keywords "performance," "process priorities," "pagefile," and "Task Manager."

Application Subsystem Architecture

16

Terms you'll need to understand:

√ Environment subsystem

√ Win32 subsystem

√ POSIX subsystem

√ OS/2 subsystem

√ Virtual DOS Machine (VDM)

√ Virtual Device Driver (VDD)

√ Windows-On-Windows (WOW)

Techniques you'll need to master:

√ Understanding the Windows NT Workstation system architecture

√ Knowing how older applications run on Windows NT Workstation

Windows NT Workstation is a 32-bit Windows operating system. In addition to supporting Win32 applications, NT can host Win16, DOS, OS/2, and POSIX applications. The range of support varies for each type of application. In this chapter, we examine the details you need to know for the Workstation exam regarding the application subsystems.

The Windows NT Environmental Subsystems

Windows NT has three environmental subsystems that provide application support (see Figure 16.1): the Win32 subsystem, the POSIX subsystem, and the OS/2 subsystem.

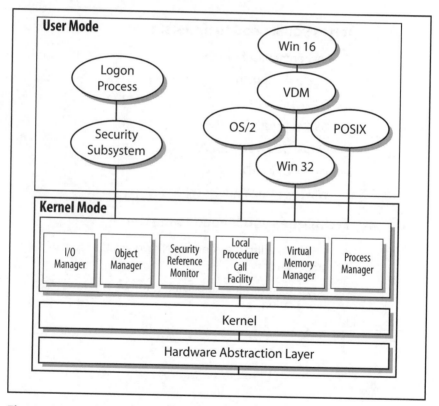

Figure 16.1 The location of the subsystems in the overall architecture of NT.

The Win32 Subsystem

The Win32 subsystem handles support for 32-bit Windows applications (Win32 applications). This subsystem is also called the "CSR" or "client/server" subsystem. Win32 applications run directly in the Win32 subsystem.

This subsystem also maintains the display settings and manages user input from all applications. Character-based screen I/O used by OS/2 and POSIX applications are mapped by their respective subsystems to functions supported by the Win32 subsystem.

The Win32 subsystem boasts the following features:

➤ **32 bit** This system is a 32-bit architecture.

➤ **Threads** Multiple execution threads are supported for each process, and these threads are scheduled preemptively.

➤ **Large address space** Each application within this subsystem is assigned a 2 GB continuous, nonsegmented address space—the actual memory used by a process is control by the Virtual Memory Manager (VMM).

➤ **Memory protection** Each Win32 application is protected and separated from every other application in the NT environment. Each application perceives itself as the only active process within the computer.

➤ **OpenGL** An industry software interface standard for 2-D and 3-D graphics.

Within the Win32 subsystem can exist VDMs or Virtual DOS Machines. These are Win32 processes that support DOS applications. VDMs are discussed in the next section.

DOS And Virtual DOS Machines (VDMs)

Windows NT supports DOS applications through Virtual DOS Machines (VDMs). A VDM is a Win32 application that creates an operational environment for DOS applications. This environment resembles a DOS-only computer and fools DOS applications into thinking that they have direct and unrestricted access to the computer hardware. Every DOS application is given its own single-threaded VDM, where it perceives itself as the only process on the computer.

However, not all DOS application can operate within NT. Those DOS applications that make direct hardware-level function calls are not allowed to continue functioning. Only those applications that NT can intercept hardware calls through the use of Virtual Device Drivers (VDDs) can continue operation within a VDM. Therefore, DOS support is limited to the programming method of the application itself.

There are four components used to create and control VDMs:

➤ **NTVDM.EXE** The protected mode executable that translates DOS resource requests into Win32 requests.

➤ **NTIO.SYS and NTDOS.SYS** The NT equivalents of IO.SYS and MSDOS.SYS. These operate within the VDM in real mode.

➤ **VDMREDIR.DLL** The redirector that directs file system and I/O requests to the Win32 subsystem.

The default environment found within a VDM can be configured by modifying the CONFIG.NT and AUTOEXEC.NT files. These are the equivalent to the CONFIG.SYS and AUTOEXEC.SYS files found on MS-DOS machines. However, fine-tuning for each DOS application can be performed through the executable's properties. In effect, you are modifying the app's Program Information File (PIF), which appears as a shortcut for the application. The next time you need to use the DOS app, use the new shortcut to launch the application and your customized settings will be used.

The Properties dialog box for a DOS application has four additional tabs not found on Win32 applications. Basic familiarity with these tabs is the only requirement for the Workstation exam; these settings are the same as those found on Windows 95 (the Windows 95 exam focuses heavily on these settings).

The four tabs for the DOS Properties dialog box are:

➤ **Font** Font type of bitmap or True Type is selected along with the font's size for the DOS window.

➤ **Memory** The memory environment is defined, including XMS (expanded), EMS (extended), and DMPI (protected).

➤ **Screen** Sets the window size, toolbar visibility, and performance emulation.

➤ **Misc** A conglomeration of options: screen saver, suspend, mouse control, and reservation of Windows shortcut key sequences.

Each time a DOS application is launched, a VDM is created. When a DOS application terminates, the VDM is not destroyed by NT and its memory and system pointers are maintained. When a subsequent DOS application is launched, it assumes the existing VDM. Therefore, if multiple DOS applications are launched concurrently and then existed, some system resources will be tied up in maintaining each of the VDMs. VDMs are only destroyed by terminating the VDM process itself or rebooting NT.

Within a VDM, a WOW environment can exist that supports Win16 applications. This is discussed in the next section.

Win16 And WOW

Windows 16-bit applications (Win16 applications) are supported through a DOS application called Windows-On-Windows (WOW). WOW executes within a VDM, which itself runs as a Win32 process. This configuration is used to mimic the Windows 3.x environment where Windows runs on top of DOS; thus, the applications are "fooled" into thinking they are operating within a Win16 environment. All Win16 applications operate within a single instance of WOW, unlike DOS apps, which operate within separate VDMs. This mimics the Windows 3.x environment where Win16 apps share a memory space and computer resources. Therefore, just like on Windows 3.x, Win16 applications can interact and interfere with other Win16 applications. If a Win16 application fails or corrupts the system resources of a WOW, this will not affect the operation of NT itself or any other VDMs or Win32 processes.

All applications within a Win16 WOW environment operate in a cooperative, multitasking environment—each app controls processing time until it chooses to release control. However, because WOW is within a VDM, which itself is a single-threaded Win32 process, the entire WOW environment is preemptively multitasked with all other Win32 threads.

WOW is constructed within a VDM, and the components involved in this creation are:

➤ **KRNL386.EXE** A modified version of Windows 3.1 that functions under NT. Most of the system functions are passed to the Win32 subsystem by this component.

➤ **USER.EXE** A modified version of the Windows 3.1 USER.EXE that directs API calls to the Win32 subsystem.

➤ **GDI.EXE** A modified version of the Windows 3.1 GDI.EXE that renders graphic calls into Win32 calls.

➤ **WOWEXEC.EXE** Establishes the Windows 3.1 emulation within a VDM.

Win16 applications are launched within the same instance of WOW by default. However, it is possible to launch Win16 applications in their own individual instances of WOW by modifying their PIFs or indicating this parameter from a Run instruction or command prompt. When multiple WOWs are in use, Clipboard data from one WOW app cannot be transferred into another WOW app because they no longer share resource space.

The OS/2 Subsystem

Windows NT provides a low level of OS/2 support for the purpose of complying with government purchase regulations. The support is only for OS/2 1.x applications. There is no support for the popular 2.x+ GUI applications with which most OS/2 users are familiar. An extension component enables some graphics support for the launching of Presentation Manager. The OS/2 subsystem operates alongside the Win32 subsystem, but some system calls are sent to the Win32 subsystem instead of directly to the Executive Services.

The OS/2 subsystem is constructed with the following components:

➤ **OS2SS.EXE** The main component of the OS/2 subsystem. It adapts services provided by Win32 and the NT Executive Services to the OS/2 environment.

➤ **OS2SRV.EXE** Launches OS/2 applications.

➤ **OS2.EXE** A Win32-based program that passes the name of OS/2 applications and any command-line parameters to OS2SRV.EXE.

➤ **NETAPI.DLL and DOSCALLS.DLL** Windows NT files that support OS/2 program APIs.

Some applications are compiled to function within DOS or OS/2—they are called "bound applications." Such programs will be launched into the OS/2 subsystem unless the FORCEDOS.EXE utility is used to force the bound application to be launched into a VDM.

The POSIX Subsystem

Windows NT provides a low level of POSIX support for the purpose of complying with government purchase regulations. The support is only for POSIX.1 character-based applications. Like the OS/2 subsystem, the

POSIX subsystem runs alongside and makes some system calls through the Win32 subsystem.

The POSIX subsystem is constructed with the following components:

➤ **PSXSS.EXE** The main component of the POSIX subsystem. It starts when the first POSIX application is loaded.

➤ **POSIX.EXE** Similar to OS2.EXE, POSIX.EXE is a Win32-based program that passes information between the Executive Services and the subsystem it supports.

➤ **PXSDLL.DLL** Handles communication between each POSIX application and the POSIX subsystem. This Dynamic Link Library (DLL) contains support for the C routines that POSIX applications expect.

To establish the POSIX 1.-compliance of Windows NT, the following support was added to the POSIX subsystem:

➤ **Case-sensitive naming** NTFS supports the case-sensitive naming of files though the preservation of file name case. This means that files named Text.txt, TEXT.txt, and text.txt are all different within the POSIX subsystem. Windows NT still views these files as the same, because by default it is not case sensitive.

➤ **Hard links** NTFS also supports the storage of multiple file names for a single file, called hard links.

➤ **POSIX.1 library compliance** POSIX.DLL supports POSIX library complacence for applications making C program calls.

Windows NT has a very limited support of POSIX. Therefore, most Unix applications will not operate under the POSIX subsystem.

Exam Prep Questions

Question 1

> Windows NT provides support for what types of applications?
> [Check all correct answers]
>
> ❏ a. POSIX
>
> ❏ b. Win16
>
> ❏ c. DOS
>
> ❏ d. MacOS
>
> ❏ e. Win32
>
> ❏ f. OS/2
>
> ❏ g. Solaris

Windows NT provides application support for POSIX, Win16, DOS, , Win32, and OS/2. Therefore, answers a, b, c, e, and f are correct. NT does not provide support for MacOS or Solaris applications. Therefore, answers d and g are incorrect.

Question 2

> Which subsystem do all the application subsystems interact with in some form?
>
> ○ a. WOW
>
> ○ b. VDM
>
> ○ c. Win32
>
> ○ d. POSIX
>
> ○ e. OS/2

The Win32 subsystem is used or interacted with by all the subsystems within Windows NT. Therefore, answer c is correct. WOW, POSIX, and OS/2 are only used by their respective applications. Therefore, answers a, d, and e are incorrect. VDM is used by WOW, but not by the other subsystems. Therefore, answer b is incorrect.

Question 3

> Which of the following subsystems employ the use of threaded execution? [Check all correct answers]
>
> ❑ a. Win32
>
> ❑ b. WOW/Win16
>
> ❑ c. VDM/DOS
>
> ❑ d. POSIX
>
> ❑ e. OS/2

All the subsystems within NT are executed through threads. Therefore, answers a, b, c, d, and e are correct. Even though a VDM (and subsequently WOW) uses only a single thread, it is still a threaded execution.

Question 4

> How large is the memory address space assigned to each process by the Win32 subsystem?
>
> ○ a. 32 MB
>
> ○ b. 2 MB
>
> ○ c. 4 GB
>
> ○ d. 2 GB

The Win32 subsystem assigns a 2 GB address space to each process it launches. Therefore, answer d is correct.

Question 5

> All DOS applications are launched within a single VDM.
>
> ○ a. True
>
> ○ b. False

The correct answer is b, false. Each DOS application is launched within its own VDM.

Question 6

> How can the DOS environment of VDMs be modified? [Check all correct answers]
>
> ❑ a. By changing the DOS executable's PIF
>
> ❑ b. By editing the CONFIG.NT
>
> ❑ c. Through the VDM Manager
>
> ❑ d. Through Environment tab in the System applet
>
> ❑ e. By altering AUTOEXEC.NT

DOS VDM environments can be modified by altering the PIF, CONFIG.NT, and AUTOEXEC.NT. Therefore, answers a, b, and e are correct. There isn't a VDM Manager, and the System applet does not affect VDMs. Therefore, answers c and d are incorrect.

Question 7

> What other two subsystems are required or used by WOW? [Check two answers]
>
> ❑ a. Win32
>
> ❑ b. VDM
>
> ❑ c. POSIX
>
> ❑ d. OS/2

The WOW subsystem is launched within a VDM, which is itself launched within Win32. Therefore, answers a and b are correct. POSIX and OS/2 are not associated with WOW in any way. Therefore, answers c and d are incorrect.

Question 8

> If a Win16 application corrupts its memory space and hangs, NT will need to be rebooted to restore the system.
>
> ○ a. True
>
> ○ b. False

This statement is false, so the correct answer is b. A Win16 application will only cause other Win16 applications within the same WOW to fail, it will not affect NT or any other separate subsystem. Stalled Win16 applications are resolved by terminating the WOW environment.

Question 9

OS/2 and POSIX support are included in NT, but at what level?

- ○ a. Complete support for both systems as available at the release of NT
- ○ b. Full graphical support
- ○ c. Text-only level or version 1

OS/2 and POSIX support is limited to text only or version/level 1. Therefore, answer c is the only correct answer.

Question 10

Which of the following is not true about Win16 applications?

- ○ a. Operates within a VDM
- ○ b. Can be launched in a separate memory space
- ○ c. All system calls are handled through the Win32 subsystem
- ○ d. Direct hardware-level resource requests are possible

Win16 applications operate within a VDM and can be launched in a separate memory space. Also, all system calls within Win16 application are processed by the Win32 subsystem. Therefore, answers a, b, and c are incorrect. **Win16 applications cannot make direct hardware-level resource requests**—this is a limitation of VDM and NT itself. Therefore, answer d is correct.

Need To Know More?

Perkins, Charles, Matthew Strebe, and James Chellis: *MCSE: NT Workstation Study Guide.* Sybex Network Press, San Francisco, CA, 1997. ISBN 0-7821-1973-5. Chapter 15 discusses the application support through subsystems found in Windows NT.

Search the TechNet CD (or its online version through www.microsoft.com) and *the Windows NT Workstation Resource Kit* CD using the keywords "subsystem," "Win32," "Win16," "WOW," "VDM," "OS/2," and "POSIX."

Booting Windows NT

Terms you'll need to understand:

✓ Boot

✓ Boot up

✓ Bootstrap

✓ Bootstrap loader

✓ ARC names

✓ ARC path names

✓ MBR (Master Boot Record)

✓ BOOT.INI

✓ NTLDR

✓ NTDETECT.COM

✓ NTBOOTDD.SYS

✓ Boot partition or boot drive

✓ System partition or system drive

Techniques you'll need to master:

✓ How to edit the BOOT.INI file

✓ How to interpret and construct Advanced RISC
  Computer (ARC) device and path names

✓ How to troubleshoot the Windows NT boot sequence

Starting up a computer from scratch involves a lot more work, as well as many more parts, than might immediately be expected. Because a computer that won't boot is a dead computer, it's essential to understand the Windows NT boot process and where that process can go awry.

In this chapter, we walk you through the Windows NT boot process, explain the important pieces, and explore some things that can derail this process. Along the way, you'll get to know more about how computers work, in general. You'll also learn what's involved in fully completing Windows NT's intricate boot process in order to pass that section of the Workstation exam.

Bootstrapping A Computer

When you boot a computer that has Windows NT installed, the machine goes through a number of steps before an operating system (OS) can be selected. And if Windows NT is selected, a number of additional steps follow before the login prompt dialog box appears.

The initial phase, called the bootstrap process, covers the steps necessary to turn a computer from a lump of inert metal and plastic into a device that is ready to accept and react to input. For ordinary PCs, this consists of the following steps:

1. **Power-on the computer, or initiate startup** This one is easy—it requires only that the computer be plugged in and that you turn the power switch to "on." For Windows NT, the startup process also can be initiated when you click Restart The Computer in the Shut Down Windows dialog box (Start|Shut Down), or when you select the Shutdown tab followed by Shutdown And Restart through the Windows NT Security dialog box, which is always available by entering Ctrl+Alt+Del while Windows NT is running.

2. **Power-On Self-Test (POST) processing** Once the computer begins its startup process, it performs a number of built-in diagnostics and hardware tests to make sure all its components are working properly. This is driven by firmware on the motherboard through the BIOS (and might involve other BIOSs such as those typically found on graphics adapters) once the on-board BIOS completes its checks. This produces all the messages and status information that flash on your screen while the computer is going through the hardware check stages of startup. POST also determines how much RAM is available on the machine and checks to make sure essential peripherals (keyboard, mouse, and so on) are present and connected.

3. **Initial startup process** Once the hardware has been checked out, the initial startup process exhausts the on-board diagnostics and self-check capabilities of most computers. At this point, some real software must be read from disk to continue the boot process, which requires that an OS establish a runtime environment for the computer to be loaded.

If you are booting from a floppy, the first sector on the disk contains the Partition Boot sector; if you are booting from a hard disk, the first sector contains the Master Boot Record (MBR) and the partition table. These records contain the information that allows the computer to obtain boot information; they also provide a map for how the hard disk (or floppy) is physically arranged.

The MBR is probably the most important record on any hard disk. It contains the partition table that describes a disk's physical layout and arrangement, and it includes a small program that examines the partition table and identifies the system partition. The program then locates the system partition's starting address on disk (sector 0) and loads a copy of the Partition Boot sector into memory.

Once this step is complete, the program transfers execution to another program, usually an operating system loader, run from code included in the Partition Boot sector just loaded. This partition is identified in the partition table by being marked as the "active partition," which indicates that it is the partition to which control should next be passed during the boot process.

 Warning! It's essential to recognize that the files that reside in the system partition on a drive are the files needed to boot a computer and some operating systems, whereas the files that reside in what Microsoft calls "the boot partition" on a drive are those files needed to run Windows NT. Therefore, the boot files—that is, NTLDR, BOOT.INI, NTDETECT.COM, and so on—reside in the system partition, whereas the Windows NT OS files—including NTOSKRNL.EXE and the Windows NT Kernel—reside on the boot partition. Get it?

4. **Boot loader process** When the Partition Boot Sector code is loaded, a program runs that brings up a designated operating system—or, as with Windows NT's NTLDR program, it provides a menu of load choices. This starts an execution sequence for full-blown programs from files on-disk (as opposed to code embedded in the MBR or a Partition Boot Sector). This ultimately results in the complete loading of an operating system, after which the computer will be ready to run applications or services on demand.

 Windows NT also runs on RISC CPUs as well as on generic PCs. The boot process differs for RISC machines to some degree. We'll point out these differences in tips as we step through the rest of this process. The primary difference, as far as the bootstrap process is concerned, is that once a RISC computer completes its POST routines, built-in firmware selects a startup disk by reading a boot precedence table from nonvolatile RAM on the machine. This identifies the system partition (where the boot files reside) and indicates if a floppy may be used as an alternative boot selection. The information in nonvolatile RAM also indicates where the OSLOADER.EXE program, which loads Windows NT on a RISC system, resides as well as the folder that contains the OS to be booted.

This marks the point at which the bootstrap process is complete, and the point at which activities specific to the OS to be booted begin. Once NTLDR is loaded into memory, it is possible to choose an OS (or multiple versions of the same OS, one of which is definitely Windows NT). The steps that follow assume Windows NT is selected as the operating system to boot:

1. **Selecting the OS** When NTLDR executes, it reads another important Windows NT boot file, BOOT.INI, which we discuss in detail later. BOOT.INI provides information about choices of operating systems, defines their locations on-disk, and assigns some important default characteristics for the load process. This information makes it possible to boot a Windows NT machine without requiring user intervention; therefore, keyboard input is not strictly required to start up a Windows NT machine. We now will choose a version of Windows NT in the loader menu to begin the process of loading Windows NT.

 At this point in the process for RISC machines, the program that loads is named OSLOADER.EXE. It performs all the functions supplied for PCs by NTLDR, NTDETECT.COM, and BOOTSECT.DOS.

2. **Detecting hardware** Now the Windows NT program NTDETECT. COM executes. This is a hardware recognition program that collects a list of currently installed components and returns the information to NTLDR. NTLDR will not run, however, unless you select a version of Windows NT on the boot loader screen (or the default selection is Windows NT and the timer times out). The following message appears:

```
NTDETECT V1.0 Checking Hardware . . .
```

3. **Choosing a load configuration** Once NTDETECT finishes its job, the boot loader resumes control and the following message appears:

```
OS Loader V4.0

Press spacebar now to invoke Hardware Profile/
   Last Known Good Configuration menu.
```

The boot loader waits several seconds to give you time to press the spacebar. If it isn't pressed and only one hardware profile is defined for the computer (which is typical, except for laptops), the boot loader loads Windows NT's default configuration. Otherwise, you can elect to use an alternative hardware profile here (for laptops, this usually means selecting Networked or Detached hardware profiles) or switch to the Last Known Good Configuration menu, which permits you to boot Windows NT using the Registry values defined the last time the machine booted successfully.

4. **Loading the Windows NT Kernel** Once the configuration or Registry versions have been identified (or chosen by default, as is most often the case), the next step is to load the OS Kernel for Windows NT. A sequence of periods appears on screen as the boot loader loads NTOSKRNL.EXE and the Hardware Abstraction Layer (HAL.DLL) into memory.

 On RISC machines, OSLOADER.EXE handles everything through this step. It concludes by loading the appropriate version of NTOSKRNL.EXE and HAL.DLL for the CPU in use. The remaining steps are identical, whether the machine is a PC clone or a RISC computer.

5. **Initializing the Kernel** When the PC's screen turns blue and displays a message similar to the following:

```
Microsoft (R) Windows NT (TM) Version 4.0 (Build 1381)
1 System Processor (64 MB Memory)
```

This indicates that the Kernel has initialized properly and has taken control. At this point, Windows NT is running the computer.

During Kernel initialization, the following tasks are completed:

➤ Initializing low-level device drives loaded with the Kernel in the preceding step

➤ Loading and initializing other device drivers as needed

➤ Running diagnostic or setup programs such as CHKDSK before loading services

➤ Loading and initializing all services identified with automatic startup in the OS configuration

➤ Creating the paging file for temporary storage and swap space

➤ Starting all subsystems needed for Windows NT (such as the Win32 subsystem, security subsystem, and possibly the OS/2 or POSIX subsystems)

6. **Logging on** When Kernel initialization is complete, the Begin Logon dialog box appears (this contains the message "Press Ctrl+Alt+Delete to log on"). Once a successful logon occurs, Windows writes the values in the Registry to a special backup file that provides the data needed to invoke the Last Known Good Configuration boot option the next time the machine starts up (a successful logon is required to make this change because numerous Registry values will not be updated until the first actual logon occurs).

The Windows NT Boot Components

The most important components of the Windows NT boot process are worth memorizing:

➤ **BOOT.INI** This is the PC information file that describes Windows NT boot defaults as well as operating system locations, settings, and menu selections. This file resides in the root directory of the system partition.

➤ **BOOTSECT.DOS** This MS-DOS boot sector file is used if NTLDR offers the option to boot to some other Microsoft (or near-equivalent) operating system, such as DOS or Windows 95. This file resides in the root directory of the system partition.

➤ **NTDETECT.COM** This is the PC hardware detection program that gathers equipment and configuration information prior to booting Windows NT (to make sure the stored configuration agrees with the detected one). This file resides in the root directory of the system partition.

➤ **NTLDR** This is the PC operating system loader program, that loads Windows NT or another designated operating system and then relinquishes control once loading is complete. This file resides in the root directory of the system partition.

➤ **NTOSKRNL.EXE** This is the executable file for Windows NT that includes all the basic capabilities and components necessary to establish a working run-time environment. This file resides in the \Winnt_root\system32 directory on the boot partition.

➤ **OSLOADER.EXE** This is the OS loader program for RISC computers, which performs the same functions as NTLDR does for Intel-based systems.

One other PC-based Windows NT boot file that sometimes crops up in test questions is NTBOOTDD.SYS. It must be present when a SCSI drive, with its on-board BIOS disabled, is used as the system partition or the boot partition on a Windows NT system. This file replaces the functions the on-board BIOS would normally provide with a software-based driver. Like the other boot files, NTBOOTDD.SYS resides in the root directory of the system partition.

ARC Names And Attached Hard Drives

To fully understand the ins and outs of the BOOT.INI file, which drives much of NTLDR's behavior during the Windows NT boot process, it is essential to understand what Microsoft calls "Advanced RISC Computer (ARC) names" (and sometimes, ARC path names). ARC represents a common naming convention used within disk controller software to specify the unique combination of disk controller, disk drive, and disk partition that identifies the system and boot partitions for Windows NT. These names appear in the BOOT.INI file and must sometimes be edited, particularly during recovery from failure of the primary member of a mirrored or duplexed drive pair.

ARC names not only provide a method to specify the type and location of the disk controllers, drives, and partitions in use, but they also include pointers to files and directories. Such names typically take one of two forms:

```
scsi(0)disk(0)rdisk(0)partition(1)\path
multi(0)disk(0)rdisk(0)partition(1)\path
```

Here's a breakdown of the terms involved:

➤ **scsi(*) or multi(*)** Normally, most ARC names begin with "multi(*)"; "scsi(*)" appears only when a SCSI controller with its on-board BIOS disabled is in use. **multi(*)** is used for other hard disks of all kinds, including IDE, EIDE, ESDI, and SCSI (where the on-board BIOS is enabled, as is most often the case). The (*) indicates the address of the hardware adapter from which to boot, numbered ordinally, beginning with zero. Controller numbers begin at zero; therefore, the card closest to bus slot zero on the motherboard is the first controller and is assigned the controller number of zero; the next card is the second controller and is assigned the controller number of one, and so on.

➤ **disk(*)** This portion of the name applies only when the **scsi(*)** keyword appears. In that case, the value of (*) indicates the SCSI bus ID (usually 0 to 6) for the drive where the designated files reside. If the ARC name begins with the **multi(*)** keyword, the value of **disk(*)** is always **disk(0)**.

➤ **rdisk(*)** This portion of the name applies only when the **multi(*)** keyword appears. It either indicates the SCSI logical unit number (LUN) for the drive or selects the position in the chain of hard disks attached to the controller where the designated files reside. Here again, numbering begins with zero; therefore, the first drive in the chain is named **rdisk(0)**, the second **rdisk(1)**, and so on.

➤ **partition(*)** This portion of the name indicates the disk partition that contains the designated files. Unlike the other numbering schemes in

ARC names, partition numbers begin with one; therefore, the first partition is **partition(1)**, the second is **partition(2)**, and so on.

Please note that for PCs, a maximum of four partitions per drive is allowed. But one of those partitions can be something called an "extended partition," which simply means that more than one logical drive can be created within that partition. The other three (or four, if no extended partition exists) are called primary partitions and can have only one logical drive per partition.

There are two important things to remember about primary and extended partitions. First, only a primary partition can be a system partition (where boot files reside and initial boot phases occur), but Windows NT system files (the boot partition) can reside on a logical drive within an extended partition. Second, on a drive with primary and extended partitions, the extended partition is always numbered the highest. If a test question indicates that NT files reside on an extended partition and a new primary has been defined, this means the partition number for the extended partition increases by one as a result of that new definition.

➤ **\path** Indicates the directory (or subdirectory) on the partition where the operating system files can be found. The default path for Windows NT is \winnt.

Working with ARC names requires understanding the rules by which they're to be applied or interpreted. Remember that **scsi(*)** appears only for SCSI controllers with their on-board BIOSs disabled, and that numbering for **scsi(*)**, **multi(*)**, **disk(*)**, and **rdisk(*)** starts with zero, but numbering for **partition(*)** starts with one. Also, remember that when **multi(*)** appears, **disk(0)** is the only valid value, and that when **scsi(*)** appears, **rdisk(0)** is likewise the only valid value. These three rules, properly applied, will see you through the ARC name questions.

Managing The BOOT.INI File

You can make changes to BOOT.INI from the Startup/Shutdown tab of the System applet or by using a text editor. If problems occur as a result of these changes, always make backup a copy of the file to a floppy. Here's an example of a typical BOOT.INI file (without most of the many possible bells and whistles):

```
[boot loader]
timeout=30
default=multi(0)disk(0)rdisk(0)partition(3)\WINNT
[operating systems]
multi(0)disk(0)rdisk(0)partition(3)\WINNT="Windows NT
Workstation Version 4.00"
multi(0)disk(0)rdisk(0)partition(3)\WINNT="Windows NT
Workstation Version 4.00 [VGA mode]" /basevideo /sos
C:\ = "MS-DOS"
```

Note that this file is divided into two sections labeled **[boot loader]** and **[operating systems]**. The **[boot loader]** section supplies the **timeout** interval after which the default operating system to load (defined in the **default=** line that follows **timeout**) loads automatically. The **[operating systems]** section supplies the complete menu of operating system choices NTLDR displays after the program loads. You can disable the timer before it elapses by striking any arrow or letter key on the keyboard. Then, you can wait as long as you like to make your menu selection.

Using The Control Panel

Using the System applet Control Panel to change BOOT.INI is definitely the safest method, but it doesn't expose everything you might need to access. The System applet includes a Startup/Shutdown tab that permits you to choose a default boot selection as well as to set the interval for the delay before the default boot selection is automatically invoked. This delay time corresponds to the **timeout** value in the **[boot loader]** section of the file shown previously. Also, the value assigned to the **default=** statement in that section defines the ARC name for the default OS to be loaded.

Using A Text Editor

BOOT.INI is a plain, pure-ASCII file that should be edited with a plain text editor, such as Notepad or an equivalent program. As with any initialization file, be careful when editing it. Anything between quotation marks in the **[operating systems]** section of the file is fair game, but it is vital that you be careful if you must edit an ARC name. If you configure the BOOT.INI file incorrectly, Windows NT might not boot. That's why you should always create an Emergency Repair Disk (ERD) before making any changes to BOOT.INI; also, you should be sure to have a set of Windows NT boot disks on hand.

BOOT.INI has the following DOS attributes: Read-Only, System, and Hidden. You will need to turn off the Read-Only attribute to make changes to the file, and you'll probably want to turn off the Hidden attribute as well. It's necessary to restore the file to Read-Only after editing, so be sure to remember this step before you try to reboot.

Troubleshooting The Windows NT Boot Process

There are a lot of ways things can break down and interfere with the Windows NT boot process. Here, we recount those problems—and their fixes—that you're most likely to encounter when dealing with boot problems. While you're troubleshooting, remember that hardware problems are always possible (if not also vexing and unpleasant), and sometimes the computer won't boot because a component has failed, not because of the kinds of software and configuration difficulties we recount here.

That's why the first things to do with a PC that won't boot Windows NT is to insert a DOS boot disk. If the machine will boot DOS, it's easy to run DOS-based diagnostics to check the hardware. This eliminates many potential avenues for problems from further consideration. The next step is to boot the system from a set of Windows NT boot floppies—if this works, it proves the machine will still boot Windows NT, no matter how badly the current configuration is mangled or disturbed.

The next step is to try to boot using the Last Known Good Configuration boot option. If this works, it indicates the problem lies in changes made to the system since the last time it booted successfully. This should narrow the field considerably and let you focus on the most likely causes of the problems. If you can't get to this point, you'll have to get the hardware working before you can proceed.

Common Boot-Related Problems, Causes, And Fixes

Here's a litany of potential woes, with possible causes and definite fixes:

> ➤ **I/O Error Accessing Boot Sector File** This type of error can occur when a power failure or fluctuation interrupts file system activity or software installation. Sometimes, this occurs when installing another OS over a Windows NT installation. The symptom will be a BIOS-level error message from the computer indicating that the boot sectors are damaged or that the drive is unavailable. The only way to repair this is to boot the PC from a DOS floppy and run the **FDISK/MBR** command to rebuild the MBR.

➤ **Corrupted Partition Tables** This generally won't happen unless you attempt to use some operating system other than Windows NT, or another operating systems compatible with the IBM/Microsoft partitioning scheme, to create or manipulate partitions on a drive. For obvious reasons, Unix can be a culprit. If this happens, a backup is your best bet—you'll have to reformat the drive, reestablish the partitions, and restore the data. If no data was written to the drives following their partition changes, it might be possible to restore the partition table to its prior state and attempt to carry on from there. However, this can be an unbelievable exercise in frustration.

➤ **BOOT: Couldn't Find NTLDR** This error message indicates that NTLDR is corrupt or missing. This can sometimes pop up if the wrong partition has been made active in Disk Administrator, but it is usually remedied by copying a good copy of NTLDR onto the root of the errant drive.

➤ **NTDETECT V1.0 Checking Hardware...** If this message appears repeatedly, it means NTDETECT.COM is corrupted or missing. In most cases, putting a fresh copy of the program onto the root of the errant system partition will do the trick.

➤ **Windows NT Could Not Start Because The Following File Is Missing Or Corrupt: \<winnt root>\system32\ntoskrnl.exe** This indicates any number of problems, but it generally means NTLDR couldn't find the NT operating system Kernel file needed to complete the OS load. The most frequent cause of this problem is when allocation of free space on a Windows NT drive results in a change to the partition number for the boot partition where the Windows NT system files reside. Properly assigning the partition number for the boot partition usually fixes this problem.

➤ **Could Not Read From The Selected Boot Disk...** This indicates that something is amiss with the boot partition. It could be that a drive is missing or malfunctioning (unlikely, but possible). Otherwise, the disk partition specified in an ARC name might not contain a file system that's recognizable to the NTLDR program. In that case, check to see if partition allocations have changed lately or if someone has been tinkering with BOOT.INI. Restoring the malfunctioning drive or correcting the ARC name should fix the problem.

➤ **STOP: 0x000007E: Inaccessible Boot Device** A STOP error is as fatal as it gets; Windows NT won't go any further until you fix the problem. This error occurs most frequently when a SCSI controller that fails to adhere completely to the SCSI standard is installed in a Windows NT machine. It can also occur if you add a SCSI controller to an NT machine that boots from an IDE hard disk. In that case, make sure no SCSI device is set to SCSI ID 0; otherwise, disable booting from the SCSI drive(s). This prevents the SCSI controller from attempting to boot the disk and stops NTDETECT.COM from assigning the SCSI adapter a bus number equal to zero, which might cause BOOT.INI to point to the wrong partition.

Multiboot Configuration Issues

Windows NT can exist on a system that hosts multiple operating systems. NT Workstation can exist without problems on a computer with Windows 95, Windows For Workgroups, Windows 3.x, or DOS. For such a dual-boot to exist, it is recommended that you install the Microsoft non-NT OS first and then install NT onto a different partition. The resultant BOOT.INI file will contain the two standard lines for NT's normal and safe boot modes as well as a third entry for the alternative operating system, which is usually labeled "MS-DOS" by default. Keep in mind that non-NT OSs will not be able to read any data stored on NTFS volumes.

NT can also be installed in a multiboot configuration with other OSs, but the ease of installation and operation will vary. The only non-Microsoft OS mentioned on the certification exam is OS/2. It is shipped with its own version of a boot manager. When NT is installed onto an OS/2 system, the OS/2 boot manager is disabled in favor of the NT boot manager. You can revert to the OS/2 boot manager by activating the small OS/2 boot manager partition through Disk Administrator. If this change is made, the OS/2 boot manager will be displayed. If DOS or Windows is selected, the NT boot manager is then displayed.

To remove an alternative OS from the boot manager, simply edit the BOOT.INI file and delete the ARC name\path entry.

Exam Prep Questions

Question 1

A Windows NT PC is configured with two 2.2 GB EIDE hard drives, with both drives attached to a controller built into the motherboard. Each disk contains a single primary partition; the Windows NT system files reside on disk 1, and the boot files reside on disk 2. Which of the following ARC names correctly identifies the system disk?

- ○ a. multi(1)disk(1)rdisk(0)partition(0)
- ○ b. multi(0)disk(1)rdisk(0)partition(1)
- ○ c. multi(0)disk(0)rdisk(0)partition(0)
- ○ d. multi(1)disk(0)rdisk(0)partition(0)
- ○ e. multi(0)disk(0)rdisk(1)partition(1)

The options for the first element in an ARC name are **scsi** or **multi**, but scsi applies only to a genuine SCSI drive whose on-board BIOS has been disabled. Because **multi(*)** appears at the start of all five choices, all of them are correct to that point. The number that follows **multi** within parentheses is the ordinal number of the disk controller to which the drive (or drives) is attached. Ordinal numbers start with 0. Only one controller is mentioned in the question, which immediately rules out answers a and d because they allude to a second controller—as denoted by **multi(1)**—to which neither drive in the preceding question is attached. The **disk(*)** element in an ARC name designates the SCSI bus number for a SCSI drive with its BIOS disabled, and it is always zero for a non-SCSI disk. This eliminates answer b from further consideration. The **rdisk(*)** element in an ARC name indicates the SCSI logical unit number (LUN) or selections for the drive that contains the operating system. The **rdisk(*)** element is always set to zero when an ARC name starts with **scsi**—because this one starts with **multi**, it indicates the position in the order in which drives are attached to the controller. Furthermore, the question indicates that the NT system files are on the first disk, and boot files are on the second disk. Knowing that rdisk numbers begin with zero, this means the NT system files live on the drive named **multi(0)disk(0)rdisk(0)partition(1)**, and the boot files live on the drive named **multi(0)disk(0)rdisk(1)partition(1)**. One small trick to ARC names is that although **scsi**, **multi**, **disk**, and **rdisk** all numbered ordinally starting with zero, partition numbers start with one. Therefore, any valid ARC name will never have zero as a value for **partition(*)**, eliminating answers c and d from consideration. **Because each partition mentioned in this question is the only one on its drive, it must be partition(1); therefore, answer e is the correct choice. Here's the real trick in this question: Boot files reside on the system partition on an NT machine. This means the correct answer is the ARC name for the drive that contains the boot files, or answer e.** Note that the correct ARC name for the first disk, where the Windows NT system files reside, does not appear as an option in the list of answers.

Question 2

> Jane has just installed a new device driver for her UPS on her Windows NT client, and now the machine will not boot properly. What is the easiest way to get the system to boot so the driver problem can be fixed?
>
> ○ a. Add the /NoSerialMice option to the BOOT.INI file.
>
> ○ b. Run the emergency repair process to restore the Windows NT Registry.
>
> ○ c. Boot Windows NT from the Emergency Repair Disk (ERD).
>
> ○ d. Select the Last Known Good Configuration option when it appears during the next reboot.

First, we can dispense with a couple of red herrings: Answer a has nothing to do with getting an unbootable Windows NT machine running for troubleshooting purposes (even if it might be the fix that's finally enacted for a UPS that resets a PC when its serial port is probed). And, because it's impossible to boot from the ERD, answer c is bogus. Answer b sounds tempting, but it raises interesting questions about how the emergency repair process knows what to fix in the Registry, and how it can change the behavior of possibly damaged or mismatched driver software. It, too, is bogus. **Answer d is the only option that really makes sense because it reverts NT to the working configuration that held the last time it booted successfully. Because this ignores anything changed since then—such as the errant UPS driver that may (or may not) be causing the problem—it brings the machine back up so Jane can try again from a relatively pristine state.**

Question 3

> Which ARC name in the following list correctly indicates that Windows NT boot files reside on the fourth partition on a SCSI disk drive whose on-board BIOS is disabled, with a SCSI bus ID of 1 on the first SCSI controller on the NT machine?
>
> ○ a. scsi(0)disk(0)rdisk(0)partition(3)
>
> ○ b. scsi(0)disk(1)rdisk(0)partition(4)
>
> ○ c. scsi(0)disk(1)rdisk(1)partition(4)
>
> ○ d. multi(0)disk(0)rdisk(0)partition(4)

The secret to answering this question lies in knowing how to "unpack" its contents and what values to assign based on the information it contains. Partitions are numbered ordinally starting from one, so any correct answer must end in **partition(4)**. This automatically disqualifies answer a. Any SCSI hard disk with its on-board BIOS disabled must begin with the string **scsi(*)**. This automatically disqualifies answer d. Likewise, if the **scsi(*)** keyword begins an ARC name, the value for **rdisk** will always be zero; this disqualifies answer c.

By the process of elimination, b must be the right answer. By breaking down the question, we discover that:

➤ The first SCSI controller with BIOS disabled translates into "scsi(0)".

➤ The SCSI bus ID provides the value for "disk(*)": whenever the BIOS is disabled, which translates into "disk(1)".

➤ Because the BIOS is disabled, "rdisk(*)" is always "rdisk(0)".

➤ The value for partition equals its number on the drive; therefore, "partition(*)" translates into "partition(4)".

Only b matches the entire string.

Question 4

> Of the choices in the following list, what is the most likely cause of the following Windows NT error message at boot time?
>
> "Boot: Couldn't find NTLDR
>
> Please insert another disk"
>
> ○ a. An incorrect hard disk partition is set to active.
>
> ○ b. NTLDR is missing or corrupt.
>
> ○ c. An unbootable floppy was left in the A drive.
>
> ○ d. The designated system disk is damaged or inaccessible.

The most common cause of this error message, by far, is powering down a Windows NT machine with a nonbootable floppy in the floppy drive. Because many PCs' BIOSs try to boot from any floppy inserted during bootup, this error occurs whenever you forget to remove a floppy before the machine is powered back up. Therefore, answer c is the most likely. Answers a, b, and d are possible, but nowhere near as likely to provoke this error message. When you see this error message, look for (and remove) a floppy and try again.

Question 5

> Windows NT can exist in a multiboot configuration with OS/2.
>
> ○ a. True
>
> ○ b. False

NT can exist in a dual-boot system with OS/2. Therefore, answer a is correct.

Question 6

> When the System Administrator at XYZ Corp. tries to boot a newly reconfigured Windows NT machine, she gets an error message that reads:
>
> "I/O Error accessing boot sector file multi(0)disk(0)rdisk(0)partition(2): \bootsect.dos"
>
> What is the most expedient way to fix this problem?
>
> ○ a. Boot from the Last Known Good Configuration.
>
> ○ b. Start the computer from the Windows NT boot disks and copy BOOTSECT.DOS from another machine.
>
> ○ c. Boot the computer from the Emergency Repair Disk and follow the prompts.
>
> ○ d. Start the computer from the Windows NT boot disks and insert the Emergency Repair Disk when prompted.

Here, full-blown repair is needed because BOOTSECT.DOS stores partition information that is specific to the computer where it is generated. Because the machine won't boot completely, the Last Known Good Configuration option never appears; this eliminates answer a. Any copy of this file from another machine is useless; this disqualifies answer b. Because the ERD is not bootable, answer c is bogus. This leaves only answer d, where the NT boot disks permit the system to boot completely and the ERD can then regenerate a new BOOTSECT.DOS.

Question 7

> Which of the following files must appear in the system partition of an Intel PC-based Windows NT machine if that machine uses one or more SCSI drives with their on-board BIOSs disabled? [Check all correct answers]
>
> ❑ a. BOOT.INI
>
> ❑ b. NTLDR
>
> ❑ c. NTOSKRNL.EXE
>
> ❑ d. NTBOOTDD.SYS
>
> ❑ e. OSLOADER.EXE
>
> ❑ f. BOOTSECT.DOS

The files that always appear in the system partition on a PC running Windows NT are BOOT.INI, NTDETECT.COM, BOOTSECT.DOS, and NTLDR. When a drive with its on-board BIOS disabled is used as the boot or system partition, an additional file, NTBOOTDD.SYS, is also required. Therefore, answers a, b, d, and f are correct. Answer e applies only to RISC machines (that is, non-Intel CPUs) running Windows NT; answer c names a file that appears in the default directory where the Windows NT system files reside (usually specified as winnt_root\system32 or as the common default—winnt\system32).

Question 8

XYZ Corp. has just added a new IDE hard drive and controller to a Windows NT machine. The machine continues to boot from its SCSI drive, which has its BIOS disabled. Each drive has only a single primary partition. Of the following options, which is the correct ARC name for the machine's boot partition?

○ a. scsi(0)disk(0)rdisk(0)partition(1)

○ b. scsi(0)disk(1)rdisk(0)partition(0)

○ c. scsi(1)disk(0)rdisk(0)partition(1)

○ d. scsi(1)disk(1)rdisk(0)partition(1)

○ e. scsi(0)disk(0)rdisk(1)partition(1)

Once again, a working knowledge of ARC name construction comes in handy. Because the drive in question is SCSI, but its on-board BIOS is disabled, the ARC name must begin with **scsi(*)**. Because there is only one SCSI controller and numbering begins with zero, it must begin with **scsi(0)**; this disqualifies answers c and d immediately. For ARC names that begin with **scsi(*)**, only the **disk(*)** keyword is significant. In such cases, **rdisk(*)** is always **rdisk(0)**; this disqualifies answer e. Here again, disks are numbered by their SCSI bus numbers, starting with zero. By default, "disk(0)" is the correct value (because no replacement bus number was specified); this disqualifies answer b (and d). By the process of elimination, this leaves answer a, which can be constructed as follows:

➤ "scsi(*)" becomes "scsi(0)" because the BIOS is disabled, and it is the first and only SCSI controller.

➤ "disk(*)" becomes "disk(0)" because that's the default assignment and no overriding values were supplied.

➤ "rdisk(*)" must be "rdisk(0)" because the BIOS is disabled on a SCSI controller; therefore, this value is ignored.

➤ "partition(*)" becomes "partition(1)" because it is the first and only partition on the drive, and partition numbering begins with one.

Question 9

After modifying the Registry, a Windows NT machine will no longer boot. What is the easiest way to get the machine to boot?

○ a. Start the computer from the Windows NT boot disks and restore the Registry from a backup.

○ b. Start the computer from the Windows NT boot disks and select the Emergency Repair option.

○ c. Start the computer from the Emergency Repair Disk and follow the prompts.

○ d. Choose the Last Known Good Configuration option when it appears during boot up.

The easiest approach to this kind of problem, be it caused by untoward edits to the Registry or by installation of drivers or new system components, is to choose the Last Known Good Configuration option during bootup. Therefore, answer d is correct. Answers a and b might produce the same results eventually, but they're not nearly as easy (and perhaps not as up-to-date as the Last Known Good Configuration). Answer c is wrong because you can't boot from the ERD.

Question 10

> While Windows NT is booting, the following error message appears right after the Last Known Good Configuration prompt:
>
> "Windows NT could not start because the following file is missing
>
> or corrupt:
>
> \Winnt_root\system32\ntoskrnl.exe.
>
> Please reinstall a copy of the above file."
>
> You're certain this file is present even though the boot process cannot locate it. What's the most likely cause of this error message?
>
> ○ a. Missing NTLDR
>
> ○ b. Missing BOOTSECT.DOS
>
> ○ c. Missing NTDETECT.COM
>
> ○ d. Missing BOOT.INI

The most common cause of this error is setting an invalid partition as active in Disk Administrator—that is, one that does not include any of the requisite Windows NT boot files. When this happens, none of these files is present on the designated boot partition. **However, it's really the absence of BOOT.INI that makes the difference because it's the file that indicates where the other files are located. Therefore, the correct answer is d.** This message will also appear if the ARC name for the NTOSKRNL.EXE file is incorrect in BOOT.INI (which is sometimes specified as the **default=** entry in the **[boot loader]** section, and always in at least two entries in the **[operating systems]** section).

Need To Know More?

 Perkins, Charles, Matthew Strebe, and James Chellis: *MCSE: NT Workstation Study Guide*. Sybex Network Press, San Francisco, CA, 1997. ISBN 0-7821-1973-5. Chapter 16 has complete details on the boot process of NT, including altering the BOOT.INI and multiboot configurations.

 Search the TechNet CD (or its online version through www.microsoft.com) and the *Windows NT Workstation Resource Kit* CD using the keywords "boot," "BOOT.INI," "boot troubleshooting," and "ARC names."

Troubleshooting

Terms you'll need to understand:

- √ Troubleshooting
- √ Boot Failures
- √ NTLDR
- √ NTOSKRNL
- √ BOOT.INI
- √ BOOTSECT.DOS
- √ NTDETECT.COM
- √ Event Viewer
- √ Last Known Good Configuration (LKGC)
- √ Registry
- √ Emergency Repair Disk (ERD)
- √ Dr. Watson
- √ Kernel Debugger

Techniques you'll need to master:

- √ Understanding the trouble-shooting process
- √ Troubleshooting media errors, domain controller communi cation difficulties, stop message errors or halt on blue screen, hardware problems, and dependency failures
- √ Recognizing installation failures
- √ Troubleshooting boot failures
- √ Using NT's built-in repair tools

The arena of troubleshooting NT is both extensive and immense. In this chapter, we focus on the troubleshooting issues that appear on the Workstation exam, including installation failures, repair tools, printing solutions, and other pertinent issues. Not all the troubleshooting details are listed in this chapter; some useful troubleshooting details can be found in the chapters that focus on these topics, such as printing and booting.

Installation Failures

During the initial installation of Windows NT, five common types of errors can occur: media errors, domain controller communication difficulties, STOP message errors or halt on blue screen, hardware problems, and dependency failures. The following is a short synopsis of each type of error:

> **Media errors** Media errors are problems with the distribution CD-ROM, the copy of the CD-ROM hosted on a network drive, or the communications between the installation and distribution files. The only way to resolve a media error is to attempt to switch media, such as switching from one server's CD-ROM to another or copying the CD-ROM files to a network drive. If media errors are encountered, always restart the installation from the beginning.

> **Domain controller communication difficulties** Not being able to communicate with the existing domain controller prevents the current installation from joining the domain. This error is often due to a mistyped name, a network failure, or because the domain controller is offline. Verify the viability of the domain controller directly and with other workstations (if present).

> **STOP message errors or halt on blue screen** STOP messages and halting on the blue screen during installation are usually caused by using the wrong driver for a controller card. If any information about an error is presented to you, try to determine if the proper driver is being used. If not (or if you can't tell), double-check your hardware and the drivers required to operate them under NT.

> **Hardware problems** Hardware problems should occur only if you failed to verify your hardware with the Hardware Compatibility List (HCL) or if a physical defect has surfaced in previously operational devices. In such cases, replacing the device is the only solution. However, it is not uncommon for a device to be improperly configured or installed. Always double-check your hardware setup before purchasing a replacement.

➤ **Dependency failures** Dependency failures are when one or more dependent services fail due to the absence of a foundation service, hardware, or a driver. An example of a dependency failure is when the Server and Workstation services fail because the NIC fails to initialize properly. If NT even boots with such errors, you should check the Event log.

Now that we have covered some caveats pertaining to installation, let's move on to discuss NT's built-in repair tools.

Repair Tools

Fortunately, Windows NT does not leave you high and dry when you encounter errors. It has a handful of invaluable tools to repair and correct operational difficulties. In the next few sections, we detail how to use the Event Viewer, Last Known Good Configuration, Registry, and Emergency Repair Disk (ERD).

Event Viewer

The Event Viewer, located in Programs|Administrative Tools, is used to inspect the three logs automatically created by NT. These logs are:

➤ **System** Records information and alerts about NT's internal processes

➤ **Security** Records security-related events

➤ **Application** Records NT application events, alerts, and system messages

Each log records a different type of information, but all the logs collect the same information about each event: date, time, source, category, event, user ID, and computer. Also, each event recorded has, at worst, an error code number or, at best, a detailed description with a memory HEX buffer capture.

Most system errors, including STOP errors that result in the blue screen, are recorded in the System log. This allows you to review the time and circumstances around a system failure.

Last Known Good Configuration

The Last Known Good Configuration (LKGC) is a recording NT makes of all the Registry settings that existed the last time a user successfully logged on to the server. Every time a logon is completed, NT records a new LKGC.

If a system error occurs or the Registry becomes corrupted so that booting or logging in is not possible, the LKGC can be used to return to a previously operational state. The LKGC is accessed during bootup when the message "Press the spacebar to boot with the Last Known Good Configuration" displays. A menu will appear from which you can select to load using the LKGC (by pressing L) or other stored configurations.

The Registry

Editing the Registry by hand should be the last resort. A single, improperly configured Registry entry can render an NT installation unusable. There are two Registry editing utilities: REGEDIT and REGEDT32. Both of these utilities must be launched from the Run command or a DOS prompt. REGEDIT displays all the hives of the Registry in a single display window, and the entire Registry can be searched at one time. REGEDT32 displays each of the five hives in separate display windows, but it offers more security- and control-related functions.

It is a good idea to regularly back up your Registry. This can be done using:

➤ NT Backup

➤ Disk Administrator (**SYSTEM** key only)

➤ Either Registry editing tool (REGEDIT or REGEDT32)

➤ The REGBACK utility from the *Windows NT Workstation Resource Kit*

The best times to make a backup are just before and after any significant changes are made to your system, such as hardware installation, software installation, or service pack application. If NT fails to operate properly but boots up, you can attempt a repair by restoring the Registry from a backup.

You should note a few things about working with the Registry. When you edit the Registry, you are working with it in memory. This means the instant you make a Registry change, it goes into effect. However, in some cases, a reboot is required to correct memory settings and launch applications to fully comply with the changes. It is always a good idea to reboot after editing the Registry. Also, when a key of the Registry is saved (or backed up), you capture all the subcontents of that key. This is important to remember when restoring portions of the Registry from backup. All subkeys below the point at which restoration occurs will also be overwritten by the saved version. All changes made since the backup will be lost in the sections restored.

Emergency Repair Disk

Emergency Repair Disk (ERD) is the miniature first-aid kit for NT. This single floppy contains all the files needed to repair system partition and many boot partition problems. The ERD is most often used to repair or replace files that are critical to NT's boot process. An ERD is usually created during installation, but additional and updated ERDs can be created using the RDISK.EXE utility. At the Run command, **RDISK /S** forces NT to save all current Registry settings in memory to \Winnt\System32\ Config. You are then prompted for a preformatted disk. The ERD contains the files listed in Table 18.1.

The ERD does not contain the entire Registry, but just enough to fix the most common errors. To use the ERD to make repairs, you need the three setup disks used to install NT. The repair process is depicted in the following steps:

1. Reboot the computer using the Windows NT setup disks 1 and 2.

2. Select "R" for repair. A menu appears containing the following options:

   ➤ Inspect Registry files

   ➤ Inspect startup environment

   ➤ Verify Windows NT system files

   ➤ Inspect boot sector

Table 18.1 The contents of an ERD.	
File	**Contents**
SYSTEM._	HKEY_LOCAL_MACHINE\SYSTEM compressed
SOFTWARE._	HKEY_LOCAL_MACHINE\SOFTWARE compressed
SECURITY._	HKEY_LOCAL_MACHINE\SECURITY compressed
SAM._	HKEY_LOCAL_MACHINE\SAM compressed
NTUSER.DA_	Default profile, compressed
AUTOEXEC.NT	%winntroot%\system32\autoexec.nt
CONFIG.NT	%winntroot%\system32\config.nt
SETUP.LOG	List of installed files and their checksums
DEFAULT._	HKEY_USERS\DEFAULT compressed

3. Deselect any options you do not wish to use; then continue.

4. Insert disk 3 and the ERD when prompted.

Boot Failures

Boot failures are problems during the NT startup after a successful installation has completed. Some of the more common boot failures are presented in the sections that follow. NT's boot process is covered in depth in Chapter 17.

NTLDR Error Message

If the NTLDR executable is missing or if a floppy is in the A drive, the following error message is displayed:

```
BOOT: Couldn't find NTLDR. Please insert another disk.
```

If the NTLDR is damaged or missing, you must use the ERD to repair or replace it. If a floppy disk is in the drive, eject it and continue the boot process.

NTOSKRNL Missing Error Message

If the NT Operating System Kernel (NTOSKRNL) is corrupt or missing, or if the BOOT.INI points to the wrong partition, an error message like the following appears:

```
Windows NT could not start because the following
file is missing or corrupt:
\winnt root\system32\ntoskrnl.exe
Please re-install a copy of the above file.
```

This error can be resolved by repairing the NTOSKRNL file using the ERD repair process. Or, if the BOOT.INI is wrong, you can edit it to correct the problem (see the discussion on ARC names in Chapter 6).

BOOT.INI Missing Error Message

If BOOT.INI is not present, the NTLDR attempts to load NT from the default \winnt directory of the current partition. If this fails, an error message similar to the following appears:

```
BOOT: Couldn't find NTLDR. Please insert another disk.
```

To alleviate this problem, replace the BOOT.INI file from a backup or use the ERD to repair it.

BOOTSECT.DOS Missing Error Message

If the BOOTSECT.DOS file is not present to boot to MS-DOS or another operating system (not NT), the following error message appears:

```
I/O Error accessing boot sector file
multi(0)disk(0)rdisk(0)partition(1):\bootsect.dos
```

This indicates that the BOOT.INI file has been changed, the partition numbering has changed, or the partition is missing, inactive, or inaccessible. To repair or replace the BOOTSECT.DOS file, use the ERD repair procedure.

NTDETECT.COM Missing Error Message

If the NTDETECT.COM file is not present, the following error message appears:

```
NTDETECT V1.0 Checking Hardware...
NTDETECT failed
```

This error must be repaired with the ERD repair process.

Printing Solutions

When you're working with printers, there seems to be an infinite number of issues to resolve before normal operation can be restored after an error. Many printer problems are simple or obvious, so always check the obvious solutions before moving on to more complicated ones. Here is a short list of tasks you can perform when digging for a printer solution:

➤ Always check the physical aspects of the printer—cable, power, paper, toner, and so on.

➤ Check the logical printer on both the client and the server.

➤ Check the print queue for stalled jobs.

➤ Reinstall the printer driver to be sure it hasn't become corrupted.

➤ Attempt to print from a different application or a different client.

➤ Print using Administrator access.

> ➤ Stop and restart the spooler using the Services applet.

> ➤ Check the status and CPU usage of SPOOLSS.EXE using the Task Manager.

> ➤ Check the free space on the drive hosting the spooler file and change its destination.

A number of topics don't fall into any one category; the following sections discuss this hodgepodge of troubleshooting considerations.

Miscellaneous Troubleshooting Issues

Topics included here encompass permissions problems, re-creating setup disks, the Master Boot Record, and other troubleshooting issues.

Permissions Problems

If you suspect a permissions problem, use the Administrator account or temporarily add the user account to the Administrators group. Double-check group memberships for conflicting access levels—especially No Access. Check the access control list (ACL) on the object in question for group and No Access assignments. Check the permissions on the share if appropriate. Check user, group, or computer policies for access restrictions.

Re-Creating The Setup Disks

If you need a new set of installation floppies, run the WINNT.EXE (or WINNT32.EXE) program from the installation CD-ROM with the /ox parameter. This creates the three floppies without initializing the actual installation process. However, you'll need to preformat the disk beforehand.

Master Boot Record

If the Master Boot Record (MBR) fails on the system partition (the section of the disk that contains BOOT.INI, NTLOADER, and NTDETECT), the ERD will not help with its restoration. Instead, you'll need to use the first disk from DOS 6.0 (or higher). Executing **FDISK / MBR** re-creates the MBR and allows the system to boot.

Dr. Watson

Dr. Watson is NT's application error debugger. It detects application errors, diagnoses the error, and logs the diagnostic information. Most of the information gathered by Dr. Watson is useful only when working with a Microsoft technical professional to diagnose an application error. Data captured by Dr. Watson is stored in the DRWTSN32.LOG file. Dr. Watson can also be used to create a binary crash dump file of the memory where the failing application operates.

Dr. Watson launches itself automatically whenever an application error occurs. However, to configure Dr. Watson, you can launch it by executing DRWTSN32 at the command prompt or in the Run dialog box. Dr. Watson's configuration options are fairly obvious; the only two that might cause some confusion are Dump Symbol Table and Dump All Thread Contexts, which are discussed in the following:

➤ **Dump Symbol Table** Adds the corresponding symbol data to the dump file, greatly increasing its size.

➤ **Dump All Thread Contexts** Forces a dump file to be created for all active threads, not just those owned by the failed application.

BOOT.INI Switches

To improve the bootup's troubleshooting capabilities, you can use one of the following switches after each OS line in the BOOT.INI file (remember those have the ARC name followed by the displayable name in quotes):

➤ **/BASEVIDEO** Boots using the standard VGA video driver.

➤ **/BAUDRATE=**n Sets the debugging communication baud rate when using the Kernel Debugger. The defaults are 9,600 for a modem and 19,200 for a null modem cable.

➤ **/CRASHDEBUG** Loads the debugger into memory, where it remains inactive unless a Kernel error occurs.

➤ **/DEBUG** Loads the debugger into memory to be activated by a host debugger connected to the computer.

➤ **/DEBUGPORT=** com$x$ Sets the debugging COM port.

➤ **/MAXMEM:n** Sets the maximum amount of RAM Windows NT can use.

➤ **/NODEBUG** Indicates that no debugging information is being used.

➤ **/NOSERIALMICE=[COM*x* | COM*x*,*y*,*z*...]** Disables serial mouse detection of the specified COM port(s).

➤ **/SOS** Specifies to display each driver name when it is loaded.

VGA Mode

If you set your video driver to something that prevents a readable display, you can select VGA Mode from the boot menu to boot with the standard VGA driver loaded. Then, you can modify the display drivers to correct the problem.

NTDETECT Debugged

If NTDETECT fails to detect the proper hardware, it might be corrupted or damaged, or your hardware might not be functioning properly. A debugged or checked version of NTDETECT is stored on the CD-ROM in the Support\Debug\I386 directory. First, rename NTDETECT.COM to NTDETECT.BAK; then copy the file named NTDETECT.CHK to the system partition and rename it NTDETECT.COM. Now, you can reboot. This version of NTDETECT gives a verbose display of all detection activities to help you isolate the problem. NTDETECT.COM has the attributes of Hidden, System, and Read-Only set. You need to deselect these attributes before renaming the file and then reset them after the renaming process. Once you've solved the hardware detection problem, return the original NTDETECT from NTDETECT.BAK or the ERD.

ESDI Hard Drives

Some ESDI hard drives are not supported by NT. ESDI hard drives are pre-IDE-type storage devices that have the capability of being low-level formatted with various sector values per track. Due to special formatting geometry and drive controllers, NT may be capable of accessing cylinders beyond 1,024. If NT has direct access to the cylinders above 1,024, only NT (and not DOS) can access these areas. If the controller performs a transparent translation for these cylinders, both NT and DOS can access above 1,024 cylinder areas.

Determining whether NT can even use an ESDI disk cannot be done until an installation is attempted. If NT fails to install properly on an ESDI disk, a "Fatal System Error:0x0000006b" message will be displayed after NTLDR starts. When this occurs, you can deduce that NT does not support the ESDI drive.

Now that we've wrapped up many troubleshooting loose ends, let's look at some advanced troubleshooting issues.

Advanced Troubleshooting

In addition to the tools and utilities listed earlier in this chapter, there are two more troubleshooting mechanisms that require a professional support engineer to interpret them. These mechanisms—blue screen and memory dump—are listed here only for your general understanding.

Blue Screen

No matter what "they" tell you, NT has general protection faults (GPFs), but they aren't called that. When a GPF occurs under NT, the blue screen "of death" appears. This is a test display of the STOP message error. Lots of details are included on this screen, such as the location of the error, the type of error, and whether a memory dump is created. Unfortunately, most of the data will appear in hexadecimal or a strange acronym shorthand you won't be able to read.

Memory Dump

A memory dump is the act of writing the entire contents of memory to a file when a STOP error occurs. The contents of this file can be inspected to determine the cause of the failure. Memory dumps are configured on the Startup/Shutdown tab of the System applet. The options are:

➤ Write The Error Even To The System Log

➤ Send An Administrative Alert

➤ Write A Dump File

➤ Automatically Reboot

The default location and name of the memory dump file is %WINNTROOT%\MEMORY.DMP. The DUMPEXAM.EXE utility can be used to view the contents of a memory dump file. However, most of the contents will require a Microsoft technical professional to interpret them.

Exam Prep Questions

Question 1

> Which of the following can be corrected by the repair process
> using the three installation disks and a recent Emergency Repair
> Disk? [Check all correct answers]
>
> ❑   a. Boot sector corruption
>
> ❑   b. Unable to locate Master Boot Record
>
> ❑   c. NTLDR not found
>
> ❑   d. Corrupt NTOSKRNL

The ERD repair process can often correct boot sector problems, replace
the NTLDR, and repair the NTOSKRNL. Therefore, answers a, c, and d
are correct. The MBR cannot be repaired with the ERD or the installation
floppies—that requires a DOS setup disk. Therefore, answer b is incorrect.

Question 2

> Your NT Workstation experiences a STOP error due to a runaway
> process from a custom application developed in-house. Where
> can information about this error be found once the machine has
> been rebooted?
>
> ○   a. Kernel Debugger
>
> ○   b. Performance Monitor
>
> ○   c. Event Viewer
>
> ○   d. NT Diagnostics

The Kernel Debugger is a troubleshooting tool found on NT Server, not
NT Workstation. Also, it can view STOP error information only when
specifically configured and installed on two connected machines. Therefore, answer a is incorrect. The Performance Monitor and NT Diagnostics
cannot record any information about a STOP error. Therefore, answers b
and d are incorrect. The Event Viewer can be used to view the System log
where all STOP errors are recorded. Therefore, answer c is correct.

Question 3

Which two parameter switches are present by default on the VGA Mode selection ARC name line in the BOOT.INI file? [Check all correct answers]

- ❏ a. **/NODEBUG**
- ❏ b. **/BASEVIDEO**
- ❏ c. **/NOSERIALMICE**
- ❏ d. **/SOS**
- ❏ e. **/VGAVIDEO**

The parameters /NODEBUG and /NOSERIALMICE are not present on the VGA Mode line by default. Therefore, answers a and c are incorrect. **The parameters "/BASEVIDEO" and "/SOS" are present on the VGA Mode line by default. Therefore, answers b and d are correct.** The parameter /VGAVIDEO is not a valid parameter. Therefore, answer e is incorrect.

Question 4

The **SYSTEM** Registry key contains errors. You do not have a recent ERD, but you do have a copy of the **SYSTEM** key itself on floppy. Which of the following programs should you use to restore the **SYSTEM** key from the floppy?

- ○ a. Disk Administrator
- ○ b. The System applet
- ○ c. User Manager
- ○ d. The three NT setup disks

The Disk Administrator is the correct utility to use to restore the "SYSTEM" key if you have a stored copy. Therefore, answer a is correct. The System applet and User Manager do not offer Registry restoration options. Therefore, answers b and c are incorrect. Because no ERD is available, the setup disks cannot be used.

Question 5

> Your NT Workstation has recently been experiencing numerous STOP errors. In order to help pinpoint the problem, where should you configure NT so that a memory dump will occur before the system reboots?
>
> ○ a. The Network applet's properties
>
> ○ b. The recovery option in Dr. Watson
>
> ○ c. The Tracking tab of the Task Manager
>
> ○ d. On the Startup/Shutdown tab of the System applet

The Network applet does not offer memory dump configuration options. Therefore, answer a is incorrect. Dr. Watson is used to perform memory dumps on application faults, not for NT's system itself. Therefore, answer b is incorrect. The Task Manager does not have a Tracking tab nor does it offer memory dump options. Therefore, answer c is incorrect. **The Startup/ Shutdown tab of the System applet is the location of the memory dump options for NT. Therefore, answer d is correct.**

Question 6

> After installing a new SCSI driver, you discover that NT will not successfully boot. No other changes have been made to the system. What is the easiest way to return the system to a state where it will boot properly?
>
> ○ a. Use the repair process with the ERD
>
> ○ b. Use the Last Known Good Configuration
>
> ○ c. Configure a memory dump
>
> ○ d. Boot to DOS and run the setup utility to change the installed drivers

The ERD repair process will restore the system so that it can boot; however, this requires a recent ERD and all three installation disks. In addition, this process can take at least 30 minutes. Therefore, answer a is incorrect. **The LKGC is the fastest way to return to a bootable configuration, especially because only a single change was made to the system. Therefore, answer b is correct.** A memory dump will not only be useless to resolving this problem, it cannot even be configured due to the inability to boot. Therefore, answer c is incorrect. There is no DOS setup utility; that utility was available only for Windows 3.x. Therefore, answer d is incorrect.

Question 7

During the boot process, you receive the following error message after the Last Known Good Configuration prompt:

"Windows NT could not start because the following file is missing or corrupt: \winnt root\system32\ntoskrnl.exe. Please reinstall a copy of the above file."

What are the possible explanations for this error? [Check all correct answers]

❑ a. NTOSKRNL.EXE is missing

❑ b. BOOT.INI points to the wrong partition

❑ c. NTOSKRNL.EXE is corrupt

❑ d. BOOT.INI file is missing

All these explanations can result in the given error message. Therefore, answers a, b, c, and d are all correct. When the boot process cannot find NTOSKRNL.EXE, it does not indicate if the problem is with the file itself, its location, or the pointers to it.

Question 8

Which of the files on the ERD lists the files installed during setup and the checksums of each of these files?

○ a. INSTALLED.DAT

○ b. CONFIG.NT

○ c. DEFAULT._

○ d. SOFTWARE._

○ e. SETUP.LOG

Trick! question

The file INSTALLED.DAT is not present on an ERD. Therefore, answer a is incorrect. The files CONFIG.NT, DEFAULT._, and SOFTWARE._ are all on an ERD, but they do not contain installed file and checksum information. Therefore, answers b, c, and d are incorrect. **The file SETUP.LOG is the only file on the ERD that lists the files installed during setup and their corresponding checksums. Therefore, answer e is correct.** To get this right, you must not only know which files are present on the ERD, but also which ones provide checksum information.

Question 9

> Your NT Workstation experiences yet another STOP error. Fortunately, you enabled the memory dump option through the System applet. What utility can you use to view the contents of the DMP file?
>
> ○ a. Event Viewer
>
> ○ b. Debug Inspector
>
> ○ c. DUMPEXAM.EXE
>
> ○ d. NT Diagnostics

The Event Viewer and NT Diagnostics cannot be used to view the contents of a memory dump file. Therefore, answers a and d are incorrect. The Debug Inspector does not exist. Therefore, answer b is incorrect. **Only DUMPEXAM.EXE can be used to view the contents of DMP files. Therefore, answer c is correct.**

Question 10

> Which of the following are valid ways to make full or partial backups of the Registry? [Check all correct answers]
>
> ❑ a. Create an ERD using the **rdisk /s** command
>
> ❑ b. Use NT Backup
>
> ❑ c. Copy all the contents of the \Winnt\System32\Config directory
>
> ❑ d. Use the Disk Administrator
>
> ❑ e. Use REGEDT32

All these methods are valid ways to create full or partial backups of the NT Registry. Therefore, answers a, b, c, d, and e are all correct. However, note that the files stored in \Winnt\System32\Config are only as current as the last reboot or the execution of "rdisk /s".

Need To Know More?

Perkins, Charles, Matthew Strebe, and James Chellis: *MCSE: NT Workstation Study Guide*. Sybex Network Press, San Francisco, CA, 1997. ISBN 0-7821-1973-5. Chapter 17 has extensive coverage of NT troubleshooting techniques.

Searching the TechNet CD (or its online version through www.microsoft.com) and the *Windows NT Workstation Resource Kit* CD using the keyword "troubleshooting" will result in numerous hits on relevant materials. However, for more focused searching, use keywords associated with the topic in question, such as "boot," "installation," "printing," "Emergency Repair Disk," or "Registry."

Sample Test

The sections that follow provide numerous pointers for developing a successful test-taking strategy, including how to choose proper answers, how to handle ambiguity, how to work within the Microsoft framework, how to decide what to memorize, and how to prepare for the test. This chapter also provides a number of questions that cover subject matter that's likely to appear on the Microsoft Windows NT Workstation exam. Good luck!

Questions, Questions, Questions

You should have no doubt in your mind that you're facing a test full of questions. Each exam consists of 50 to 60 questions. You'll be allotted 90 minutes to complete the exam. Remember, questions come in four basic types:

➤ Multiple choice with a single answer

➤ Multiple choice with multiple answers

➤ Multipart with a single answer

➤ Make a selection on a graphic

Always take the time to read a question twice before selecting any answer. Also, be sure to look for an Exhibit (or Graphic) button, which brings up graphics and charts you'll need to consult in order to understand a question, provide additional data, or illustrate user interface details. You'll find it difficult to answer such questions if you don't examine the exhibits.

It's easy to assume that a question demands only a single answer. However, a lot of questions require more than one answer. In fact, there are even some questions for which all answers should be marked. Read each question carefully enough to determine how many answers are needed; also, look for additional instructions when marking your answers. These instructions are usually in brackets, immediately after the question itself.

Picking Proper Answers

Obviously, the only way to pass an exam is to select correct answers. However, the Microsoft exams are not standardized, like SAT and GRE exams—they are more diabolical and convoluted. In some cases, questions are so poorly worded that deciphering them is nearly impossible. In such cases, you may need to rely upon the process of elimination. There is almost always at least one answer out of a set of possible answers that can be eliminated because of any of the following scenarios:

➤ The answer doesn't apply to the situation.

➤ The answer describes a nonexistent issue.

➤ The answer is already eliminated by the question text.

Once obviously wrong answers are eliminated, you must rely on your retained knowledge to eliminate further incorrect answers. Look for items that sound correct but refer to actions, commands, or features that do not apply to or appear within the described situation.

After this elimination process, if you still face a blind guess for two or more answers, reread the question. Try to picture the situation in your mind's eye and visualize how each of the possible remaining answers might alter that situation.

After you can no longer eliminate incorrect answers but remain unclear about which of the remaining possible answers is correct, it's time to guess! An unanswered question scores no points, but a guess gives you some chance that the choice you make is correct. However, don't be too hasty when making blind guesses—wait until your final round of reviewing marked questions before making guesses. Guessing should always be your last resort.

Decoding Ambiguity

Microsoft exams have a reputation for including questions that are difficult to interpret, confusing, or outright ambiguous. In our experience with numerous exams, we fully understand why this reputation is so prevalent. The Microsoft exams are difficult because they are designed to limit the number of passing grades for those who take the tests.

The only way to beat Microsoft at its own game is to be prepared. You'll discover that many exam questions test your knowledge of things that might not be directly related to the issue raised in a question. This means that the answers offered—even incorrect ones—are as much a part of the skills assessment as the question itself. If you don't know most aspects of Windows NT Workstation well, you might not be able to eliminate obviously wrong answers because they relate to NT topics other than the subject or subjects addressed by the question.

Questions often give away their answers, but you have to be smarter than Sherlock Holmes to find the clues. Often, subtle hints appear in the text in such a way that they seem like irrelevant information. You must inspect and successfully navigate each question to pass the exam. Look for small clues that seem incidental, such as time stamps, group names, configuration settings, and even local or remote access methods. Small details can point out the right answers; but if you miss them, you may find yourself facing a blind guess.

Another common source of difficulty in the certification exams is vocabulary. Microsoft has an uncanny ability for naming some utilities and features cogently, yet it creates completely inane or arbitrary names for others—especially for those dealing with printing and remote access. Be sure to brush up on the key terms presented in the appropriate chapters for these topics. You might also want to review the glossary before taking the test.

Working Within The Framework

Test questions appear in random order. Many similar elements or issues repeat in multiple questions. It's not uncommon to observe that the correct answer to one question is a wrong answer for another. As you take the test, make time to read each answer, even if you find the correct one immediately. Incorrect answers can spark your memory and help on other questions.

You can revisit any question as many times as you like. If you're uncertain about the answer to a question, mark that question in the box provided, and you can return to it later. Also, mark questions you think might help you answer other questions. We usually mark 25 to 50 percent of the questions on exams we've taken. The testing software is designed to help you track your answers to every question, so use those capabilities to your advantage. Everything you want to see again should be marked; then, the test software can help you return to marked items easily.

What To Memorize

How much material you must memorize for an exam depends on your ability to remember what you've read and experienced. If you're visually oriented and can see the drop-down menus and dialog boxes in your head, you won't need to memorize as much as you would if can't visualize those things. These tests stretch your recollection skills through questions that require you to name or select specific commands, or to know the locations for menu entries and dialog boxes in NT utilities.

Important types of information to memorize include:

➤ The order of steps in setup or configuration.

➤ Features or commands found in pull-down menus and configuration dialog boxes.

➤ Applications found by default in the Start menu.

➤ Applets in the Control Panel.

➤ Names and functions of the five main Registry keys.

If you work your way through this book while sitting at an NT Workstation machine, you should have little or no problem interacting with most of these important items. Or, you can use The Cram Sheet that's included with this book to guide your rote memorization of key elements.

Preparing For The Test

The best way to prepare for the test—after you've studied—is to take at least one practice exam. We've included such an exam in this chapter. Give yourself 90 minutes to take the test. Also, keep yourself on the honor system and don't cheat by looking at text that appears elsewhere in the book. Once your time is up or you finish, check your answers against the "Answer Key," which follows this chapter.

For additional practice, visit Microsoft's Training And Certification Web pages at www.microsoft.com/train_cert/ and download the Self-Assessment Practice Exam utility.

Taking The Test

Relax. Once you sit down in front of the testing computer, there's nothing more you can do to increase your knowledge or preparation. Take a deep breath, stretch, and attack the first question.

Don't rush; there's plenty of time to complete each question and to return to skipped or marked questions. If you read a question twice and remain clueless, mark it and move on. Easy and hard questions are dispersed throughout the test in random order. Don't cheat yourself by spending too much time on difficult questions early on that prevent you from answering easy questions positioned near the end of the test. Work your way through the entire test quickly, as a first pass. Then, before returning to marked questions, evaluate the amount of time remaining by the number of such questions. As you answer questions, remove their marks (unless you want to revisit them). Continue to review all remaining marked questions until your time expires or you complete the test.

That's it for pointers. Here are 55 questions to practice on.

Sample Test

Question 1

Using the Task Manager, what are the possible priority settings you can make for an active application? [Check all correct answers]

❑ a. Low

❑ b. Realtime

❑ c. System

❑ d. Normal

❑ e. Pause

❑ f. High

Question 2

Windows NT fails to boot after you have modified the Registry. What is the quickest and simplest way to get the machine to boot?

○ a. Start the computer from the Windows NT boot disks and restore the Registry from a backup.

○ b. Start the computer from the Windows NT boot disks and select the Emergency Repair option.

○ c. Start the computer from the Emergency Repair Disk and follow the prompts.

○ d. Choose the Last Known Good Configuration option when it appears during bootup.

Question 3

A new application is installed onto your Windows NT Workstation. You attempt to use this new application, but it conflicts with your existing word processor. The conflict causes both programs to terminate prematurely. Which audit event type should be tracked to obtain information about the conflict and to determine which programs are affected?

○ a. File And Object Access

○ b. Security Policy Changes

○ c. Restart, Shutdown, And System

○ d. Process Tracking

○ e. Application Activity

Question 4

A normal user, who is a member of the Users group, is able to set what priority levels for processes?

❑ a. Realtime (24)

❑ b. High (13)

❑ c. Normal (8)

❑ d. Low (4)

❑ e. System (32)

Question 5

At XYZ Corp., a handful of NetWare 3.11 clients remain in use. These machines need access to files on a newly installed Windows NT subnet. To support such access without changes to existing clients, which of the following services and/or protocols must be available on Windows NT? [Check all correct answers]

❑ a. Gateway Service For NetWare (GSNW)

❑ b. Client Service For NetWare (CSNW)

❑ c. File And Print Services For NetWare (FPNW)

❑ d. The NWLink protocol

Question 6

One of the new interns used your computer over the weekend. She left a note stating that she attempted to install a new application but it didn't work, so she deleted all the files she thought belonged to the new software. She left the machine powered off, so you try to start it up. During the boot process, you receive the following error message after the Last Known Good Configuration prompt:

"Windows NT could not start because the following file is missing or corrupt:
:\winnt root\system32\ntoskrnl.exe.
Please reinstall a copy of the file."

What are possible explanations for this error? [Check all correct answers]

❑ a. NTOSKRNL.EXE is missing.

❑ b. BOOT.INI points to the wrong partition.

❑ c. NTOSKRNL.EXE is corrupt.

❑ d. BOOT.INI is missing.

Question 7

You want to improve the performance of name resolution over a RAS connection. If static name resolution is used, what is the proper location of the HOST and LMHOSTS files to optimize lookup time?

○ a. Both HOST and LMHOSTS should be stored on the RAS clients.

○ b. HOST should be stored on the RAS server, and LMHOSTS should be stored on the RAS clients.

○ c. Both HOST and LMHOSTS should be stored on the RAS server.

○ d. HOST should be stored on the RAS clients, and LMHOSTS should be stored on the RAS server.

Question 8

Where do the configuration options reside that can save a memory dump file in the event of a STOP error?

○ a. The Network applet

○ b. The recovery option in Dr. Watson

○ c. The Tracking tab of the Task Manager

○ d. On the Startup/Shutdown tab of the System applet

Question 9

After installing a new application, the instructions state that you must manually modify the PATH statement so that the software will function properly. How can this be accomplished?

○ a. Edit the PATH.BAT file

○ b. Modify the PATH variable on the Environment tab of the System applet

○ c. Edit the CONFIG.NT file

○ d. Edit the PATH value in the Registry located in the \HKEY_LOCAL_MACHINE\CurrentControlSet\System\ key

Question 10

Threaded execution is employed by which NT Workstation sub-systems? [Check all correct answers]

❏ a. Win32

❏ b. WOW/Win16

❏ c. VDM/DOS

❏ d. POSIX

❏ e. OS/2

Question 11

Your Windows NT Workstation computer has two hard drives—
one for NT system files and a second for your data files. You recently added more RAM to the machine to bring it up to 128 MB.
What changes should be made to your pagefile?

- ○ a. No change to the pagefile size is recommended, but it
  should be placed on the data drive.
- ○ b. The pagefile should be increased to 140 MB and placed
  on the data drive.
- ○ c. The pagefile should be increased by 12 MB.
- ○ d. The pagefile should be increased to 140 MB.

Question 12

You need to set up two new Web sites to be hosted by a single
installation of Peer Web Services. Each Web site will require its
own directory, a unique URL, and a unique IP address. What
should you do to implement this configuration? [Check all correct answers]

- ❑ a. Install RIP For IP on the PWS server.
- ❑ b. Assign each of the IP addresses to be used to the NIC in
  the PWS server and then associate each IP address with
  the appropriate Web directory.
- ❑ c. Set up the DHCP Relay Agent.
- ❑ d. Configure DNS so it contains the FQDN for each site and
  correlates that name to its IP address.
- ❑ e. Configure WINS by adding the NetBIOS names and IP
  addresses of the sites to the static list of sites.

Question 13

If your network has only a single printer, how can you configure the system so your executives' print jobs will print before other users' documents?

- ○ a. Create a separate logical printer, assign rights to the Executive group, and set the printer priority to 1.

- ○ b. Create a separate logical printer, assign rights to the Executive group, and set the printer priority to 99.

- ○ c. Create a separate logical printer for the Executive group and configure the printer to start printing immediately.

- ○ d. Create a separate logical printer for the Executive group and configure the printer to print directly to the physical print device.

Question 14

A Windows NT PC is configured with two 2.2 GB EIDE hard drives, with both drives attached to a controller built into the motherboard. Each disk contains a single primary partition; the Windows NT system files reside on Disk 1, and the boot files reside on Disk 2. Which of the following ARC names correctly identifies the system disk?

- ○ a. multi(1)disk(1)rdisk(0)partition(0)

- ○ b. multi(0)disk(1)rdisk(0)partition(1)

- ○ c. multi(0)disk(0)rdisk(0)partition(0)

- ○ d. multi(1)disk(0)rdisk(0)partition(0)

- ○ e. multi(0)disk(0)rdisk(1)partition(1)

Question 15

On a network that contains multiple versions of NetWare, some clients are configured for NetWare 2.2, whereas others are con- figured for NetWare 4.11. Among other protocols, NWLink is used on this network. NetWare 2.2 clients use an 802.3 raw frame type, whereas NetWare 4.11 clients use the 802.2 frame type. What kinds of information must be supplied in the NWLink IPX/SPX Properties dialog box to allow the same Windows NT workstation to recognize both flavors of NetWare clients on this network?

O a. Select Auto Frame Type Detection and add the clients' IPX network numbers and frame types to the frame type configuration list.

O b. Select Manual Frame Type Detection and add the network numbers and frame types for both 2.2 and 4.11 clients to the frame type configuration list.

O c. Select only Auto Frame Type Detection; the rest is automatic.

O d. Select Manual Frame Type Detection and add the 2.2 clients' network numbers and frame types to the frame type configuration list.

Question 16

Several users complain that after repeated tries, their documents never print. You open the print queue for the suspect printer. There you see all the print jobs, but you're unable to delete them. What is the next step in resolving this problem?

O a. Verify that the Pause printing option is not checked on the print server.

O b. Delete the stalled printer from the print server, create a new printer, and tell your users to resend their jobs to the new printer.

O c. Delete all files from the spool folder on the print server and tell your users to resend them.

O d. Stop the spooler service and then restart it.

Question 17

One feature of NT is its capability to hide or isolate complicated, behind-the-scenes activity from users and applications. What NT component is responsible for the operating system's redirection and network processes?

- ○ a. NetBIOS Extended User Interface (NetBEUI)
- ○ b. Multiple Universal Naming Convention Provider (MUP)
- ○ c. InterProcess Communications (IPC)
- ○ d. Internetwork Packet eXchange/Sequenced Packet eXchange (IPX/SPX)

Question 18

User MaryJane is a member of the Accounting, Managers, and Print Operators groups. For a share named Marketing, these groups have the following share permissions:

- Accounting: Change
- Managers: Read
- Print Operators: Full Control

In addition, MaryJane's NTFS permissions for the Marketing directory and its contents are Read. What is MaryJane able to do with files from the Marketing directory when she accesses them through the share?

- ○ a. Nothing, she has no access.
- ○ b. Read and Execute.
- ○ c. Read, Write, Execute, and Delete.
- ○ d. Read, Write, Execute, Delete, Change Permissions, and Take Ownership.

Question 19

Using the Disk Administrator, you create a new partition from free space on a SCSI hard drive. The new drive appears in the Disk Administrator display. What should you do next to create new storage space?

○ a. Assign a drive letter

○ b. Select Configuration|Save

○ c. Format

○ d. Commit Changes Now

Question 20

Which of the following components belong to the Windows NT Kernel? [Check all correct answers]

❑ a. HAL

❑ b. Executive Services

❑ c. Security Reference Monitor

❑ d. Logon process

❑ e. I/O Manager

❑ f. User applications

Question 21

A user's job description has changed. She no longer uses one single computer, but moves around the organization as her project requires. What applet in Control Panel can help this user maintain her profile no matter where she logs on?

○ a. System

○ b. Network

○ c. Regional Settings

○ d. User Manager

Question 22

What files should be placed on a boot disk to boot Windows NT?
Assume the drive controller is SCSI and does not support BIOS
translation. [Check all correct answers]

- ❏ a. NTDETECT.COM
- ❏ b. BOOT.INI
- ❏ c. NTLDR
- ❏ d. WINA20.386
- ❏ e. NTBOOTDD.SYS

Question 23

An LMHOSTS file contains what type of information?

- ○ a. A static list of NetBIOS names mapped to IP addresses
- ○ b. A dynamic list of NetBIOS names mapped to IP addresses
- ○ c. A static list of FQDNs mapped to IP addresses
- ○ d. A dynamic list of FQDNs mapped to IP addresses

Question 24

Why would a user want to connect to a remote printer share rather
than create a new printer on his or her Windows NT Workstation?

- ○ a. More options for scheduling accessibility
- ○ b. Local spooling of print jobs
- ○ c. The print driver does not have to be manually installed
- ○ d. Local print queues

Question 25

DHCP is used for what purpose?

- ○ a. To maintain a dynamic relationship database between IP addresses and NetBIOS names
- ○ b. To route IP packets across routers to other subnets
- ○ c. To assign IP addresses to clients
- ○ d. To resolve FQDNs into IP addresses

Question 26

Sixteen-bit Windows on 32-bit Windows (WOW) is not a stand-alone subsystem. What other two Windows NT subsystems support the WOW environment? [Check two answers]

- ❑ a. Win32
- ❑ b. VDM
- ❑ c. POSIX
- ❑ d. OS/2

Question 27

What steps might be required to install a new SCSI-based tape device? [Check all correct answers]

- ❑ a. Reboot
- ❑ b. Install SCSI controller drivers through the SCSI Adapters applet
- ❑ c. Use the Add New Hardware applet
- ❑ d. Detect the tape device through the Tape Devices applet

Question 28

What activities can a user sitting at an NT Workstation computer attached to a network perform if the PDC fails? [Check all correct answers]

❑   a. Log on locally to the Workstation

❑   b. Maintain a current active session on the network

❑   c. Change his or her password

❑   d. Log on to the network

Question 29

You need to create user accounts for 12 new employees. All will have the same level of user access and permissions as the existing BobSmith account. You decide to make copies of Bob Smith's user account to create these accounts for the new users. What pieces of information are reset or left blank when you copy a user account? [Check all correct answers]

❑   a. User Must Change Password At Next Logon

❑   b. User Name

❑   c. Account Disabled

❑   d. Password Never Expires

❑   e. Profile Settings

❑   f. Password

❑   g. Group Memberships

Question 30

Your dial-up connection to the office network is not functioning as it should. Where can you find information related to RAS problems to aid in troubleshooting? [Check all correct answers]

❑ a. Event Viewer

❑ b. DEVICE.LOG

❑ c. Dr. Watson

❑ d. MODEMLOG.TXT

❑ e. NT Diagnostics

Question 31

Which of the following ARC names indicates the third partition of the fourth SCSI drive on the second controller that has its BIOS disabled?

○ a. multi(1)disk(3)rdisk(0)partition(3)

○ b. multi(1)disk(0)rdisk(3)partition(3)

○ c. scsi(1)disk(3)rdisk(0)partition(3)

○ d. scsi(1)disk(3)rdisk(0)partition(4)

Question 32

Everything within the NT environment is an object. Which of the following are object attributes? [Check all correct answers]

❑ a. Data

❑ b ACL

❑ c. Services

❑ d. Name

Question 33

IPC (or InterProcess Communications) provides NT with fast, efficient communication channels among its own components.
Which of the following are supported IPC elements? [Check all
correct answers]

❏ a. NetBIOS

❏ b. MPR

❏ c. NetDDE

❏ d. Windows Sockets

❏ e. RPC

Question 34

By booting from the three boot/setup floppies for Windows NT
Workstation, selecting R at the menu for Repair, and supplying a
recent Emergency Repair Disk—which of the following problems
can be corrected? [Check all correct answers]

❏ a. Boot sector corruption

❏ b. Unable to locate Master Boot Record

❏ c. NTLDR not found

❏ d. Corrupt NTOSKRNL

Question 35

Windows NT Workstation can participate as a member of a
workgroup. Which of the following are characteristics of
workgroups? [Check all correct answers]

❏ a. No central control

❏ b. Share-level security

❏ c. Requires a PDC

❏ d. All user accounts must be created on each member

❏ e. Recommended for more than 10 users/computers

Question 36

Your boot drive fails. To build a boot floppy from another functional NT machine, what files should you copy onto the floppy? Assume the computer with the failed drive uses a SCSI drive with its onboard BIOS disabled. [Check all correct answers]

❑ a. BOOT.INI

❑ b. NTLDR

❑ c. NTOSKRNL.EXE

❑ d. NTBOOTDD.SYS

❑ e. OSLOADER.EXE

❑ f. BOOTSECT.DOS

Question 37

The standard permissions for directories and files are quite similar. Which of the following is not a standard file and directory permission?

○ a. Read

○ b. List

○ c. Create Directory

○ d. Change

○ e. Add

Question 38

It is your responsibility to install Windows NT Workstation on 50 new, identical computers located in the tech support wing of your building. Which tools, files, and/ or utilities might you use to automate and deploy this process? [Check all correct answers]

❑ a. Setup Manager

❑ b. UNATTEND.TXT

❑ c. Uniqueness Database File

❑ d. WINNT.EXE or WINNT32.EXE

Question 39

Your organization has several salespeople who travel from city to city every week. They want to connect to the office LAN to keep tabs on quotas, prices, and stock levels. Therefore, they want to connect to the LAN as if they were in their own offices. However, they can only gain access by establishing a PPP connection using RAS. What NT networking activities are supported over such a connection? [Check all correct answers]

❏ a. Printer share access

❏ b. Named pipes

❏ c. WinSOCK API applications over TCP/IP

❏ d. InterProcess Communications (IPC)

❏ e. User logon authentication

Question 40

You need to install help desk systems hosted by Windows NT Workstation onto 35 newly purchased, identical machines. The help desk system has six installation routines, a database add-on, two patches, and a service update. You want to use SYSDIFF to create a special installation data file so that each computer will be installed with NT and the complicated help desk application with a single command line of WINNT.EXE. What SYSDIFF command should you use to establish this scenario?

○ a. sysdiff /dump difference_file dump_file

○ b. sysdiff /apply /m [/log:log_file] difference_file

○ c. sysdiff /inf /m [/u] difference_file oem_root

○ d. sysdiff /snap [/log:log_file] snapshot_file

Question 41

> Windows NT Workstation, when the TCP/IP protocol is installed, has several TCP/IP tools and utilities. Which of the following can report on your connection to a remote system? [Check all correct answers]
>
> ❑ a. IPCONFIG
>
> ❑ b. TRACERT
>
> ❑ c. FINGER
>
> ❑ d. PING
>
> ❑ e. Telnet

Question 42

> You open the BOOT.INI file to edit it. Which two parameter switches are present on the VGA Mode selection? [Check two answers]
>
> ❑ a. /NODEBUG
>
> ❑ b. /BASEVIDEO
>
> ❑ c. /NOSERIALMICE
>
> ❑ d /SOS
>
> ❑ e. /VGAVIDEO

Question 43

> The Windows NT Workstation architecture provides support for which types of applications? [Check all correct answers]
>
> ❑ a. POSIX
>
> ❑ b. Win16
>
> ❑ c. DOS
>
> ❑ d. Mac OS
>
> ❑ e. Win32
>
> ❑ f. OS/2 1.1 (character mode)
>
> ❑ g. Solaris

Question 44

With CSNW installed on an NT Workstation computer, which of the following NetWare command-line utilities can be launched from your Workstation?

O a. SLIST

O b. LOGOUT

O c. SYSCON

O d. CAPTURE

O e. ATTACH

Question 45

On your Windows NT Workstation computer, you establish a direct access file transfer area for users on your network. The range of clients that require access to this area include PCs running DOS, Windows 3.1x, Windows 95, and Windows NT, as well as Macintoshes, and Unix machines. You create a 50 MB partition on your Windows NT Workstation. You do not want to impose any access restrictions on the volume, but instead leave policing of the area up to its users. What file system is recommended for such use by Microsoft?

O a. FAT

O b. NTFS

O c. HPFS

O d. VFAT

Question 46

> Your organization requires callback security on all RAS connections made into the office LAN. However, you have an important technician who travels across the country regularly who must periodically establish a connection. How can you configure her account so that she is able to gain access while also supporting your organization's security?
>
> ○ a. Set the callback security to No Call Back for her account only.
>
> ○ b. nable callback security with Set By Caller selected.
>
> ○ c. Set the callback security to Preset To with her home phone number.
>
> ○ d. Set the callback security to Roaming and give her the page number to configure the callback number remotely.
>
> ○ e. Turn on the callback Caller ID capture.

Question 47

> You map a drive to a newly created network share using the following command:
>
> Net use H: \\devel3\documents
>
> A user deposits a file for you in the document share named RESULTS.TXT. What additional setting must be made to grant you access to the RESULTS.TXT file?
>
> ○ a. Set the Read permission on the Documents folder to your user account
>
> ○ b. Your user account must be added to the Everyone group
>
> ○ c. None, Full Control to all users is the default on all new shares
>
> ○ d. A new group must be created and your account added as a member

Question 48

You recently purchased a UPS to protect your computer from power failures and spikes. You have taken the precaution of adding the /NOSERIALMICE parameter to your BOOT.INI file. After charging the UPS and attaching it to the correct serial port, you boot your NT Workstation computer. You test your configuration by unplugging the UPS from the wall. After five minutes, the UPS battery is drained, cutting off power to your computer. NT did not shut down gracefully, even though you heard repeated beeps from the UPS. What is the best explanation for this behavior?

○ a. The UPS drivers were not installed through the Devices applet.

○ b. The voltages were reversed in the UPS applet.

○ c. NT is not compatible with UPS devices.

○ d. The UPS variables were not defined in the System applet on the Environment tab.

Question 49

You suspect that some member of the Marketing group is accessing a directory that he should be prevented from reaching. You aren't sure who it is, but you do know which directory is involved. What feature of NT will let you track who gains access to this directory?

○ a. NTFS file activity logging

○ b. Event auditing

○ c. Event Viewer

○ d. Account lockout

Question 50

You've obtained an HP network interface print device and plan to use your Windows NT Workstation computer as the print server for this new device. However, you are unable to locate any option to install a port for this printer. Why?

○ a. PostScript printing is enabled on the print device and must be disabled.

○ b. You didn't install the print driver on the print server.

○ c. The print processor is corrupt and must be fixed.

○ d. The DLC protocol is not installed on the print server.

Question 51

Your NT Workstation computer is in an isolated TCP/IP network with no routing and no external connections. After assigning an IP address to this machine, what additional parameter must be specified to enable proper communication?

○ a. The subnet mask

○ b. The default gateway

○ c. The DHCP server IP address

○ d. The WINS server IP address

Question 52

You want to upgrade from Windows NT Workstation 3.51 to 4. Your main data directory, H:, is an HPFS volume. After NT 4 is installed, you can use the CONVERT.EXE utility to convert H: from HPFS to NTFS.

○ a. True

○ b. False

Question 53

The binding order for protocols can significantly affect performance between a client and server. Where should this binding order be modified to improve network communications?

○ a. On the domain controllers only

○ b. On the workstations only

○ c. On the servers only

○ d. On both the workstations and servers (including the domain controllers)

Question 54

Your NT Workstation computer is configured to create a memory dump file each time a STOP error occurs. What utility can you use to view the contents of the DMP file?

○ a. Event Viewer

○ b. Debug Inspector

○ c. DUMPEXAM.EXE

○ d. NT Diagnostics

Question 55

You need to change permission settings for several NTFS directories in the wake of a security breach. Which of the following choices represent valid ways to perform this task? [Check all correct answers]

❏ a. The CACLS command utility

❏ b. Moving the file to a new partition

❏ c. The Share properties tab

❏ d. Taking ownership

❏ e. The Permissions button on the Security properties tab

Answer Key

1.	a,d,e,f	20.	a,b,c,e	38.	a,b,c,d
2.	d	21.	a	39.	a,b,c,d,e
3.	d	22.	a,b,c,e	40.	c
4.	b,c,d	23.	a	41.	b,d
5.	c,d	24.	c	42.	b,d
6.	a,b,c,d	25.	c	43.	a,b,c,e,f
7.	a	26.	a,b	44.	c
8.	d	27.	a,b,d	45.	d
9.	b	28.	a,b,d	46.	b
10.	a,b,c,d,e	29.	a,b,c,f	47.	c
11.	b	30.	a,b,d	48.	b
12.	b,d,e	31.	c	49.	b
13.	b	32.	a,b,d	50.	d
14.	b	33.	a,c,d,e	51.	a
15.	b	34.	a,c,d	52.	b
16.	d	35.	a,b,d	53.	b
17.	b	36.	a,b,d	54.	c
18.	b	37.	c	55.	a,b,e
19.	d				

Here are the answers to the questions presented in the sample test in Chapter 19, "Sample Test."

Question 1

Low, High, Normal, and Pause are the four selections that appear on the Applications tab. Therefore, answers a, d, e, and f are correct. Realtime is only available on the Process right-click, pop-up menu. Therefore, answer b is incorrect. System is not a valid priority setting. Therefore, answer c is incorrect.

Question 2

The easiest approach to this kind of problem—be it caused by untoward edits to the Registry or installation of drivers or new system components—is to choose the Last Known Good Configuration option during bootup. Therefore, the correct answer to this question is d. Answers a and b may produce the same results eventually, but they're nowhere near as easy (and perhaps not as up-to-date as the Last Known Good Configuration). Answer c is flat wrong, because you can't boot from the ERD.

Question 3

File And Object Access is for tracking NTFS objects such as files and printers. Therefore, answer a is incorrect. Security Policy Changes tracks modifications to security and policies. Therefore, answer b is incorrect. Restart, Shutdown, And System tracks system restarts. Therefore, answer c is incorrect. Process Tracking tracks threads and process, including applications. Therefore, answer d is correct. Application Activity is not a valid selection. Therefore, answer e is incorrect.

Question 4

Only administrators can set process priority to Realtime. Therefore, answer a is incorrect. As a non-administrator, any user can set priority to High, Normal, or Low. Therefore answers b, c, and d are correct. Only the system itself can launch processes with the highest level of priority—namely, system. Therefore answer e is incorrect.

Question 5

The correct answers are c and d. Here's why: GSNW provides mediated access to NetWare services for Microsoft Network clients, so it's not required—meaning answer a should be left unchecked. Likewise, CSNW makes it possible for NT workstations and servers to obtain direct access to a NetWare server. Therefore, answer b should remain unchecked as well. File And Print Services For NetWare make an NT Server look like a NetWare server to NetWare network clients, so it's what provides file access—this means that answer c must be checked. But native NetWare 3.x clients need IPX/SPX to access real NetWare servers, or Windows NT Servers running FPNW; because NWLink is Microsoft's implementation of IPX/SPX, answer d must be checked as well.

Question 6

Any of these explanations can result in the given error message. Therefore, answers a, b, c, and d are all correct. When the boot process cannot find NTOSKRNL.EXE, it does not indicate if the problem is with the file itself, its location, or the pointers to it.

Question 7

The fastest lookup time occurs when both HOST and LMHOSTS files are stored on the local hard drive of each RAS client, because no WAN traffic need occur to resolve a resource location. Therefore, answer a is correct. All others answers are incorrect because they require storing these files somewhere other than on the client, which increases the lookup time.

Question 8

The Network applet does not offer memory dump configuration options. Therefore, answer a is incorrect. Dr. Watson is used to perform memory dumps for application faults, not for the NT system itself. Therefore, answer b is incorrect. The Task Manager does not have a Tracking tab, nor does it offer memory dump options. Therefore, answer c is incorrect. The Startup/Shutdown tab of the System applet is where memory dump options for NT appear. Therefore, answer d is the only correct answer.

Question 9

There is no such thing as a PATH.BAT file. Therefore, answer a is incorrect. The Environment tab of the System applet is the proper place to modify the PATH variable. Therefore, answer b is correct. The CONFIG.NT file is not editable by users. Therefore, answer c is incorrect. The Registry key listed for a PATH value is fictitious. Therefore, answer d is incorrect.

Question 10

All of the subsystems within NT are executed through threads. Therefore answers a, b, c, d, and e are correct. Even though a VDM, and subsequently WOW, uses only a single thread, all of these subsystems use threaded execution nevertheless.

Question 11

Microsoft recommends a pagefile be set equal in size to the amount of physical RAM on a system, plus 12 MB. Therefore, answer a is incorrect. The pagefile should be 140 MB and placed on a different drive than where the system files reside (if possible). Therefore, answer b is correct. The pagefile should be the size of physical RAM plus 12 MB. Therefore, answer c is incorrect. The pagefile should be 140 MB and placed on a drive other than the one where the system files reside. Therefore, answer d is incomplete.

Question 12

RIP For IP should not be used in this situation; also, you do not know if there is more than one NIC in the server. Therefore, answer a is incorrect. Assigning the additional IP addresses to the server's NIC is an important step. Therefore, answer b is correct. The DHCP Relay Agent does not apply to this situation. Therefore, answer c is incorrect. Because this site is within a private network, you will need both DNS and WINS to support name resolution. Therefore, answers d and e are both correct. Thus, answers b, d, and e are all correct. The trick to this question is to realize that even though NT Workstation does not host DNS or WINS servers, a Workstation machine can be the subject of a reference in a DNS or WINS server database.

Question 13

It is possible to set priorities among groups of documents by creating different logical printers for a single physical print device and then setting different priorities for each logical printer. To set printer priority, select the Scheduling tab in Printer Properties. The lowest priority is 1. Therefore, answer a is incorrect. The highest priority is 99. Therefore, b is the correct answer. There is no "start printing immediately" option. Therefore, answer c is incorrect. Any NT printer automatically prints to the print device. Therefore, d is incorrect.

. . . .

Question 14

The options for the first element in an ARC name are either **scsi** or **multi**, but **scsi** applies only to a genuine SCSI drive whose onboard BIOS has been disabled. Because **multi(*)** appears at the start of all five choices, all of them are correct to that point. The number that follows **multi** within the parentheses is the ordinal number of the disk controller to which the drive (or drives) is attached. Ordinal numbers start with 0; because there is only one controller mentioned in the question, that immediately rules out answers a and d, because they allude to a second controller (as denoted by **multi(1)**) to which neither drive in the preceding question is attached. The **disk(*)** element in an ARC name designates the SCSI bus number for a SCSI drive with its BIOS disabled, and it is always zero for a non-SCSI disk. This eliminates answer b from further consideration. The **rdisk(*)** element in an ARC name indicates the SCSI logical unit number (LUN) or selects the drive that contains the operating system. The **rdisk(*)** element is always set to zero when an ARC name starts with **scsi**—because this one starts with **multi**, it indicates the position in the order in which drives are attached to the controller. Furthermore, the question indicates that the NT system files are on the first disk, and boot files on the second disk. Because **rdisk** numbers begin with zero, this means that the NT system files live on the drive named **multi(0)disk(0)rdisk(0) partition(1)** and that the boot files live on the drive named **multi(0)disk(0)rdisk(1)partition(1)**. One small trick to ARC names is that although **scsi**, **multi**, **disk**, and **rdisk** all number ordinally, starting with 0, partition numbers start with 1. Therefore, any valid ARC name will never have zero as a value for **partition(*)**. Because each of the partitions mentioned in this question is the one and only on its drive, it must be "partition(1)." Here's the real trick in this question: Boot files reside on the system partition on an NT machine. This means that the correct answer is the ARC name for the drive that contains the boot files, or answer b. Note that the correct ARC name for the first disk, where the Windows NT system files reside, appears nowhere in the list of answers to the question!

Question 15

The secret to answering this question is to understand how automatic frame type detection works in NT. As long as the only frame type in use is 802.2, automatic detection works fine. But because older NetWare clients—especially NetWare 2.2 clients—use only 802.3 frames, Manual Frame Type Detection must be selected during the configuration process. This eliminates answers a and c from consideration. Answer d is incorrect because Manual Frame Type Detection requires entry of all frame types and network numbers in use. **Only answer b covers all these requirements; that's why it's correct.**

Question 16

There is no Pause printing option. Therefore, answer a is incorrect. There's no need to re-create the printer from scratch, so answer b is also incorrect. You should never have to involve users in the problem-solving process (other than to gather information from them). Therefore, answer c is also incorrect. **Choice d is the correct answer. This scenario is a quintessential example of a stalled print spooler. To fix the problem, select Services in Control Panel, stop the spooler service, and then restart it.**

Question 17

NetBEUI is a protocol used by NT, but it's not the unified redirector hiding interface. Therefore, answer a is incorrect. **Multiple Universal Naming Convention Provider (MUP) is the unified redirector hiding interface. Therefore, answer b is correct.** IPC is not a redirector. Therefore, answer c is incorrect. IPX/SPX is the Novell protocol that Microsoft re-created as NWLink; it is not a redirector. Therefore, answer d is incorrect.

Question 18

To calculate share and NTFS permissions combined, take the most permissive of each kind and then the least permissive of the remaining share and NTFS permissions. If No Access appears anywhere, the resulting permission will always be No Access. Of the three share permissions that pertain to Marketing by virtue of MaryJane's group memberships, Full Control is the most permissive, so that becomes her share permission. The NTFS permission is Read. **The less permissive of Read and Full Control is Read, so MaryJane's effective permission to Marketing is Read. Therefore, only answer b is correct, because Read access includes both Read and Execute.**

Question 19

It is not possible to assign a drive letter to a partition unless it is formatted. Therefore, answer a is incorrect. The Configuration|Save command stores the current configuration status as stored in the Registry to an Emergency Repair Disk, but this is not a step in creating a usable volume. Therefore, answer b is incorrect. Formatting a partition to create a volume is a required step, but this cannot be performed until the partition creation changes are committed. Therefore, answer c is also incorrect. **You must use the Commit Changes Now command to save the partition creation changes as the next step, then proceed to format the partition, and finally, assign it a drive letter. Therefore, d is correct.**

Question 20

The Kernel is host to the HAL, the Executive Services, the Security Reference Monitor, and the I/O Manager. Therefore, answers a, b, c, and e are correct. The Logon process and User applications exist in User mode. Therefore, answers d and f are incorrect.

Question 21

The User Profile tab located in the System applet is where roaming profiles are established. Therefore, answer a is correct. The Network applet is not involved in the creation of user profiles. Therefore, answer b is incorrect. The Regional Settings applet makes changes that are stored in a user profile, but roaming profiles are not managed through this tool. Therefore, answer c is incorrect. The User Manager is not a Control Panel applet. Also, it is only able to establish the path of a profile; it is not used to create profiles. Therefore, answer d is incorrect.

Question 22

NTDETECT.COM is required on the boot floppy. Therefore, answer a is correct. BOOT.INI is required on the boot floppy. Therefore, answer b is also correct. NTLDR is required on the boot floppy. Therefore, answer c is also correct. WINA20.386 is a Windows 3.x device driver that is not needed on the boot floppy. Therefore, answer d is incorrect. NTBOOTDD.SYS is the driver for SCSI translation required for non-BIOS controllers. Therefore, answer e is also correct. Thus, a, b, c, and e are all correct.

Question 23

LMHOSTS is a predecessor to WINS and is a static list of NetBIOS names mapped to IP addresses. Therefore, answer a is correct. A dynamic list of NetBIOS names mapped to IP addresses is WINS. Therefore, answer b is incorrect. The HOST file is a static list of FQDNs mapped to IP addresses. Therefore, answer c is incorrect. The DNS database, in essence, represents a dynamic list of FQDNs mapped to IP addresses. Therefore, answer d is incorrect.

Question 24

There are no additional scheduling options in either case. Therefore, answer a is incorrect. There is no local spooling of print jobs for network connection over printers; a logical printer is simply a redirector to the real print server where all spooling takes place. Therefore, answer b is incorrect. **Print drivers do not need to be installed locally on each NT Workstation that connects to a network share printer. Therefore, answer c is correct.** The logical printer used to connect to a print share will display a print queue, but it is the entire print queue for the printer as seen by the print server that is displayed. There is no individual print queue for each local machine; however, only those print jobs owned by the workstation user can be manipulated by that user. Therefore, answer d is incorrect.

Question 25

The service that maintains a dynamic relationship database between IP addresses and NetBIOS names is WINS. Therefore, answer a is incorrect. The service that routes IP packets is RIP For IP—a subject not covered on the Workstation exam. Therefore, answer b is incorrect. **The service that assigns IP addresses to clients is DHCP. Therefore, answer c is correct.** The service that resolves FQDNs to IP addresses is DNS. Therefore, d is incorrect.

Question 26

The WOW subsystem is launched within a VDM that is itself launched within Win32. Therefore, answers a and b are correct. POSIX and OS/2 are not associated with WOW in any way. Therefore, answers c an d are incorrect.

Question 27

Rebooting, the SCSI Adapters applet, and the Tape Devices applet are all required elements when installing a new SCSI-based tape device. Therefore, answers a, b, and d are correct. There is no Add New Hardware applet in NT. Therefore, answer c is incorrect.

Question 28

Without a PDC, you can still log on locally, maintain current network access, and log on to the network (through BDC authentication). Therefore, answers a, b, and d are correct. You cannot change your password because a BDC cannot modify the SAM database. Therefore, answer c is incorrect.

Question 29

The items that are reset or left blank when a user account is copied are User Must Change Password At Next Logon, User Name, Account Disabled, and Password. Therefore, answers a, b, c, and f are correct. Password Never Expires, Profile Settings, and Group Membership options remain as set in the original account. Therefore, answers d, e, and g are incorrect.

Question 30

The Event Viewer, DEVICE.LOG, and MODEMLOG.TXT can be useful troubleshooting tools for RAS problems. Therefore, answers a, b, and d are correct. Dr. Watson doesn't track RAS events; it focuses on applications. Therefore, answer c is incorrect. NT Diagnostics provides no useful RAS-related information. Therefore, answer e is incorrect.

Question 31

Answers a and b begin with **multi**, which indicates a BIOS-enabled controller. Therefore, answers a and b are both incorrect. **Answer c indicates the third partition on the fourth drive on a non-BIOS SCSI controller. Therefore, answer c is correct.** Answer d indicates the fourth partition. Therefore, answer d is incorrect.

Question 32

The data in an object is an attribute. Therefore, answer a is correct. The ACL of an object is an attribute. Therefore, answer b is correct. The services for an object are not attributes. Therefore, answer c is incorrect. The name of an object is an attribute. Therefore, answer d is correct. Thus, answers a, b, and d are correct.

Question 33

The programming interface elements of IPC are NetBIOS, NetDDE, Windows Sockets, and RPC. Therefore, answers a, c, d, and e are correct. MPR is a redirector, not an IPC element. Therefore, answer b is incorrect.

Question 34

The ERD repair process can often correct boot sector problems, replace NTLDR, and repair NTOSKRNL. Therefore, answers a, c, and d are correct. Neither ERD nor installation floppies can repair the MBR—that requires a DOS setup disk. Therefore, b is incorrect.

Question 35

Workgroups have no central control and use share-level security; also, user accounts must be created on each member. Therefore, answers a, b, and d are correct. Workgroups do not require a PDC and are recommended for 10 or fewer users/computers. Therefore, answers c and e are incorrect.

Question 36

The files that always appear in the system partition on a PC running Windows NT are BOOT.INI, NTDETECT.COM, and NTLDR. When a drive with onboard BIOS disabled is used as a boot or system partition, an additional file, NTBOOTDD.SYS, is required. Therefore, answers a, b, and d are correct. Answer e applies only to RISC machines (that is, non-Intel CPUs) running Windows NT. Therefore, answer e is incorrect. Answer c names a file that appears in the default directory where Windows NT system files reside (usually specified as winnt_root\system32, or as the common default: winnt\system32). Therefore, answer c is incorrect. Answer f names a file that appears only when DOS is present for dual-boot systems; it is not needed on the boot floppy. Therefore, answer f is incorrect.

Question 37

Read is both a directory and a file permission. Therefore, answer a is incorrect. List is a directory permission. Therefore, answer b is incorrect. **Create Directory is not a permission. Therefore, answer c is correct.** Change is both a directory and file permission. Therefore, answer d is incorrect. Add is a directory permission. Therefore, answer e is incorrect.

Question 38

All of these items can be or are involved in an automated or customized installation of NT. Therefore, answers a, b, c, and d are all correct.

Question 39

Because a RAS-connected client is no different than a direct-connected client (other than in its speed of data transfer), all standard network activities still occur over the WAN link. Therefore, all five answers are correct.

Question 40

The command "sysdiff /inf /m [/u] difference_file oem_root" enables NT and custom applications to be installed automatically with a single command. Therefore, answer c is correct. Answer a creates a contents list of a difference file; answer b applies a difference file to an installation of NT; and answer d creates an initial snapshot of NT. Therefore, a, b, and d are all incorrect.

Question 41

The IPCONFIG utility is only useful for identifying local TCP/IP configurations. Therefore, answer a is incorrect. **The TRACERT utility displays the route taken by packets to the remote system. Therefore, answer b is correct.** The FINGER utility is used to obtain user information, but it offers no connection diagnostics. Therefore, answer c is incorrect. **PING indicates whether or not a remote system is currently online. Therefore, answer d is correct.** The Telnet utility is used to establish a terminal emulation session with a remote system, but it offers no connection diagnostics. Therefore, answer e is incorrect.

Question 42

The parameters /NODEBUG and /NOSERIALMICE are not present on the VGA Mode line by default. Therefore, answers a and c are incorrect. **The parameters /BASEVIDEO and /SOS are present on the VGA Mode line by default. Therefore, answers b and d are correct.** The parameter /VGAVIDEO is not a valid parameter. Therefore, answer e is incorrect.

Question 43

Windows NT provides application support for Win32, Win16, DOS, POSIX, and OS/2 1.1 (character mode). Therefore, answers a, b, c, e, and f are correct. NT does *not* support Mac OS or Solaris applications. Therefore, answers d and g are incorrect.

Question 44

The only command-line utility on this list that works inside NT is SYSCON. Therefore, answer c is correct. All the other utilities are not supported by NT, but their functions can be performed using NT's NET command equivalents. Therefore, a, b, d, and e are incorrect.

Question 45

FAT cannot be used because it is not directly supported by NT; it is supported only through VFAT's backward compatibility options. Therefore, answer a is incorrect. NTFS isn't suitable because of the need for broad cross-platform access and the partition's size. Therefore, answer b is incorrect. HPFS is not supported in Windows NT 4. Therefore, answer c is incorrect. **VFAT is the proper file system to use, because it works well with small volumes, imposes no security restrictions, is backwards compatible with FAT, and is supported by NT. Therefore, d is the correct answer.**

Question 46

Setting the No Call Back option violates the organization's security policy. Therefore, a is incorrect. **Setting the Set By Caller option allows her to input a callback number each time she connects. Therefore, b is correct.** Setting the Preset To number does not allow her to access the network because she's never in the same place. Therefore, c is incorrect. There is no Roaming callback setting. Therefore, d is incorrect. NT has no Caller ID capture setting, but this service can be obtained from third-party software. Therefore, because this service is not required for this situation, answer e is also incorrect.

Question 47

Assigning specific permissions for the object for your user account is unnecessary. Because your account belongs, by default, to the Everyone group, and new shares offer Full Control to this group, answer a is incorrect. Your user account automatically becomes a member of the Everyone group when it's created. Therefore, b is incorrect. **No action is required because your account belongs to the domain's Everyone group with Full Control to new shares, by default. Therefore, answer c is correct.** A new group is not required to gain access to the new share. Therefore, answer d is incorrect.

Question 48

The Devices applet is not used to install drivers; also, a UPS requires no additional drivers to operate. Therefore, a is incorrect. **If the voltages that define communications from a UPS are reversed, the computer will fail to understand its signals. Therefore, answer b is correct.** NT is UPS compatible. Therefore, c is incorrect. There are no UPS variables to be defined through the System applet. Therefore, answer d is incorrect.

Question 49

NTFS file activity logging is a fault tolerance feature used to ensure the integrity of stored data; it cannot be used to track access. Therefore, answer a is incorrect. **Event auditing tracks activity around any object within**

NT. Therefore, answer b is correct. The Event Viewer is used to review the logs created by the auditing system, but it is not what does the actual tracking. Therefore, answer c is incorrect. Account lockout is the feature used to prevent compromised accounts from being used. Therefore, answer d is incorrect.

Question 50

PostScript printing has nothing to do with print device installation. Therefore, a is incorrect. You can't install a driver if NT can't recognize a print device. Therefore, answer b is incorrect. The print processor is not involved in printer installation. Therefore, answer c is also incorrect. **For Windows NT to support HP network interface print devices, you must install DLC (Data Link Control) or the LPR (line printer remote) protocol. Therefore, answer d is correct.** You can't install a printer driver if Windows NT cannot recognize the print device.

Question 51

When installing TCP/IP on a nonrouted network, the IP address and subnet mask parameters must be specified. Therefore, answer a is correct. If a default gateway is not specified, the machine can only communicate with other machines within its subnet. Because this is not mandatory on a nonrouted network, answer b is incorrect. DHCP and WINS are not mandatory for IP networks of any kind. Therefore, c and d are incorrect, as well.

Question 52

The correct answer is b, false. Because Windows NT 4 no longer supports HPFS, you'll have to obtain the ACLCONV.EXE utility from Microsoft to convert an HPFS partition into NTFS. The Windows NT 4 utility CONVERT.EXE can only transform FAT partitions into NTFS. Because NT 3.51's convert utility works with HPFS, it might be even better to convert HPFS to NTFS before installing the upgrade to NT 4.

Question 53

Because NT servers use the protocol sent to them by workstations, the binding order needs only to be changed on the workstations. Therefore, answer b is the correct choice. Network speed is affected by the binding order on the workstations, but not on servers. Therefore, answers a, c, and d are all incorrect.

Question 54

The Event Viewer and NT Diagnostics are not able to view the contents of a memory dump file. Therefore, answers a and d are incorrect. There is no Debug Inspector. Therefore, answer b is incorrect. **Only DUMP EXAM.EXE can be used to view the contents of DMP files. Therefore, answer c is correct.**

Question 55

The CACLS command-line utility can be used to change ACLs or permissions for files and folders. Therefore, answer a is correct. Moving a file to a new partition causes the file to take on the settings of its new container, thus its permissions are changed. Therefore, answer b is correct. The Share properties tab can only change permissions for a share, not NTFS permissions for files. Therefore, answer c is incorrect. Taking ownership gives users the ability to change permissions, but the act of taking ownership alters no permissions. Therefore, d is incorrect. **The Permissions button on the Security properties tab is the easiest method for changing NTFS permissions. Therefore, answer e is correct (and preferred).**

Glossary

access token—The collection of security settings generated at user login that tells Windows NT which resources a user can access as well as the extent of that access.

account policy—A file that establishes security settings, including how passwords on a domain or a workstation are used.

ACL (access control list)—The attribute list for all system objects. It defines which users and groups have what level of access to each object.

ACLCONV.EXE—A Microsoft conversion utility that converts HPFS volumes (from LAN Manager, LAN Server, or Windows NT 3.51 or earlier NT versions) to an NTFS equivalent.

administrative alert—An alert generated by Windows NT Workstation Performance Monitor when it detects a problem in the NT system environment.

administrative tools—A group of tools and utilities provided by Windows NT that controls the management and configuration of components such as user rights, system security, and disk drives.

administrator account—A default account created by Windows NT that has full access and full control over the entire system.

ANSI (American National Standards Institute)—The U.S. representative on the International Standardization Organization (ISO), a worldwide standards-making body. ANSI creates and publishes standards for networking, communications, and programming languages.

API (Application Programming Interface)—A set of interface subroutines that define the methods for programs to access external services.

AppleTalk—Apple Computer's networking protocols and software used for network communication with Macintosh computers.

Application log—This utility documents events noted by the NT system and user applications. It also records their warnings and error messages. The Application log is located in the Event Viewer.

ARCNet (Attached Resource Computer Network)—An inexpensive and flexible network architecture created by Datapoint Corporation in 1977. It uses the token-passing channel access method.

ARP (Address Resolution Protocol)—A protocol in the TCP/IP suite used to associate logical addresses to physical addresses.

ASCII (American Standard Code for Information Exchange)—A way of coding that translates letters, numbers, and symbols into digital form.

AT.EXE—A utility used on a batch file with the NTBACKUP link that schedules the batch file to run at a specific time. AT.EXE schedules commands to be run by the scheduling service in Windows NT.

AUTOEXEC.BAT—A DOS batch file that is launched when a computer is started or booted.

Backup Browser—Computers on an NT network that maintain a duplicate list of the network's resources and act in a similar way within the Browser Service as BDCs act for domain control.

Backup Operators—A built-in group in Windows NT that has the permission to log on to a domain and back up a particular server or workstation.

basevideo—A command-line parameter switch used on the BOOT.INI file. It forces NT to boot using 16-color VGA video at 640×480. This setting appears by default on the ARC name line identified by "[VGA mode]".

BDC (Backup Domain Controller)—A backup server that protects the integrity and availability of the SAM database. BDCs are not able to make any changes or modifications, but they can use the database to authenticate users.

BIOS (Basic Input/Output System)—A system that houses the buffers used to transfer information from a program to the hardware devices receiving the information.

BOOT.INI—One of the files placed on the system partition that contains the location of the system files for each OS installed on the machine. The locations are listed using ARC names.

BOOTSECT.DOS—An NT file used at bootup to determine which of multiple operating systems should be booted.

bottleneck—The effect of trying to force too much information through a system with inadequate bandwidth, causing the system to slow significantly.

Browser Service—An NT utility that maintains a list of network resources within a domain, and provides lists of these domains, servers, and resource objects to any Explorer-type interface that requests it (e.g., browse lists).

cache—A specified area of high-speed memory used to contain data that is going to be or recently has been accessed.

CACLS command—A command used to display or modify the ACL.

CDFS (Compact Disk File System)—A special read-only file system supported by both Windows 95 and Windows NT 3.51 and higher. CDFS permits easy access to CDs within these operating systems.

client/server subsystem—A Win32 subsystem that handles support for 32-bit Windows applications (Win32 applications). Also called the CSR.

computer name—The name of a computer on a LAN that is specific to an individual workstation or server.

Control Panel—In Windows, this is the area where you modify system settings, such as fonts, screen color, SCSI hardware, and printers, among others.

CONVERT.EXE—A utility in Windows NT that converts FAT volumes to NTFS equivalents.

CPU (Central Processing Unit)—The "brains" of your computer. This is the area where all functions are performed.

dependency failures—When one or more dependent services fail due to the absence of a foundational service, hardware, or driver.

DHCP (Dynamic Host Configuration Protocol)—A service that enables the assignment of dynamic TCP/IP network addresses, based on a specified pool of available addresses.

DHCP Relay Agent—Intercepts the DHCP broadcasts then transmits the broadcasts directly to the DHCP server.

disk administrator—An administration application in the Administrative Tools group that lets an administrator create and delete stripe sets and various disk partitions, change the assignment of drive letters, and display facts about a partition's size and setup.

disk controller—A piece of hardware that controls how data is written and retrieved from the computer's disk drive.

disk duplexing—A fault tolerance method used by Windows NT that uses a duplicate physical and logical drive on a separate hard disk where the drive is connected to the system via a separate controller. If the original drive or controller fails, the system continues to operate using the duplexed drive.

disk partition—A portion of a hard disk that acts like a physically separate unit.

disk striping—A fault tolerance method used by Windows NT that stores data across multiple physical storage devices.

DLC (Data Link Control)—A protocol used to interoperate with IBM mainframes and provide connectivity to network-attached print devices.

DLL (Dynamic Link Libraries)—Small executable program routines or device drivers stored in separate files and loaded by the OS when called upon by a process or hardware device.

DMB (Domain Master Browser)—In Windows NT networks, a browser that communicates resource lists across subnets within the same domain.

DMP file—A memory dump file with the extension .DMP.

DNS (Domain Name Service)—A system used to resolve host names into IP addresses.

domain—A group of computers and peripheral devices that shares a common security database.

domain controllers—A computer that authenticates domain logons as well as manages the Security Accounts Manager (SAM) database.

DOS (Disk Operating System)—Software that regulates the way a computer reacts with its floppy or hard disks.

DUN (Dial-Up Networking)—A utility found in the RAS Phone book|Programs|Accessories folder of the Start menu that controls the dial-out capabilities of RAS.

election packet—The electronic communication used by a browser (Master, Backup, or Potential) to initiate a new selection of a Master Browser when the current Master Browser is no longer accessible or when a new machine goes online.

encryption—A method of coding data in which a person has to have a decoding key to decipher the information.

ERD (Emergency Repair Disk)—A miniature first aid kit for NT. This single floppy contains all the files needed to repair system partition and many boot partition related problems.

ESDI (Enhanced Small Device Interface)—A pre-IDE type storage device that is low-level formatted with various values of sector per track.

Ethernet—The most widely used type of LAN, originally developed by Xerox.

exabytes—One million gigabytes.

Exam Preparation Guides—Guides that provide information specific to Microsoft Certified Professional exams to help students prepare for the exam.

Exam Study Guide—Short for *Microsoft Certified Professional Program Exam Study Guide*, it contains information about more than one of the Microsoft Certified Professional exams.

FAT (File Allocation Table)—A table originally used by the DOS file system to keep information about the properties, location, and size of files being stored on a disk.

fault tolerance—The ability of a computer to work continuously, even when there is a system failure.

firewall—A barrier between two networks made of software and/or hardware that permits only authorized communication to pass.

firmware—A type of software that becomes part of the hardware function after it has been saved into a Programmable Read-Only Memory chip (PROM).

FQDN (fully qualified domain name)—The complete site name of an Internet computer system.

FTP (File Transfer Protocol)—A protocol that transfers files to and from a local hard drive to an FTP server located elsewhere on another TCP/IP-based network (such as the Internet).

GDI (Graphics Device Interface)—Provides network applications with a system for presenting graphical information. The GDI works as a translator between an application's print request and a device driver interface (DDI) so a job is rendered accurately.

Gopher—An Internet service that provides text-only information, most suited to large documents with little or no formatting or images.

GSNW (Gateway Service For NetWare)—A service that enables Windows NT servers to map a drive to a NetWare server and provides access to NetWare server resources for Windows NT workstations (via a gateway).

GUI (Graphical User Interface)—A computer interface that uses graphics, windows, and a trackball or mouse as the method of interaction with the computer.

HAL (Hardware Abstraction Layer)—In the NT operating system, it creates a bridge between the computer's operating system and hardware.

hard drive—Permanent storage area for data. It is also called the hard disk.

hardware—The physical components of a computer system.

HCL (Hardware Compatibility List)—A list that comes with Windows NT Server that tells you what hardware is compatible with the software. The most updated versions of this list can be found on the Microsoft Web site or on the TechNet CD.

HOST file—A static list of FQDNs mapped to IP addresses.

HPFS (High Performance File System)—The first PC-compatible file system that supported LFNs. Like FAT, HPFS maintains a directory structure, but it adds automatic sorting of the directory and includes support for special attributes to better accommodate multiple naming conventions and file-level security.

HTTP (Hypertext Transfer Protocol)—This is the World Wide Web protocol that allows for the transfer of HTML documents over the Internet or intranets that respond to actions, like a user clicking on hypertext links.

IDE (Integrated Device Electronics)—A type of storage device interface where the electronics required to operate the drive are stored on the drive itself, thus eliminating the need for a separate controller card.

IIS (Internet Information Server)—A Web Server software by Microsoft. It is included and implemented with Windows NT Server.

instructor-led course—Usually held in a classroom setting, a course led by an instructor.

Internet—The collection of TCP/IP-based networks around the world.

intranet—An internal private network that uses the same protocols and standards as the Internet.

I/O Manager—The module in the Executive Services that oversees all input and output. It acts like a proxy by intercepting an application's requests and directing commands to the appropriate hardware drivers.

IP address—Four sets of numbers separated by decimal points that represent the numeric address of a computer attached to a TCP/IP network, such as the Internet.

IPC (InterProcess Communications)—Within an operating system, it is the exchange of data between applications.

IPX (Internetwork Packet eXchange)—A network and transport-layer protocol developed by Novell, most commonly associated with NetWare networks.

IPX/SPX (Internetwork Packet eXchange/Sequenced Packet eXchange)—The name of Novell's NetWare protocol that was reinvented by Microsoft and implemented in Windows NT under the name "NWLink". This protocol is fully compatible with Novell's version and, in many cases, is a better implementation than the original.

ISDN (Integrated Services Digital Network)—A dedicated form of digital communication that has a bandwidth of 128 Kbps.

job function expert—A person who knows just about everything about a particular job function and the software products/technologies related to that job. Typically, a job function expert is performing the job, has recently performed the job, or is training people to perform the job.

Kernel—The essential part of an operating system that provides basic services.

LAN (Local Area Network)—A network confined to a single building or geographic area and comprised of servers, workstations, peripheral devices, a network operating system, and a communications link.

Last Known Good Configuration—A recording made by NT of all the Registry settings that existed the last time a user successfully logged in to a server.

leased lines—Communications connections that are provided to consumers by third-party communications carriers for a fee.

LFN (long files names)—File names of up to 256 characters.

LMHOSTS—The predecessor to WINS, it is a static list of NetBIOS names mapped to IP addresses.

Local procedure call facility—The module in the Executive Services manager that maintains communications user applications and environmental subsystems.

lockout—In Windows NT security, it is a feature used to prevent compromised accounts from being used.

logical partitions—The segments created when a physical hard drive is divided. Each segment can be used independently of the others, including belonging to separate volumes and hosting different file systems. Most logical partitions have a drive letter assigned to them and can be referred to by an ARC name.

logical printers—The software component used by NT to direct print jobs from applications to a print server. A physical printer can be serviced by numerous logical printers.

logoff—The process by which a user quits using a computer system.

logon—The process by which a user gains access or signs onto a computer system.

logon scripts—Files that consist of a set of network commands that must be carried out in a particular order.

LPD (Line Printer Daemon)—Originally a Unix component, it receives documents from LPR clients and sends them to a printer. An LPD is essentially a print server.

LPR (Line Printer Remote)—A command-line utility provide by Widows NT used for directing and monitoring print jobs aimed for Unix host printers.

Master Browser—A tool used to maintain the main list of all available resources within a domain (including links to external domains).

MB—The abbreviation for megabyte, 1,024 kilobytes.

MBR (Master Boot Record)—A BIOS bootstrap routine used by low-level, hardware-based system code stored in Read-Only Memory (ROM) to initiate the boot sequence on a PC.

MCI (multiple-choice item)—An item within a series of items that is the answer to a question (single-response MCI) or one of the answers to a question (multiple-response MCI).

MCP (Microsoft Certified Professional)—An individual who has taken and passed a series of certification exams, thereby earning one or more of the following certifications: Microsoft Certified Trainer, Microsoft Certified Solution Developer, Microsoft Certified Systems Engineer, or Microsoft Certified Product Specialist.

MCPS (Microsoft Certified Product Specialist)—An individual who has passed at least one of the Microsoft operating system exams.

MCSD (Microsoft Certified Solution Developer)—An individual who has taken and passed a series of certification exams, thereby classified as qualified to create and develop business solutions using the Microsoft development tools, technologies, and platforms.

MCSE (Microsoft Certified Systems Engineer)—An individual who has taken and passed a series of certification exams, thereby classified as an expert on Windows NT and the Microsoft BackOffice integrated family of server software. This individual can also plan, implement, maintain, and support information systems associated with these products.

MCT (Microsoft Certified Trainer)—An individual who has taken and passed a series of certification exams, thereby qualified by Microsoft to instruct Microsoft Education courses at sites authorized by Microsoft.

Microsoft certification exam—A test created by Microsoft to verify the mastery of a software product, technology, or computing topic.

Microsoft Certified Professional Certification Update—A newsletter for Microsoft Certified Professional candidates and Microsoft Certified Professionals.

Microsoft official curriculum—Microsoft education courses that support the certification exam process and are created by the Microsoft product groups.

Microsoft Roadmap To Education And Certification—An application based on Microsoft Windows that takes you through the process of determining your certification goals and planning how you can achieve them.

Microsoft Sales Fax Service—A service provided by Microsoft where you can obtain Exam Preparation Guides, fact sheets, and additional information about the Microsoft Certified Professional program.

Microsoft Solution Provider—An organization not directly related to Microsoft that provides integration, consulting, technical support, and other services related to Microsoft products.

Microsoft TechNet Technical Information Network—A service provided by Microsoft that provides helpful information via a monthly CD-ROM disk. TechNet is the primary source of technical information for people who support and/or educate end users, create automated solutions, or administer networks and/or databases.

MOLI (Microsoft Online Institute)—An organization that offers training materials, online forums, user groups, and online classes.

motherboard—A term that refers to the main circuit board in a computer system.

MPR (Multi-Protocol Router)—A device that converts various email formats.

MRI (multiple-rating item)—An item that gives you a task and a proposed solution. Every time a task is given, an alternate solution is provided, and the candidate must choose the answer that gives the best results produced by one solution.

MSDN (Microsoft Developer Network)—The official source for Software Development Kits (SDKs), Device Driver Kits (DDKs), operating systems, and programming information associated with creating applications for Microsoft Windows and Windows NT.

multilink PPP—The combining of the bandwidth of multiple physical links, which increases the total bandwidth that can be used for a RAS connection.

NDA (nondisclosure agreement)—A legal agreement signed by both Microsoft and a vendor that renders certain rights and limitations.

NetBEUI—A simple network layer transport protocol that was developed to support NetBIOS networks.

NetBIOS—Originally developed by IBM in the 1980s, it provides the underlying communication mechanism for some basic NT functions, such as browsing and interprocess communications between network servers.

Netstat—A utility that displays TCP/IP status and statistics.

NetWare—A popular network operating system from Novell.

Network Dynamic Data Exchange—An API developed by Microsoft that supports DDE applications over a network.

NFS (Network Filing System)—A popular distributed file system on Unix networks.

Network Monitor—A tool used for investigating network-related problems.

Network Neighborhood—Within Explorer or My Computer, this is the area in which you access other computers on the network.

NIC (Network Interface Card)—An adapter card used to connect a computer to a network.

NMA (Network Monitor Agent)—A network service tool that gathers counter readings from network related objects.

NOS (network operating system)—A specialized collection of software that gives a computer the ability to communicate over a network and to take advantage of a broad range of networking services. Windows NT is a network operating system available in Workstation and Server versions; Windows 95 and Windows For Workgroups also include built-in network client and peer-to-peer capabilities.

NT (Network Termination)—Part of the network connection device in an ISDN network.

NT Diagnostics—NT's GUI rendition of MSD (Microsoft Diagnostics). NT Diagnostics provides detailed system configuration information from the NT Registry.

NTBACKUP.EXE—A backup utility that is shipped with Windows NT.

NTDETECT.COM—A hardware recognition program that collects a list of currently installed components and returns the information to NTLDR.

NTFS—A naming file system used in Windows NT.

NTLDR file—The executable program launched by the boot files that load the NT Kernel. The name is a shortened version of "NT Loader."

null modem cable—An RS-232 cable used to enable two computers within close proximity to communicate without a modem.

NWLink—Microsoft's "clean room" implementation of Novell's IPX/SPX protocol suite for NetWare networks.

Object Manager—The module in the Executive Services that controls activities related to objects, such as use, naming, removing, tracking, and security of objects.

OS (operating system)—A software program that controls the operations of a computer system.

OSLOADER.EXE—The OS loader program for RISC computers. This program provides all of the services and information provided by NTDETECT.COM, BOOTSECT.DOS, NTDETECT.COM, and NTLDR on PCs. It resides wherever the nonvolatile RAM location data indicates.

OSR2—The only current Microsoft operating system that supports FAT32.

page faults—A counter that should be measured when you suspect there is not enough memory in the system.

pagefile—The file used by the Virtual Memory Manager to temporarily store segments or pages of memory to hard disk.

partition—A portion of a hard disk or memory.

password—A word used by an individual to gain access to a particular system or application.

PDC (Primary Domain Controller)—The central storage and management server for the SAM database.

Performance Monitor—A graphical application that lets you set, graph, log, and report alerts. It is also referred to as PerfMon.

peripheral devices—Hardware device, such as keyboard, mouse, and so on, connected to a computer.

Phonebook entry—A collection of settings used by RAS to establish a connection with a remote dial-up server. A Phonebook entry contains details such as phone number, name, password, protocol settings, and encryption type.

POSIX—An operating system type that complies with the IEEE Std 1003.1 standard. NT supports only POSIX.1.

POST (Power-On Self-Test)—The set of internal diagnostic and status-checking routines a PC and its peripheral devices go through each time the computer is powered on.

power users—A user group found on NT Workstation. Also, a user who is well versed in the operation and modification of a computing system—someone who pushes an operating system to its limits.

PPP (Point-To-Point Protocol)—An industry standard protocol used to establish network-protocol-supporting links over POTS lines using modems.

PPTP (Point-To-Point Tunneling Protocol)—Enables "tunneling" of IPX, NetBEUI, and TCP/IP inside PPP packets in such a way as to establish a secure link between a client and server over the Internet.

printer—Typically refers to the logical printer (software component) within the NT environment as opposed to the physical printing device.

Process monitor—The module in the Executive Services that manages process activities, such as creation, deletion, and tracking.

protocols—In networking, this is a set of rules that define how information is transmitted over a network.

PWS (Peer Web Services)—NT Workstation's equivalent of NT Server's Internet Information Server.

RAS (Remote Access Service)—A Windows NT service that provides remote network communication for remote clients over telecommunication lines. RAS connections are different from standard, direct-network connections only in relation to speed.

Registry—The hierarchical database that serves as a repository for hardware, software, and OS configuration information.

REXEC—The TCP/IP connectivity command that executes commands on a remote system running the rexecd service.

RIP (Routing Internet Protocol)—A router protocol that enables communication between routers on a network to facilitate the exchange of routing tables.

RISC (Reduced Instruction Set Computer)—A set of processor instructions that speeds up processing by using simple computer instructions. Also, a type of computer platform.

RPC (Remote Procedure Calls)—A network interprocess communications mechanism.

SAM (Security Accounts Manager)—The security database of NT that maintains a record of all users, groups, and permissions within a domain. The SAM is stored on the PDC and duplicated on the BDCs.

SCSI (Small Computer System Interface)—A standard interface defined by ANSI that provides high-speed connections to devices such as hard drives, scanners, and printers.

security—A manner of protecting data by restricting access to authorized users.

Security reference monitor—The module in the Executive Services that handles logon procedures, user authentication, access validation, and the security subsystem in the User mode.

Server Manager—The NT administration utility where computer accounts are managed.

Server Operators—The built-in group whose members can manage domain servers.

SID (Security ID)—A code assigned to users, groups, and computers by NT to identify them. Even when the name of an object changes, NT recognizes the object by its SID. Every SID is unique.

SLIP (Serial Line Internet Protocol)—An older industry standard for RAS communication links. SLIP is included with NT only for establishing connections with Unix systems that do not support the newer PPP standard.

SMS (Systems Management Server)—A Microsoft product used for high-end management and administration of an enterprise-level network.

SMTP (Simple Mail Transfer Protocol)—The Internet protocol used to distribute email from one mail server to another over a TCP/IP network.

SNA (System Network Architecture)—A communications interface used to establish a link with IBM mainframes and AS/400 hosts.

SNMP (Simple Network Management Protocol)—A protocol used to monitor remote hosts over TCP/IP network.

spooler—A software component of the print system that stores print jobs on a hard drive while they wait in the print queue.

SQL Server—A Microsoft product that supports a network-enabled relational database system.

stripe set—A hard disk construct where segments of data are written in sequence across multiple drives.

subnet—A portion or segment of a network.

tape drives—Devices used for backing up data that employs metal film cassettes for storage.

TAPI (Telephony Application Programming Interface)—An interface and API that defines how applications can interact with data/fax/voice devices and calls.

TCP/IP—The most widely used protocol in networking today because it is the most flexible of the transport protocols and is able to span wide areas.

Telnet—A terminal emulation utility used to interact with remote computers.

UDF (Uniqueness Database File)—A script file used in conjunction with the UNATTEND.TXT file to specify different computer specific details without having to create a unique UNATTEND.TXT for each machine.

UDP (User Datagram Protocol)—A TCP/IP component that transmits data through a connectionless service but does not guarantee the delivery or sequencing of sent packets.

UNC (Universal Naming Convention)—A standardized naming method for networks taking the form of *servername**sharename*.

Unix—An interactive time-sharing operating system developed in 1969 by a hacker to play games. This system developed into the most widely used industrial-strength computer in the world and ultimately supported the birth of the Internet.

UPS (Uninterruptible Power Supply)—A semi-intelligent, rechargeable battery system that protects a computer from power failures and fluctuations.

user account—The collection of information, such as name, password, group memberships, access privileges, and user rights, stored by NT about a specific network user. User accounts are managed through the User Manager For Domains utility.

user name—The human-friendly name of a user account. The user name is one of two items of data used to log on to NT. NT does not recognize an account by the user name, but rather by the SID.

user profiles—The collection of desktop and environmental settings that define the work area of a local computer.

user rights—Settings that define the ability of a user to access a computer or a domain.

users group—This is another term for "group."

VDM (Virtual DOS Machine)—A Win32 application that creates an operational environment for DOS applications.

VFAT (Virtual File Allocation Table)—This file system is currently supported by Windows 95, Windows NT 3.51, and Windows NT 4. VFAT provides 32-bit Protected Mode access for file manipulation.

VGA (Video Graphics Array)—A PC display standard of 640x480 pixels, 16 colors, and a 4:3 aspect ratio.

Virtual Memory Manager (VMM)—The module in the Executive Services that maintains and controls physical and virtual memory.

VMM (Virtual Memory Manager)—The executive service within NT's Kernel that manages physical and virtual (swap or pagefile) memory.

VPN (Virtual Private Networks)—A WAN, provided by a common communications carrier, that works like a private network; however, the backbone of the network is shared with all of the customers in a public network.

WAN (Wide Area Network)—A network that spans geographically distant segments. Often the distance of two miles or more is used to define a WAN; however, Microsoft equates any RAS connection as establishing a WAN.

Web server—A computer connected to the Internet or a intranet that stores Web documents and displays them upon request.

Windows Sockets—An API that provides a standard for application interaction with transport protocols, such as TCP/IP over PPP.

WinLogon utility—A utility that displays the logon dialog box and sends the inputted data to the security manager.

WINMSD (Windows NT Diagnostics)—A Windows NT utility that gives you a shallow insight into the current configuration of the NT software and the hardware it is operating on.

WINS (Windows Internet Name Service)—A Windows network service used to resolve NetBIOS names to IP addresses.

workgroups—A collection of networked computers that participate in a peer-to-peer relationship.

WOW (Windows on Windows)—The DOS application that supports Windows 16-bit applications WOW executes within a VDM, which itself runs as a Win32 process.

Write permissions—This setting grants the ability to create or modify files and directories.

WWW (World Wide Web)—An information-distribution system hosted on TCP/IP networks. The Web supports text, graphics, and multimedia. The IIS component of NT is a Web server (which can distribute Web documents).

Index